The Poetry of
Robert Graves

MICHAEL KIRKHAM

The Poetry of
Robert Graves

New York
OXFORD UNIVERSITY PRESS
1969

ACKNOWLEDGEMENTS

The poems quoted in their entirety in this book are copyright by Robert Graves © 1921, 1927, 1931, 1933, 1938, 1944, 1955, 1961, 1964, 1965. They are reprinted by permission of Robert Graves and Collins-Knowlton-Wing, Inc.

PRINTED IN GREAT BRITAIN

TO MY WIFE

AND IN MEMORY OF

I. R. BROWNING

Preface

I FIRST presented a view of Graves's poetry—as a blend of romantic and realistic impulses—in an essay entitled 'Incertitude and the White Goddess' published in *Essays in Criticism* (Volume XVI, Number 1, 1966). This book was originally planned as a more detailed and precise exposition of the view outlined there but grew into something larger. Apart from a few sentences, however, there is little actual quotation from that source. Acknowledgements are due to the editors of *The Minnesota Review* for permission to use my essay on 'The Poetic Liberation of Robert Graves', which appeared in their issue Volume VI, Number 3, 1966, as the basis of Chapter 6.

Laura Riding (now Mrs Laura Jackson), whose influence was described in the article, objected in a later number that I had underestimated and simplified (if I have understood her correctly) her role in Graves's intellectual life. Simplification is likely, if only because my sketch of her thought was derived from only one of her published works, *The World and Ourselves* (1938). I have not been able to revise for inclusion in Chapter 6 those portions of the article to which she has taken exception, but she will note that in Chapter 4 I have given further attention to her ideas, as expressed in *Anarchism Is Not Enough* (1928). This by no means exhausts the subject of her 'influence', but a thorough investigation would have taken more space than was available to me. Her influence on the thematic materials and practice not only of Graves but of other poets in the 'thirties and since surely deserves a book to itself. As for her second charge: I think Mrs Jackson mistook caution, dictated by the limits of an outsider's biographical knowledge, for underestimation. In fact, I admire her work and, as is clear from this study, estimate its influence on Graves's poetic outlook more highly than have previous commentators.

In the course of the book I refer occasionally to the opinions of

G. S. Fraser, J. M. Cohen, Donald Davie, Ronald Gaskell, Douglas Day and Daniel Hoffman. The books and periodical articles where these are to be found are named in the Introduction. The Bibliography, for which I am largely indebted to Fred Higginson's complete bibliography of Graves, contains works by but not about him.

I have especially to thank Robert Graves himself for allowing me to quote from his work.

M.K.

Contents

Introduction

SINCE the early 'twenties Robert Graves has managed to support himself by his writings. His range is extraordinarily wide: the work he has done includes, besides poetry, reviewing, criticism, translation (from German, Spanish, Latin and Greek), polemical essays, humour, some exceptionally learned historical novels and fantasies, mythography, studies in the origins of religion and of the Old and New Testaments, biography and autobiography. He is, surely, the best contemporary writer in English of a lucid, plain but well-bred prose—a verdict which G. S. Fraser has also reached; but still primarily he is a poet. It is certain that he has now lost interest in being an objective critic; his novels are firstly attempts to solve historical puzzles and only secondarily works of imagination (moreover he seems to have stopped writing them); the mythological studies, though of considerable interest and value in their own right, are by-products of, and sources for, his poetry. In everything he writes he maintains standards of professional competence, but he classes his prose works as those that earn him a living and regards poetry as his vocation. In his conception of the good life poetry has a unique role: poetic thought is the most precise instrument for the uncovering of truth.

In the following pages I have confined myself to an historical and critical examination of the poetry. The two critics who have so far published full-length studies of Graves have each covered a wider area of his work. J. M. Cohen in his volume *Robert Graves* (Writers and Critics series, 1960) attempted a general though brief survey; Douglas Day's *Swifter than Reason* (1963), larger and more reliable, was an assessment of the poetry and criticism together. Day's book also provided useful biographical information. The time for a thorough detailed investigation of the poetry alone, therefore, was certainly overdue. In pursuing such an investigation I have tried to

I

keep biographical reference to the absolute minimum and have cited Graves's prose works only where they directly illuminate the themes and attitudes of the poetry. Obviously, for example, his various writings concerning the White Goddess and, recently, the Black Goddess—both of whom are central figures in the poetry—are essential reading for the student of his poetry, and not only of his later poetry. But for this purpose Graves's writings hardly take precedence over those of Laura Riding, whose personality, ideas and poetic practice had a revolutionary effect on Graves as a man and a writer during the late 'twenties and throughout the 'thirties, leaving an impression that can be traced in the style and thought of his subsequent work. Consequently I have given as much space to an exposition of her ideas as I have to an outline of the White Goddess Theme. Critics have not ignored the part played by Laura Riding in the transformation that Graves's poetry underwent during the years 1926 to 1939, but seem to have been unaware that it involved not merely his poetic technique and critical opinions but his whole intellectual, moral and religious outlook.

Graves began writing verse at school before the First World War —his published juvenilia date from 1910—and he has been producing poems without intermission ever since. Far from showing signs of diminishing powers, the poems written between the publication of *Collected Poems 1959* and his latest collection in 1965 are more numerous than those written in any previous period of comparable length and are as serious and as surprising as anything he has published. His total output is not, however, represented in any single collection. Each of the five collections so far published has, in fact, been a critical *selection* of his previous work, in which those poems not suppressed were likely to appear in a considerably revised form. I can think of no poem that has suffered by emendation; almost always, in fact (I agree with Douglas Day), the poems subjected to this process have been improved in style and clarity. Very occasionally, however—it is the case, for example, with 'The Lands of Whipperginny' (revised as 'The Land of Whipperginny') and 'Pure Death'—the mood of a poem has also been tampered with, to suit the changed sympathies of the later poet. While the critic may approve, this nevertheless detracts from a collection's value as 'the poet's spiritual autobiography', the presentation of which in Graves's own opinion, as stated in the Foreword to *Poems and Satires 1951*, should be the purpose of any volume of collected poems; moreover, it is possible to prefer the original poem, as I prefer, despite its harshness and comparative awkwardness, the more painful early version of 'Pure Death'. The critical standards by which he promotes and relegates poems are even more questionable. In 1938, introducing his second collection, he was able to write with fair accuracy: 'I have suppressed whatever I felt misrepresented my poetic seriousness *at the time when it was written*' (my italics). But this is no longer true. *Collected Poems 1965*, for instance, omits one of the best poems of his first period, 'An English Wood', while retaining that merely charming favourite of the early anthologies (and no more characteristic than 'An English Wood') 'The Troll's Nosegay'; and 'Recalling War', an important example of the mood and manner of his second period, has been excluded—as is evident from a passage in *Poetic Craft and Principle* about the 'poetic virtues' displayed by the soldiers of the First World War—solely because his attitude to war has changed.

The habit of rewriting, with the result that the majority of the poems that have survived more than one collection now exist in several versions, poses another problem for the critic. The actual volume of Graves's published verse makes the task of identifying the principles of development in it a challenging one; but there is also the textual problem—which version of a poem should be quoted? Inevitably the poems of any one collection, whether their originals were written in 1914 or more recently, tend to have a uniform look; so much so, in fact, that readers usually underestimate the amount of change in technique, theme and moral attitude that has taken place during a half-century of unflagging poetic output. To trace the lines of development in his poetry it is essential to read it chronologically, and throughout this study I have quoted the earliest versions, except where comparison with later versions illustrates Graves's changing intentions or where, occasionally, rewriting has clarified the thought of a poem without actually deviating from the spirit of the original.

In surveying the work of any poet the critic has several tasks which are not easily performed concurrently. He must both indicate, by representative quotation and summary, the variety of the poet's achievement, and stress the unifying factors that define his total poetic character; he must map out the different paths (displaying them separately and together) along which the poetry develops without giving the impression that this development is simply a steady progress forward (in Graves's 'struggle to be a poet' there are, as he points out in the Foreword to *Collected Poems 1938*, 'anticipations and regressions'); finally, literary history should accompany but remain distinct from the evaluation of what is *at each stage* best in the poet's work. This last is the heaviest of the critic's responsibilities, for it is difficult not to suggest that the introduction of a new controlling attitude, when it at the same time implies in the rejection of a previous attitude a greater self-consciousness, does not *ipso facto* create a better poetry. The possibilities of confusion are increased by the fact that certain developments, technical and moral, are indeed improvements in the quality of the poetry. One must distinguish the two kinds of development—as I hope I have succeeded in doing.

While Graves's poetic progress cannot be described as a steady advance—there have been cul-de-sacs and digressions—yet a sequence can be discerned in it. His career falls naturally into four periods, the end of each coinciding with the publication of four out of five of his *Collected Poems*; but it has been my aim in this survey to draw attention as much to the continuity between them as to the differences in approach that separate them.

The first period, stretching from 1916 to 1926, was one of confusion. After a false start its two main themes, war—with its aftermath of neurasthenia—and romantic love, came to the fore in his third volume, *Country Sentiment* (1920), and dominated his poetry until the end of the period. It was a time of restless experiment in ways of absorbing, psychologically and technically, the impact of the two experiences. On the whole, during these years, they rarely received the full, honest, impersonal realization for which he strove; he was too much at the mercy, as he records in his preface to

Whipperginny (1923), of 'unceasing emotional stress'. At first he contrived in his poems merely to escape from conflict into a literary or folk world of pastoral and simplified emotion; in the second half of this period, however, he sought relief in a more sophisticated self-deception: turning from the inner drama, which has always been his true subject, he applied himself to the exposition in a studiously flat, discursive style of certain theories centring on the abstract *idea* of conflict. The informing intention was antiromantic and self-disciplinary, and the most memorable poems in *Poems 1914–1926* are generally the later ones; but a very large proportion of them were external and pedestrian; some, again, were irresponsibly cynical, others—though these are altogether more attractive—practised an irony that was too elegantly detached.

The next twelve years, concluding with the publication of *Collected Poems 1938*, were the period of Laura Riding's influence. Her example and personal criticism were largely responsible for the compression, rhythmic tautness and rigorously intellectual approach characteristic of Graves's verse now. His poems achieved impersonality and intellectual control, not through the avoidance of personal involvement, but, at first, by a savagely self-critical, often self-mortifying attitude towards his emotions and by restricting themselves to the expression of such negative responses as scorn, aggression, scepticism and bitterness. During the 'thirties he relaxed this posture, and poems celebrating a new kind of love (romantic without being sentimental), a theme treated once or twice at the very end of his first period, became more frequent. His writing answered to a new conception of poetry and the proper subject-matter of poetry that had taken shape during his discussions with Laura Riding. A basic premise of her thought was that the poets were left with but a single task—'the determination of values'. Poetry was for him now not psychotherapy, as it had been, but the most direct means of apprehending reality. His new themes were his own earlier romanticism and present moral short-comings, the falsity of social values, truth to self, and the evaluation of contemporary civilization. He came to see himself as having two poetic roles—that of moralist on the one hand and of love poet on the other, the two roles brought into close relationship by Graves's view of love as the source of the highest values. At the same time this period saw the stabilizing of a previous tendency to use emblem, allegory, fable and symbol rather than direct statement and comment aided by metaphor. Elements of the bizarre, humour, wit and irony were added to complete the impersonalizing process.

The third period, extending from 1938 to 1959, was dominated by the mythology of the White Goddess. Except in a few satires Graves's sole theme was the man-woman relationship. The Goddess symbolizes the feminine principle, woman in all her attributes, and the myths tell the story of the inevitable suffering that the poets who choose to serve her must undergo. Yet in that service Graves discovered the spiritual values on which until recently he has based his view of life. In this poetry the romantic images of a few early poems, and the emotional involvement with his subject characteristic of his first period, combined with the technical discipline, intellectual control, moral insight and self-knowledge acquired during the Laura Riding years to produce a romantic poetry laced with toughness and scepticism. It was during these two decades that Graves first succeeded in maintaining a *general* balance—achieved previously in only the exceptional poem—between a romantic desire for the impossible and miraculous, a state beyond conflict, and a realistic awareness of its impossibility.

The period ended with the publication in 1959 of his fourth *Collected Poems*. Since then four more volumes of poetry and another collection have appeared. This remarkable productivity signifies the beginning of yet another phase. Graves now celebrates the Black Goddess of Wisdom, who in early Jewish, Orphic and Sufi mystery cults brought to the few who, having suffered continuous death and recreation at the White Goddess's hand, had fully served their apprenticeship to her, knowledge of a final certitude in love. Incertitude had been hitherto the essential fact in Graves's experience of the relationship with woman; here is a new reality of love, that transcends the needs of physical expression, the *accomplishment* of the impossible and the miraculous. Behind the experience rendered in these poems and the imagery in which it is embodied there are the

teachings and traditional stories of Sufism, a Wisdom-cult of uncertain origin which is known to have attracted adherents from all
religions, especially from among poets (much of its literature is in
poetic form), since the time of Mohammed; Graves has evidently
discovered in Sufism a way of thought closely resembling his own.

This summary of Graves's career necessarily leaves out much that
is important in his development. Interpreted in one way, for example, his first two periods tell the story of his search for a theme.
The postwar neurasthenia which for a time psychologically crippled
Graves was responsible for deflecting him, after a brief, unsuccessful
spell as a war poet, from public to personal themes: he turned his
attention to the problems of realizing poetically the violent emotional
disturbances that afflicted him. At the same time his neurasthenia
was partly responsible for the urgency with which he also turned, at
first as an escape, to romantic love as a theme. The neurosis was an
accident of circumstance but one that has had a long-standing effect
on Graves's work. It not only accounts for the desperate quality of
his early love poetry, but it has made a permanent impression on his
personality and therefore on the nature of his love poetry ever since:
his emotional life, as he records it, swings violently between the
extremes of ecstasy and anguish. At every stage in his development
this unbalance has been the focal point of much of his writing. The
longing for some stabilizing certainty has been, perhaps, the chief
moral compulsion behind his poetry, the basis of his kind of romanticism, as an undeluded awareness of the actual prevailing uncertainty has provided the counterbalancing scepticism and moral
realism also characteristic of his mature work. In his second period
Graves extended his range by expressing through his verse a complete
system of values—attacking the falsities and hollowness of an
exclusively social reality and declaring a personal reality based on
truth to self and mental vigilance; but the love theme was still
central. Supporting this position was a conception of love as a moral
testing, of woman as man's judge, and specifically an idealization of
Laura Riding's moral and intellectual qualities. The White Goddess
mythology of the next period gave rise to a love poetry of a peculiar
kind, in which the personal reality was celebrated as a *creation*

solely of the man-woman relationship, and the phases of love were represented as a cyclic religious experience.

Of course Graves's development was also a growth in technical discipline—from the early prettiness, sentimentality and prolixity through the spare, taut, intellectual style of his second period to the more relaxed, emotionally more complex but strictly controlled verse of the early mythological poems, and so on. This growth roughly paralleled the poet's progress towards a viable moral and intellectual position. His experiences as a soldier had destroyed the simple Christian faith of his very earliest poems, and in the years immediately following the war he made no attempt to put anything in its place. But as early as 1921 the results of his studies in psychology, anthropology and the history of religion were being felt in his writing; in the phase that ensued he set himself to work out in his verse an attitude of (then fashionable) ethical relativism, while in his criticism he outlined a parallel scheme of extreme aesthetic relativism. This attitude ran counter to his deepest instincts and was poetically unfruitful. It lingered as a flavour in the early volumes of his second period, but the bitterness of these poems was in marked contrast with the studied neutrality of those that had preceded them and was a sign, rather, of his discontent with life lived in a moral vacuum. His work during this period showed a steady advance towards the acceptance, and a progressively more assured expression, of a consistent world-view and absolute moral standards. The White Goddess Myth made possible a different kind of poetry but the world-view and the standards embodied in it were essentially the same.

In yet another interpretation the history of Graves's changing style is the history of his various, more or less successful attempts to find an impersonal medium for personal, often distressing themes. The early, abortive experiments with the forms of ballad and nursery rhyme can be understood as part of this sustained effort. With a few exceptions his folk poems failed in their purpose because they were simplifications rather than impersonalizations of his conflicts. They were followed, in turn, by cynical, 'philosophical' and classically restrained poems, most of which were more successful in suppressing than expressing the poet's emotions. But, as I have already noted, the most satisfying strategy—the externalizing of the inner drama through allegory and symbol—Graves had discovered early in his career. During his second period he wrote almost entirely in this mode, enlarging the element of impersonation (the assumption of personae) and, by the practice of an austere, mocking, ironic, off-hand manner, the degree of detachment between the poet and his material. To accommodate the more positive emotions that began to appear again in his poetry during the late 'thirties and early 'forties he revived the earlier romantic symbolism, which now found its place in a rich mythology devised to express a broader range of experience and a more highly organized scheme of more complex attitudes. The mythology, considered retrospectively, was a natural if an unexpected conclusion to Graves's search for an impersonalizing medium.

One aspect of this last development which is of especial interest is the early anticipation in images and conceits of the symbolism and themes treated, more fully, in the White Goddess poetry. Whenever this is true of poems examined in the following pages I have noted it as they have come up for discussion. It is inevitable in a chronological survey that this should entail repetition of the same points. A more serious danger is that the reader who is insufficiently acquainted with the mythological poetry should not be in a position to understand the similarities as they *are* noted. My attempted solution is a compromise. At some point in the course of considering each poem that looks forward to these later themes or symbolism I have, very briefly, outlined the relevant theme or interpreted the relevant symbol as each appears in the context of the mythology. This method gives the reader a provisional understanding of the case being presented, but he must then wait until Chapters 6 and 7 for a full exposition of the White Goddess Theme and a statement of the pattern of development which, considered together, these sporadic anticipatory poems describe.

I have tried to give prominence, without obscuring a view of the poetic sequence as a whole, to each aspect of Graves's development summarized in the preceding paragraphs, and to others not mentioned here. Another aim has been, by analyzing the most successful work of each period, to isolate those elements that together constitute what is recognizable as his poetic identity. There are several ways of defining the unique character of his best poetry. No single definition, of course, will encompass all its qualities, but perhaps the most nearly adequate is that it is an individual blend of romantic and realistic impulses—the balancing of an aspiration towards a perfect, timeless state of being where contradictions are resolved against an acute sense of the limits set by actuality. His most impressive poems, it could be argued, are those in which the contrary pulls of romantic aspiration and realistic awareness are so strong and so equal that the effect is less one of poise then of a finely maintained tension.

Very little really illuminating criticism of Graves's work has been published. In fact, only in recent years has it begun to receive much serious attention; J. M. Cohen's and Douglas Day's books and Martin Seymour-Smith's British Council pamphlet (1956) were the first indications of this more general recognition. I have not burdened this study with references to these or other critics, though I have found Dr Day's work, in particular, helpful. I have found most stimulus, however, in the following periodical articles: a pioneering essay by G. S. Fraser first published in 1947 (*Vision and Rhetoric*, 1959), a long review of *Collected Poems 1959*, by Donald Davie published in *Listen* (Spring, 1960) and reprinted in *Shenandoah* (Winter, 1962), and an essay by Ronald Gaskell published in *The Critical Quarterly* (Autumn, 1961).[1]

---

[1] Since the completion of this book in 1966, *Barbarous Knowledge* (1967), a study of myth in the poetry of Yeats, Graves and Edwin Muir by Daniel Hoffman, has been published. This offers the most perceptive criticism of Graves that I have read.

I

Fairies and Fusiliers

ROBERT GRAVES has been his own severest critic. He published the first collection of his poems in 1926, and on that occasion discarded over half of his previously published poetry and revised the rest. Discarding with the same ruthlessness and rewriting much of what remained, he published four further collections, in 1938, 1948, 1959 and 1965. He now disapproves of most of what he wrote before 1926, in criticism and poetry, and very few poems from his first collection have survived to represent the period it covers in *Collected Poems 1965*.

The weeding out has been most severe in the case of his earliest verse, published during the First World War. Out of his first two volumes, *Over the Brazier* (1916) and *Fairies and Fusiliers* (1917), only one poem survives. Some of the poems had been written while he was a schoolboy at Charterhouse—these are grouped together in the first volume; the rest while on active service as an infantry officer in France; all of them between the ages of 14 and 21. Graves's low estimate of these poems is certainly justified. The spirit that informs them is, understandably, schoolboyish—whimsical and sentimental; some show technical skill, including the one that has survived, 'In the Wilderness', but most of them are loosely organized, rhythmically banal, the imagery and the diction unadventurous; and all obey in style and subject-matter the Georgian conventions.

Typical of Georgianism at its least inspired are these lines from '1915' (*Over the Brazier*):

> Dear, you've been everything that I most lack
> In these soul-deadening trenches—pictures, books,
> Music, the quiet of an English wood.

They express a common nostalgia for the countryside as an escape from the misery of war and as a haven of cultural seclusion. The feeling is languid and imprecise, running easily to clichés like 'soul-deadening', and the verse-movement is slack. There had been a reaction against the rhetoric of the Imperialists and the affectation of the 'nineties poets in the early years of the century which, when Edward Marsh decided to publish the first anthology of *Georgian Poetry* in 1912, was almost complete. The instinct was a good one, and Edward Thomas, for instance, succeeded in his best poems in creating a verse that is faithful to 'the postures which the voice assumes in the most expressive intimate speech,' an achievement he attributed to Robert Frost;[1] but frequently the reaction resulted, as in the lines quoted, in mere prosiness.

There are also examples in his first two volumes of the conventionally romantic war-poem, a confident expression of the noble sentiments with which Rupert Brooke's name is generally associated. The bonds of friendship, Graves proclaims in 'Two Fusiliers' (*Fairies and Fusiliers*), were only knotted more tightly by the shared hardships of fighting, and by the vision of Death itself: 'we faced him, and we found/Beauty in death,/In dead men breath'. The emotion is literary. The gesture made by another poem, 'To Lucasta on Going to the Wars—for the Fourth Time' (*Fairies and Fusiliers*), as the title indicates, also derives from literature. The poem feigns a contempt for the statesmen at home and a cynical indifference about 'what wrong they say we're righting'; yet these attitudes are struck merely for the heroic swagger they permit, and are conveyed in the traditional tones of the bluff soldier:

> It is no courage, love or hate
> That lets us do the things we do;
> It's pride that makes the heart so great.

Yet this is not the whole picture. Several poems in the war-time volumes show (brashly and uncertainly as yet) recognizable signs of individuality. When, in 1938, he came to review his poetic development and tried to explain the high proportion of what might be called 'unpleasant poems' in his *Collected Poems*, the formula he chose was that they were 'the blurted confession of a naturally

[1] In a letter to Gordon Bottomley, 30 June 1915.

sanguine temperament'[1]—a confession of disappointment with the intellectual and moral confusion of the age. The reason why this is not a formula that would immediately occur to the reader of his poetry is that since the mid-twenties Graves has consistently struggled to keep his 'sanguine temperament' well under control, denying it irresponsible or sentimental expression. It finds direct expression, however, both sentimental and irresponsible, in these poems of his youth. The simplest form it takes is that of boyish gaiety—the gaiety, for instance, with which the fairy pipers and the nursery atmosphere of 'Cherry-Time' (*Over the Brazier*) are exploited; the poem is trivial but conveys real sensuous delight—'Chin to knee on the orchard wall,/Cooled with dew and cherries eating'. It finds further expression in the tone of light mockery which pervades many of the poems. This is not serious enough to qualify as satire; it is merely a slightly more sophisticated version of the natural gaiety. 'Smoke Rings' (*Fairies and Fusiliers*) provides a representative example. In imitation of Lewis Carroll's 'Father William' this is a dialogue between 'Boy' and 'Philosopher'. The 'tall and true philosopher' spends his day blowing smoke-rings and with suitable reverence the boy asks what meaning they have. The philosopher answers solemnly, with a parody of theological reasoning:

> He who ringed His awe in smoke,
> When He led forth His captive folk,
> In like manner, East, West, North, and South,
> Blows us ring-wise from His mouth.

The mildly blasphemous humour is, admittedly, that of the clever schoolboy. Disrespect for the Church, as for the politicians, was common among the soldiers in France; but, no more than 'To Lucasta on Going to the Wars—for the Fourth Time' was an attack on the politicians, can this poem be regarded as a considered attack on conventional religion. Its mood is characteristic of a much less focused irreverence in many of these poems, a vague rebellion against seriousness itself. More specifically, this was an attitude wilfully adopted in the face of his war experiences. At this time

---

[1] Foreword to *Collected Poems 1938*, p. xxiv.

Siegfried Sassoon, a friend and fellow-officer, was wanting war to be an impressive experience; Graves's reaction went beyond mere scepticism: he was convinced that the continuation of the war was a 'mad joke' of the politicians, and therefore not only would have nothing to do with Sassoon's 'fine feelings' but refused to countenance any serious attitudes towards it.

In the freakishness of these two poems we have the first immature stirrings of a personal response. They are mere glimmerings, however, of Graves's future poetic self. The response, as in 'Smoke Rings', is still largely a negative one—a scepticism about the high-flown, the complementary vices of which are cynicism and whimsicality. His style at this time was as much the product of self-denial as of a positive choice, but reveals a tendency which has been characteristic of Graves's verse at each stage of his development. He disparaged the 'fine style' of Sassoon's earliest poems, and this judgement was in accord with his own practice. All the Georgians, it is true, aspired to simplicity of language, a simplicity that frequently deteriorated into childishness. But in practising it himself and though prone to the same lapses, Graves was not being merely fashionable: he was being true to his own poetic instincts, which have always encouraged him to avoid rhetoric and keep close to the language of plain feeling. He had, presumably, read the other Georgian poets, but the strongest influence on his verse came through ballads, folk-songs and nursery rhyme, and he had independently modelled his style on the language of these rather than on that of his contemporaries.

By refusing to involve himself in the serious themes of war and by avoiding the sonorities of the 'fine style', Graves at least managed to escape the worst vices of war-poetry—the self-deceptions of idealistic patriotism and the insincerities of inflated language. Even Wilfred Owen did not always escape the latter. But Graves has no poems to compare with, say, Owen's 'Dulce et Decorum Est' or Sassoon's 'To Any Dead Officer', positive attempts by a shocking use of realism to dispel the 'noble' image of war. Owen's aim is to make the reader share his helpless pity and sense of responsibility for the soldiers' suffering, Sassoon's, more simply, to engage his anger against the callous politicians and an ordinary fellow-feeling for the soldier: these poems are anti-heroic in the interests of a deeper truth about war; Graves is anti-heroic because he rejects the whole experience of war. In 'Assault Heroic' (*Fairies and Fusiliers*), whose title in quotation marks is ironic, the poet falls asleep in the trenches and dreams once again of fighting—but in a medieval setting. His enemies, behind their castle battlements, hoot and jeer at him like children. Like a child himself he defies them with his 'sharp tongue-like sword', and when they throw stones and pour down boiling oil he is able magically to transform the first into lumps of gold and the second into a refreshing shower of dew. On waking up, at the climax of this triumph, he finds that a new attack has started. The poem has no serious critical point of view; it is merely a burlesque description of strutting heroism, in which conflicts between nations are assimilated to the ridiculous antics of children. It assumes that the realities of trench-warfare are inaccessible to comment; they are there only as something to escape from and return to. Formally they are a framework for the dream, which contains the real subject: for the dream is an ironic allegory (ironic, although Graves's intention wavers a little) about heroic poetry—in particular about the poet's alleged ability to transform the painful facts of war into the comforting images of poetry:

> The stones they cast I caught
> And alchemized with thought.

Graves avoided any deep commitment of his feelings to the theme of war even in those poems which acknowledged its physical reality. His natural reaction was to make a joke of it. In July 1916 he was badly wounded. *The Times* reported that he had died, but later at his request inserted an announcement that he was alive and recovering from his wounds. In the poem he wrote about it, 'Escape', he presents his experience of a virtual death and rebirth as a dream in which the incidents only parody the reality. The period of unconsciousness is a kind of death—'I *was* dead, an hour or more'—from which the poet awakens only just in time. During this period he descends into Hades and is 'half-way down the road/To Lethe, as an old Greek signpost showed' when he returns to consciousness. With the help of 'Lady Proserpine' he retraces his steps, pursued by the shades of the dead, to where Cerberus is still guarding the entrance. Desperately thinking of ways to pass, he remembers that he has some morphia;

> Then swiftly Cerberus' wide mouths I cram
> With army biscuits smeared with ration jam;
> And sleep lurks in the luscious plum and apple.

The beast is overcome by the drug and collapses; he

> blocks up the corridor
> With monstrous hairy carcase, red and dun—
> Too late! for I've sped through.
> O Life! O Sun!

Occasionally the fantasy touches upon the poet's underlying feelings —his fear of death. The jaunty reference to the 'old Greek signpost' and the carefree account of how Cerberus is outwitted conceal it, but it is to be felt elsewhere in the poem, for instance in the description of the beast's 'carcase' blocking the light, and the desperate relief with which the poet welcomes his escape. Yet humour predominates. The poem expresses Graves's natural optimism, but at the same time betrays his inability to face either the objective horror of war or his deepest feelings about it.

It is significant that he wrote very little realistic verse. Sassoon, whose example changed the direction of Owen's writing so decisively, had no comparable influence on Graves's poetry. Graves wrote plainly and even on occasions colloquially, but made few attempts to record the brutal impact of war as felt daily in the trenches. The nearest to a realistic rendering is, perhaps, 'A Dead Boche' (*Fairies and Fusiliers*), and, as G. S. Fraser in his essay on Graves's poetry has pointed out, the strongest feeling in it is the aesthetic one of disgust:

> he scowled and stunk
> With clothes and face a sodden green,
> Big-bellied, spectacled, crop-haired,
> Dribbling black blood from nose and beard.

There is nothing here of Sassoon's generous anger or of Owen's humane self-involvement; Graves has recoiled from his subject. Such a reaction is as clearly an evasion of his experience as is the whimsicality of other poems. The extremity of this revulsion indicates a deep-seated shock to Graves's personality which he was unable to express openly in verse. Describing a similar encounter with a dead German in *Goodbye To All That*[1] he adds that 'he looked sinister in the moonlight; I needed a charm to get myself past him. The simplest way, I found, was to cross myself' (p. 267). The superstitious fear was evidently a fear of death. The physical disgust which his description of the corpse conveys in the poem is, one feels, the result of a failure to express this.

Siegfried Sassoon in *The Complete Memoirs of George Sherston* (1937) reports that 'though in some ways [Graves] was more easily shocked than I was he had...a first rate nose for anything nasty' (p. 386). The combination of unusual sensitivity and a preoccupation with the disgusting which is noticeable in a fair proportion of the poems in both volumes calls for further explanation. It cannot be attributed entirely to the poet's suppression of a natural fear. Sassoon provides a clue in a further remark about Graves: 'he seemed to want the War to be even uglier than it really was'. In order to make the shock of war more bearable he had taken to writing nursery poems—poems that imitate the tone and language of nursery rhyme—and poems about childhood. This reversion to an earlier and simpler kind of response was, without doubt, partly to find a refuge from his adult experiences. But it was also a way of expressing them—by analogy with the experiences of childhood. In *Over the Brazier* there is a group of three poems entitled 'Nursery Memories'. The occasion of the first one, 'The First Funeral', is explained in a prefatory note—'the first corpse I saw was on the German wires, and couldn't be buried'; but the poem is a record, written as from a child's point of view, of how he and his sister found the corpse of a dog in a field, how it stank and made him feel sick, and how they buried it. The poem makes war seem 'uglier than it

---

[1] 1st ed., 1929. All subsequent references are to this edition.

really was' by high-lighting what would be in a child's eyes the most important aspect of death, its disgustingness:

> His horrid swollen belly
> Looked just like going to burst.

> His fur was most untidy;
> He hadn't any eyes.

> It happened on Good Friday
> And there were lots of flies.

The main point of comparison between the corpse on the wires and that of the dog is that neither had received burial; they bury the dog, but merely 'to hide the nasty smell'. The reminder of the Crucifixion is to stress again the horror of the exposed hanging body. The poet's intention is evidently to shock, but not for the reasons that governed Owen's and Sassoon's insistence on the horrible—which were to register sympathy for the suffering it revealed and anger against those responsible. Graves rarely expresses bitterness in these poems or openly attacks anything. This is, rather, what we would now call a sick joke. The concealed motive in both cases appears to be the same: the desire for revenge against a complacent, hypocritical society to compensate for the author's distress. The method is also the same: deliberately to offend the moral and physical sensibilities of respectable people (which is the point of the nursery tone and the blasphemy). Perhaps the most unpleasant example of this strategy is 'The Next War' (*Fairies and Fusiliers*). The poet in a sneering parody of a scoutmasterly tone addresses those normal 'British boys' who play their warlike games with bows and arrows, not suspecting where they will lead:

> Another war soon gets begun,
> A dirtier, a more glorious one;
> Then, boys, you'll have to play, all in;
> It's the cruellest team will win.
> So hold your nose against the stink
> And never stop too long to think.

War is regarded as a sadistic joke, and the poet retaliates, vindictively, with a jeering use of hearty language which is itself sadistic.

Personal feeling is uncontrolled. Impelled by resentment at the psychological shock of war, Graves has abandoned the objective war for a strictly private campaign, in which mockery of solemn ideas (usually Christian), ridicule of the war-theme itself, and the nasty joke are the weapons, and the conventional, adult world is the enemy.

I have been illustrating an instinctive tendency in Graves at this time to refuse the public theme. With the advantage of knowing how his poetry was to develop we can see that, although these poems have very little positive value, in this tendency they show a vague awareness of his true poetic self. For his inspiration has always been personal—in the special sense of originating in personal conflict. These poems are, on the whole, poor not because his imagination was unable realistically to assimilate the subject-matter of war— Edward Thomas's poetry, after all, barely admits its existence—but because he could not face the emotional conflict engendered by it. He wrote personal poems, but they masqueraded as war-poems and were motivated by the desire for escape from, and impotent protest against, his experiences. He had not yet found an adequate personal theme.

The assumption underlying Graves's behaviour in his relationships with his fellow-officers and in particular with his friend Sassoon, as far as one can deduce it from his autobiography, was of a piece with his refusal to take the War seriously as a theme for his poetry. It seems that he made a clean separation between the energies used in coming to terms with his environment and the energies of thought and feeling which produced his poetry—in short, between his practical, social self and his poetic self. The assumption is similar to that which lies behind a remark he makes in his 'Postscript to *Goodbye To All That*' (*But It Still Goes On*, 1930): 'War is one of the characteristics of the crowd, with which I would not attempt to interfere, only deprecating it in so far as it interfered with me and failed to make the pleasurable most of itself' (p. 43). This only differs from the earlier attitude in being conscious and ironic; during the war Graves made the separation between his private and his public existence instinctively and practised it with less thoroughness. An interesting example is the apparent inconsistency of the views he held at different times about 'the theory of implicit obedience to orders'. He records in *Goodbye To All That* that at Charterhouse he was strongly anti-militarist and anti-authoritarian and in consequence resigned from the Officers' Training Corps; also that he spoke against the motion in a debate proposing that 'this House is in favour of compulsory military service' (p. 88). Yet later, summarizing some discussions he had with officers in France, he recalls his appreciation of arms-drill as a disciplinary institution (pp. 239–40). He notes one more change of opinion: both he and Sassoon were delighted at the reaction against military discipline that took place between the Armistice and the signing of peace (p. 353). But the inconsistency is only on the surface. Given war and the problem of maintaining a battalion 'as an effective fighting unit' and given the cessation of war, the last two views were practical responses to the external situation. Such views were reached necessarily by compromise with the changing situation. They were provisional and unaffected by his private unchanging distaste for the idea of 'implicit obedience to orders'. Another example is the position he took up when Sassoon, after showing considerable heroism in France and while suffering badly from shell-shock, decided to publicize the pacifist cause and defy the military authorities. He did everything to save Sassoon from the consequences of this action: he prevailed upon a member of parliament, a friend of his, to do all he could to prevent republication in the newspapers of a letter explaining his case that Sassoon had written to his commanding officer; he managed to avert a court martial and have a medical board arranged; finally, he gave evidence which persuaded the board to send Sassoon to a convalescent home for neurasthenics. He did all this despite the fact that he agreed entirely with his friend that the War was being prolonged unnecessarily by 'political errors and insincerities'. He did not believe in the justice, necessity or efficacy of the War, and yet he could not share Sassoon's pacifism: because as a gesture it would be ineffective, it would cause his friend suffering that he was not in a condition to bear, and it would be completely misunderstood not only by the civilians, whom they both hated, but by those people they most respected, the officers and men of their regiment (the officers, for instance, 'would only understand his protest as a lapse from good form and a failure to be a gentleman'). Later Sassoon wrote reprehending Graves for identifying himself with good form and gentlemanliness; but in doing so Graves was merely lending a provisional acquiescence to the ways of the social world because it was practical to do so. To be an idealist like Sassoon and confuse the personal world of one's beliefs and desires with the social world of action was, he considered, to be impractical. Everyone, he said, was mad but themselves and one or two others, but the only course for them to take was to return to France and just endure. The writing and publication of his autobiography in 1929 at the age of 35 was a gesture symbolizing his rejection not only of the society in which he had lived but of his past self and its participation in the purposes of that society. But in refusing as early as 1916 to identify his personal emotions with any non-personal cause he was anticipating this later detachment. Graves's position in 1929 was the rationalization and ironic refinement of an innate tendency of his personality. It was not given consistent recognition at first (my account of his attitudes during the war is taken from *Goodbye To All That* when he had become aware of the tendency), but, except for a short period in the 'twenties, it has influenced everything he has written since.

As it happened—and I have given ample illustration of this—his ways of being personal were often unsatisfactory: the poems are either irresponsible or evasive or morally unpleasant. At the same time the emotions that constituted his private poetic world were as yet immature and frequently though not invariably found sentimental expression. Principally they concern friendship, children, and the landscape near Harlech, which in Graves's mind was associated with the legends he had read in *The Mabinogion* and with a period of childhood happiness: all are themes permitting the simplest kind of response and treatment. In, for example, 'Not Dead', concerning the death of a fellow officer, the feelings the poet entertains for his friend, David, belong to the idyllic world of pastoral, not the real world of adult relationships:

All that is simple, happy, strong, he is.
Over the whole wood in a little while
Breaks his slow smile—

and this is characteristic of the regressive nature of many of these
poems. The years of childhood are idealized as a time when the
poetic vision is at its clearest and comes most spontaneously—'the
child alone a poet is' ('Babylon', *Fairies and Fusiliers*). Consequently
there are poems written from the child's point of view and others in
which the poet's relationships with children are seen as supplying
the reassurance he needs. 'Limbo' (*Over the Brazier*) is an instance
of the latter. It opens with a description of the 'horror, mud and
sleeplessness' of life in the front line; but there is a quick change of
mood as the poet turns with relief to an evocation of the scene 'miles
back':

the sunny cornland where
Babies like tickling, and where tall white horses
Draw the plough leisurely in quiet courses.

'Babies like tickling' is Graves's typically freakish addition to the
stock Georgian picture of a peaceful rural England. Another image
of peace that epitomizes the escapist trend in these volumes is connected with his memories of the Welsh country he explored as a
youth: it is of a clean, light cottage in the airy hills where he will be
able to read and write poetry undisturbed; in contrast, presumably,
with the claustrophobia of the trenches and the oppression of constant fear.

Involvement in the War was the cause of rapid maturing in Owen
and Sassoon. In some respects it had the opposite effect on Graves:
it did much to retard his development. He could not turn to account
the kind of material, descriptive and narrative, that war offers; in
fact, very few of his poems at any time have depended for their
nourishment on non-personal sources. As he came to a more confident understanding of himself as a poet, his poems became almost
exclusively symbolic enactments of an inner drama. Allegory, the
symbol and the emblem have been normal vehicles of expression in
all his verse, and these early poems are no exception. In the best of
these poems his use of them enables him to write from within his

private poetic world and at the same time avoid the sentimentality of those poems that attempt emotional directness.

A slight but successful example is the use he makes of pastoral myth in 'Faun' (*Fairies and Fusiliers*). It is a contrast between a former happiness and a present unhappiness. The first stanza tells how only yesterday 'King Faun' had been carelessly happy, safe from danger, and free; the second stanza presents his complaint:

> 'They drank my holy brook,
> My strawberries they took,
> My private path they trod.'
> Loud wept the desolate God. . .

In the first place this symbolizes the effect of a hostile world upon the poet's personality: it has despoiled the hitherto free, protected, innocent landscape of his personal feelings. 'My private path they trod' expresses plainly and succinctly his clean separation of the world of thought from the world of action; yet, limited and potentially self-pitying though this is, as a formal complaint of the traditional pastoral kind the statement of it becomes matter-of-fact and impersonal. For the faun is not merely a mouthpiece for Graves but represents on the one hand Poetry and on the other hand the theological conception of man as part-animal, part-divine. The picture of a 'desolate God' therefore is emblematic of a sacrilege committed against the spiritual part of man's nature. The use of the word 'desolate' should be noticed: its primary, mental sense applies to the faun's emotions, but in its secondary, physical sense—a literal laying-waste—it applies also to his invaded lands, and (in a poem where the majority of its neighbouring poems are about war) inevitably connects the man-god's despair with the desolation of the battle-fields in France. This opening up of a word's associations so that it becomes both precise and resonant with suggestion is characteristic of the art of Graves's mature verse.

'Goliath and David' (*Fairies and Fusiliers*) is another example of the poem which expresses the poet's experiences in a symbolic form. Here his feelings about the death of his friend, David Thomas, are given a certain sophistication by their allegorical embodiment in

23

the Old Testament story, a retelling in which David is killed. Once again the method has a generalizing effect. It makes possible an objective, critical account of the soldier's reaction to war—in this instance it is an ironic presentment of David's bragging confidence and, by implication, of the poet's own earlier optimism:

> He swears
> That he's killed lions, he's killed bears,
> And those that scorn the God of Zion
> Shall perish so like bear or lion.

The irony includes the traditional faith in God—'David, calm and brave/Holds his ground, for God will save', and when he doesn't—'God's eyes are dim, His ears are shut'. This and 'A Boy in Church' are the only poems that reflect with any seriousness Graves's own loss of faith. Impersonality is not the only benefit that this broad use of allegory bestows on the poem; paradoxically, the poet's horror of death is more strongly present in the sinister figure of the victorious Goliath (as it is also in that of Cerberus in 'Escape') than, say, in the realistic portrayal of the corpse in 'A Dead Boche':

> And look, spike-helmeted, grey, grim,
> Goliath straddles over him.

This picture has the power of emblem—depicting the cruel, gloating Death as a combination of German soldier, biblical and Celtic giant. The menacing associations of all three are focussed, again with an economy—it almost narrows down to the one word, 'straddles'—that will be the mark of Graves's mature poetry.

The best poem in these volumes, and one that relies for its success on a richer use of symbolism than that in either 'Goliath and David' or 'Faun' is 'A Boy in Church' (*Fairies and Fusiliers*). Ostensibly the poem gives us the reflections of a boy at a church service whose attention is divided between the drone of the parson's voice and the sight of the storm gathering outside the church. It is, in fact, an indirect presentment of Graves's feelings about war, symbolized by the storm. Rather as the story in 'Goliath and David' allowed him to take an objective, ironic view of his youthful optimism, so assuming the persona of a boy makes possible a critical detachment from the conflicting feelings reflected in this poem. These are dramatized in the boy's uneasy, ambivalent response on the one hand to the kind of safety that the church offers and on the other to the menace implied by the 'tossing trees' and the 'tortured copse' visible through the windows. The poem follows, stanza by stanza, the growth in the boy's awareness of his emotions. All we have at first are his immature, arrogant indifference to what goes on in the church and his merely idle interest in the scene outside. In the second stanza the restlessness of the outer scene arouses mixed feelings; he becomes conscious of experiencing at the same time admiration and fear—the 'tossing trees' and the sweep of the hill make a fine effect, but the 'shadowshow' of the 'tortured copse' is vaguely frightening. The next stanza shows that the boy's feelings about the church are similarly uncertain:

> The parson's voice runs like a river
> Over smooth rocks. I like this church:
> The pews are staid, they never shiver,
> They never bend or sway or lurch.
> 'Prayer,' says the kind voice, 'is a chain
> That draws down Grace from Heaven again.'

He likes it because, unlike the trees (and unlike the constantly shelled trenches—'lurch' implies the sickening impact of bombardment), it remains undisturbed. The comfort he derives from being there has no connection with religious piety; he finds the smooth flow of the sermon reassuring and the parson's voice 'kind', but what the voice says foolishly credulous. In the fourth stanza the boy shows boredom and, irreverently, lets his attention wander. In the last stanza he concludes that the church is a pleasant place in which to dream and let 'reason nod' and accordingly the appropriate place for an unreasonable belief in 'a forgiving God', but reality is elsewhere: 'a dumb blast sets the trees swaying/With furious zeal like madmen praying'. Here, as a result of the preceding development in the boy's awareness, the contrast between church and storm has become more sharply defined. The consolations of dreaming and 'letting reason nod', which the church has to offer him, are shown to be sentimental. At the same time the serious faith in a forgiving God is seen as a childlike, almost wilful refusal to admit the existence of the inhuman, unappeasable fury raging outside. The boy's initial curiosity about the latter, followed by an uneasy admiration for it, has matured now into a plain recognition of its horrors.

This is the most original poem in either of the first two volumes, being a successful amalgam of symbolic description, nursery rhyme simplicity ironically used, and humour. The nervous rhythms and the quick, jerky succession of impressions (for instance, in the stanza quoted) reveal beneath a casual, light-hearted tone the undercurrent of fear. It is the only poem to achieve a serious transformation of Graves's war experience into personal terms, or, except for 'Goliath and David', to treat his loss of faith in conventional religion seriously. The recognition on which it concludes is not a profound one—merely that war is a brute force and Christianity's way of meeting it irrelevant—but it is firm and undeceived. The use of a boy's consciousness, however, to reflect these attitudes, though it manages not to be sentimental, inevitably limits the quality of the emotional response expressed by the poem as a whole.

I have examined these three poems at some length because their use of symbolism anticipates the method of Graves's mature poetry. All it is necessary to say at this stage about his motives for using it is that it is a way of controlling his experience. At the same time as embodying emotions in a charged yet impersonal language it permits the mind to reflect on them at a distance. Another service it performs, which is evidently essential to Graves's caste of mind, is that it makes easy the expression of an ironic view; 'Goliath and David' and 'A Boy in Church' rely very much on it. Irony will become a common feature of his poetic style, and for this reason my survey of his beginnings would be incomplete without a mention of one other kind of poem that made its first appearance during this period: the ironic anecdote. There are two examples in *Fairies and Fusiliers*. 'Jonah', for example, tells how the 'vengeful' prophet foretold the destruction of Nineveh in forty days, but that when the Ninevites, by repenting of their sins, saved their city he resentfully left them, 'grumbling' to himself, regretting 'the glorious crash I've missed'. This fable is a pointed piece of mockery at the expense of the fire-breathing Christians who associated themselves with the aims of the First World War. It is the first, undistinguished example of a poetic genre characteristic of Graves; in conveying the poet's attitude not by direct reportage of events but indirectly through this kind of anecdote, it is obviously related to the symbolic poem.

The symbolic rendering of the inner drama, the anecdotal rendering of his moral judgements on the outer world, and the use of irony: these are the techniques that by 1917 had appeared in Graves's verse and were to be developed subsequently.

2

Love and Fear

IN JULY 1916 Graves was badly wounded in the chest and spent six months in England convalescing. When he had sufficiently recovered he asked to be sent back to his regiment in France. He saw no more fighting and soon, during the cold winter, with his lungs still weak, went down with bronchitis. For the last time he returned to England, where after another period of convalescence he was passed fit for garrison service at home. He spent the rest of the war at training camps in England and, briefly, in Ireland. In January 1918, at the age of 22, he married Nancy Nicholson, a girl of 18.

The chief legacy of his war experiences was severe shell-shock. In his autobiography he refers to it usually as neurasthenia and in his later writings sometimes as paranoia, in the general sense of a neurosis accompanied by hallucinations. He would continually meet in the streets people who had been killed in the trenches, and shells would explode about his bed at night. This kept his nerves in a permanently highly-strung condition. But the most terrifying and persistent consequence of his neurosis was his subjection to nightmares. He rarely mentions what they were about but, judging by the poems that describe them, they were not often manifestly about the war. They featured murder and apparently sexual horrors, and underlying many of them was an incomprehensible sense of guilt. There were other, less dramatic symptoms, which were perhaps more serious handicaps to his day to day existence; for instance, he was unable to use a telephone and if he met more than two new people in a day he could not sleep at night. Obviously city life was out of the question and so after his demobilization he and Nancy moved to a house in Harlech lent them by Nancy's father, where they stayed a year. Here he wrote most of the poems that were published in *Country Sentiment* (1920).

The title indicates the main theme: in his introduction to *Collected Poems 1938*, Graves summarized it as 'romantic love in a country setting'. Such a combination is a sure sign that his place was still in the ranks of the Georgian poets; several of his poems had appeared in Marsh's anthology for 1916–17 and several more were to be published in the last volume of that series, for the period 1920–22. Laura Riding and Graves enumerated the common themes of Georgianism in *A Survey of Modernist Poetry* (1927): 'it became principally concerned with Nature and love and leisure and old age and childhood and animals and sleep and other uncontroversial objects' (p. 119). The extent of his conformity was that he was pre-occupied with the first two ideas in the list and with childhood, but this did not prevent the majority of his poems from showing a by now distinct individuality.

In France Graves had used children as a way of forgetting the war; he writes in *Goodbye To All That* that immediately after his marriage his relationship with Nancy served the same purpose (p. 344). But with the birth of their first child, the regressive tendency returned. The atmosphere of childhood pervades *Country Sentiment*; it is to be felt even in the love poems, where romantic love assumes the innocent tones and rhythms of nursery rhyme, but, of course, is chiefly present in the nonsense poems and lullabies written specifically for his daughter, Jenny. 'Baloo Loo for Jenny' is tantamount to a roll-call of ancient cities in England and Scotland whose names are rich with associations in folk literature generally, ballad and song as well as nursery rhyme—Oxford, Chester, Berwick-on-the-Tweed, Stirling, Carlisle, and Edinbro'. Folk characters like 'Master Straddler' and his 'ten bold companions' play their parts in 'Hawk and Buckle'. There is even a moral tale for children in the Victorian manner, 'The Well-Dressed Children', the aim of which is to show 'how large the share of Vulgar Pride in peacock finery'. The nostalgia these poems display is less for the poet's own childhood than for the self-contained world of nursery rhyme, gay, fantastic, mysteriously evocative and made up of simple but intense sensations. The best of them is 'Allie', which has been retained in the *Collected Poems*[1] with only minor, verbal changes. It catches perfectly the spontaneous rhythms of nursery rhyme.

Allie has called in the birds:

> First there came
> Two white doves
> Then a sparrow from his nest,
> Then a clucking bantam hen,
> Then a robin red-breast.

This pattern is followed in the other stanzas; Allie calls in next the beasts and then the fish and lastly the children.

> First there came
> Tom and Madge,
> Kate and I who'll not forget
> How we played by the water's edge
> Till the April sun set.

By introducing himself as a character into this enclosed world the poet turns skilful imitation into wistful personal reminiscence. The scene suddenly springs away from the reader; framed and fixed at a distance, it becomes a miniature picture of an idyllic moment in the poet's past.

Country Sentiment shows a marked improvement in technical mpetence over his previous two volumes. The trend in them towards a plain, unrhetorical style is continued, but the part that ballads, nursery rhymes and folk songs play in its formation has become more important; they had been noticeable as a casual influence, but it is obvious that Graves has explored them more thoroughly since. In the best of these poems the influence has been completely absorbed: the ballad in 'Apples and Water' and nursery rhyme in 'Vain and Careless' have been put to quite individual use. Plainness had hitherto been, at best, a negative virtue—no more than an avoidance of the pretentious in syntax and diction: now it has developed expressiveness and, if anything, greater simplicity. It is evidently the need to find a vehicle to convey simple feelings in his

---

[1] Here and henceforward reference to the unspecific *Collected Poems* means *Collected Poems 1965* and some or all of the previous collections.

love poetry that is the force behind Graves's search for a language both intimate and modest. He achieves such a language in several poems: 'Loving Henry' is an average example, which no longer appears in his *Collected Poems*. I quote from the second stanza:

> Oh, Mary, must I say again
> My love's a pain,
> A torment most unruly?
> It tosses me
> Like a ship at sea
> When the storm rages fully.

The varying length of the lines reflects the fluctuation of feeling in the speaking voice, slowing down and quickening at the appropriate points. The imperfect rhyme frequently heard in all forms of folk literature and a part of their effect also contributes an awkward sincerity. The emotion is expressed with genuine simplicity, the lover's pain is to be felt in the mere syntax—'must I say again.. ?' and there is a sort of innocence in the touch of literary formality in 'a torment most unruly'. Yet, when all is said, it must be admitted that we have not merely simplicity of expression but also extreme simplicity of feeling. By modelling the poem's style, as also the characters, on nursery rhyme Graves has made this inevitable. His almost exclusive use of non-literary forms in this volume is to be explained, therefore, not only as a sign of the primary importance he attached to the genuine and the spontaneous (thought of as incompatible with literariness) but also, in part, as a retreat from the more complicated emotions.

Graves was attracted to the forms of folk literature by the quality, in the best examples, of bare, impersonal emotion. In his introduction to *The English Ballad* (1927), an anthology, he notes the effect on the individual ballad of continuous change; the poem, having lost its individual author and found a new one in the community, 'has all its bardic angularities smoothed away as pebbles are rounded in a stony stream' (p. 13). He makes the same claim, using the same image, for nursery rhyme in 'A Ballad of Nursery Rhyme'. But his motive for adopting a medium of expression smoothed and rounded by generations of use was not only to give a legitimate impersonality

31

to his poems but also, we might say, a way of softening the obstinate angularities of his most disturbing emotions. In 'Loving Henry', for example, the poet takes refuge (from the painful feelings described) in the conventional image of the storm-tossed ship, and elsewhere he finds an easy resolution of them in traditional folk song formulas.

Two poems in *Country Sentiment* are experiments in a freer use of iambic metre. J. M. Cohen has pointed out that they owe something to the accentual pattern of Early and Middle English verse. This is a new development in Graves's search for a plain, natural style. The verse is rougher and more heavily stressed than elsewhere in this volume and corresponds with a fiercer mood, for which his war neurosis is responsible. The first, 'Nebuchadnezzar's Fall', telling how the king for his pride was reduced to a bestial condition, is a recognizable allegory for the degrading experience of trench warfare; the second, 'Rocky Acres', is more remotely related to his neurasthenia, but the wild landscape it presents, where life is 'a hardy adventure, full of fear and shock', is at least in part symbolic of it. This poem has been much praised but, to examine only its rhythms at this point, its achievement seems to be limited.

> This is a wild land, country of my choice,
> With harsh craggy mountain, moor ample and bare.
> Seldom in these acres is heard any voice
> But voice of cold water that runs here and there
> Through rocks and lank heather growing without care.

The heaviness of the stresses and the way each line divides into two rhythmic units is certainly reminiscent of Anglo-Saxon verse. But the model is not entirely a happy one. The lines fall into a violent rocking motion which keeps the tone of the poem too rigidly declamatory, and prevents an easy flow from one line to the next, throwing such an emphasis on to the last word of the line that the rhymes clang with jarring monotony. This metrical experiment is more important for leading to a more sensitive and flexible use of blank verse and rhymed iambic pentameters in the next volume, *The Pier-Glass*.

The habit of presenting his experience obliquely in the form of allegory or symbol, which was noticeable in his previous volumes, has come to dominate the poems of this volume, almost to the exclusion of other methods, and is practised with greater skill. With few exceptions it will be the mark of Graves's poetry from now on. There is this paradox, that the source of his inspiration was more deeply personal than was the case with any of his Georgian contemporaries and yet from the start he was busy perfecting various masks or techniques for remaining detached from his emotions. His use of the themes, tones and formal conventions of folk poetry may be considered as part of the same endeavour.

It was more than the urge to escape from his war-neurosis that drew him to them. Graves has written poems modelled on ballad, nursery rhymes and folk song which display qualities of tone and rhythm and ways of approach that are valuable as devices for controlling individual experience. These qualities appealed to him because they implied attitudes that were already sympathetic. Those that he admired and imitated in, for instance, nursery rhyme—modesty, spontaneity, gaiety, wit—were ones that came naturally to a 'sanguine temperament' and which he also admired in the work of the Tudor poet, John Skelton, another early influence on his poetry. They are displayed to advantage in 'Vain and Careless', his most successful poem in the nursery rhyme manner.

> Lady, lovely lady,
>   Careless and gay!
> Once when a beggar called
>   She gave her child away.
>
> The beggar took the baby,
>   Wrapped it in a shawl,
> 'Bring her back', the lady said,
>   'Next time you call.'
>
> Hard by lived a vain man,
>   So vain and so proud,
> He walked on stilts
>   To be seen by the crowd.
>
> Up above the chimney pots,
>   Tall as a mast,

And all the people ran about
Shouting till he passed.

'A splendid match surely,'
Neighbours saw it plain,
'Although she is so careless,
Although he is so vain'.

But the lady played bobcherry,
Did not see or care,
As the vain man went by her
Aloft in the air.

This gentle-born couple
Lived and died apart.
Water will not mix with oil,
Nor vain with careless heart.

In several respects this is a characteristic expression of Graves's poetic personality. In the first place, the poem is an emblem: by which I mean here that the anecdote stands for, stands instead of, a moral proposition—that proud and careless people do not get on well together. Emblems must be distinguished from symbols. The symbol aims to bring together several associated experiences or areas of experience; the emblem aims to be entirely explicit: it represents an abstract generalization or narrows its range of association to a single area of experience. Its purpose is to make generalized experience communicable vividly and precisely. That the instances of vanity and carelessness, each an emblem in itself, come not from the poet's own life or contemporary life at all but from the folklore world of nursery rhyme is an advantage rather than not; the effect is to make the reader see the poem as a vehicle of judgement and to concentrate his attention less on the imagery, although this is striking, than on the poem's morality and especially the humour with which it is expressed. The humour is also a common element in Graves's style. It is coloured here by the nursery rhyme influence, but in its delicacy and its preposterous, dream-like logic (the man who was *so* vain he had to walk on stilts 'to be seen by the crowd') it is quite

idiosyncratic. In one other way—in being a poem of moral attitudes
—this anticipates Graves's mature poetry. These attitudes are not
necessarily made explicit. Their presence is to be felt chiefly, in this
poem, in the elegant dancing rhythms which mediate a tone of light
mockery throughout. In the first stanza, for instance, the brisk in-
souciant movement of the last two lines following hard upon the sweet
lilt of the first two adds a touch of sarcasm to the opening phrase,
'Lady, lovely lady'. As the poem develops the implications of this
tone become more precise, so that by the time we are presented, in
the penultimate stanza, with the picture of a vain man and a careless
lady who are being prevented by the incompatibility of their
'humours' from getting to know each other the effect is coolly ironic.
(Of course, this allegorizes disparities that exist within an already
established relationship.) Skilfully the poem's accumulated irony is
brought to bear on the otherwise innocuous phrase, 'this gentle-
born couple'. It is as though a moral comment held in reserve has
now been brought forward and made explicit: this is what it means
to be 'gentle-born'—to be incapable of generous self-involvement in
a relationship; the consequence of the woman's indifference and the
man's aloofness is that, metaphorically speaking, they must live and
die apart. The proverbial summary of the last two lines only rounds
off neatly an effect already achieved. By means of humorous fantasy,
modelled on nursery rhyme and sharpened by irony, Graves maintains an urbane detachment from the emotional situation contained
in the poem. Its connection with the poet's personal situation is
tenuous, and an appreciation of the poem does not depend upon
knowing it, but it seems to refer to conflict in his marriage between
the poet's pride and his wife's coolness. Pride is a theme that occurs
several times in *Country Sentiment* and occupies a central position in
the next volume, *The Pier-Glass*. 'Vain and Careless' is an attractive
poem; its limitation is the lightness with which it touches upon the
theme of personal conflict.

The folk influence continues in a group of poems modelled on
those ballads that consist entirely of dialogue. A famous instance is
'Lord Randal', which is a dialogue between mother and son; in other
cases the speakers are father and son or mother and daughter. The

situation, as in 'Lord Randal', is often tragic—by insistent questioning the mother finally elicits that he has been poisoned—and the
sparsely outlined relationship between parent and child that emerges
from the alternation of question and answer is an essential part of
that situation. Graves exploits this element in his dialogue poems.
He keeps to two stereotyped patterns of relationship. In 'After the
Play' and 'Apples and Water' the parents represent the wisdom of
experience; the message they bring to an improvidently generous
and sanguine youth is a stern one based on their knowledge of the
tragedy of life; they stand in the position of teacher to their children.
In 'The Cupboard' and 'A Frosty Night' the nature of the relationship is less easy to analyse. In each the dialogue is between mother
and daughter and the mother seems to have a potentially repressive
role to play: her questions are cruelly probing and provide glimpses
of a jealous, possessive love and a resentment against her child's
independence; the daughter is correspondingly secretive. All of
these poems dramatize the perennial conflict between the generations: between wise but arid age and spontaneous but foolish youth.
The stereotyped characters represent the opposing elements of an
inner conflict—youth the part that suffers, whether in neurasthenic
nightmares or in love, age the part that judges. In symbolizing
youth's confused rebellion as a refusal of parental authority Graves
may have been influenced by the discoveries of psychoanalysis, first
brought to his notice by the anthropologist and psychologist,
W. H. R. Rivers; a close study of folk literature could have yielded
the same insights. This conflict between generations may have had
a literal parallel in his experience but if so it does not manifest itself
in the poem.

What does manifest itself that is personal can be illustrated from
'The Cupboard', the poem that takes the least liberties with the
traditional ballad theme. The speakers in it are mother and daughter.
Three times, each time more pressingly, the mother asks her
daughter, Mary, what lies in the red mahogany cupboard with
'shining crystal handles' that stands in her chamber. To two of the
questions Mary gives evasive answers but to the third she replies
truthfully; I quote the final exchange:

Mother
What's in that cupboard, Mary?
And this time tell me true.

Mary
White clothes for an unborn baby, mother
But what's the truth to you?

The revelation is that Mary has had a lover, who perhaps has deserted her, and the bitterness of her rejoinder both reflects her distress and implies a knowledge of her mother's inability to understand or sympathize with the 'truth' asserted by such a love, indicating as it does loneliness and anguish. The tone of the mother's questions is, indeed, unsympathetic, and in this she seems to represent the traditional attitudes of society. The mahogany cupboard with 'its shining crystal handles' is an evocative symbol of tradition, against which by independently taking a lover and conceiving a child the daughter has rebelled. The story in no way allegorizes Graves's personal situation but, more subtly, is a dramatic symbol—objective correlative would be a better description—for a conflict of allegiances in him. (In *On English Poetry*, p. 123, the poet is defined as one in whom diffusion of loyalties gives rise to conflicting sub-personalities which strive for reconciliation in his poems.) The cupboard focuses opposing reactions to the established order—a fondness for its rich, glowing colours and its solid worth and the impulse to disown its old-fashioned restrictions; on the other hand, love is both an assertion of freedom and a hazardous, painful experience. These personal emotions have been successfully objectified without being denied or simplified; but the poem does not offer any solution to them, except in so much as a successful embodiment of them is a solution. At this stage of his development such honesty is an achievement, but it is a limited one: the unquestioning acceptance of emotional deadlock.

'A Frosty Night' (included in the *Collected Poems*) makes a bolder attempt to present personal conflict. 'The Cupboard' dramatizes an opposition between lover and society, and merely hints at the conflicting elements in romantic love itself; 'A Frosty Night' by taking the latter as its theme is, one feels, coming closer to the real centre of disturbance. Again the speakers are mother and daughter, but this time the mother's role is not a representative one: Graves relies less on his models for the way he presents his material. It begins in the usual way with the mother asking Alice, her daughter, why she is 'dazed and white and shaken', and the daughter answering evasively; but it is a departure from the folk-ballad tradition when the mother herself reveals Alice's secret. These last four stanzas (of which I quote two) contain the crux of the love situation.

Mother

Ay, the night was frosty,
  Coldly gaped the moon,
Yet the birds seemed twittering
  Through green boughs of June.

Your feet were dancing, Alice,
  Seemed to dance on air,
You looked a ghost or angel
  In the starlight there.

And she concludes by accusing her daughter of being in love. Giving this revelation to the mother rather than to the daughter has a startling effect. We are presented with a symbolic picture of love as a source of both frightening and ecstatic emotions, and the accusing tones in which she describes them communicate a quality of menace to the ambivalence of such an experience. The rhythmic alternation of question and answer, which gives to the poem a feeling of mounting urgency, is an admirable medium for transmitting the sense of unease that this experience of romantic love generates, the suggestion of something cruel and ominous. This poem is important as being the first to frame a conception of love that has been fundamental to his poetic thought ever since. Love has two aspects, baleful and benevolent ('ghost or angel') and the succession of one by the other is unpredictable and cannot be influenced. Out of this seed eventually grew the whole of the White Goddess mythology. The poem even makes symbolic use of the moon, which is to become the chief symbol in the mythological poems; here it evokes love in its

38

baleful aspect, in its phase of wintry unfulfilment, for which Graves's name in a poem, 'A Love Story', that immediately precedes the mythological poems, is 'Queen Famine'.

In submitting to the influence of folk-ballad, folk-song and nursery rhyme Graves was seeking to dissolve personal conflict in a traditional, generalizing situation. The situation is implicit in the form of these poems (for instance, in the dialogue form) as well as in their themes, and so the influence necessitated close, in some in- stances servile, imitation. His experiments in this mode produced some successes (the best example is 'Apples and Water', which is retained in the *Collected Poems*), but it is difficult to see where they could have led if he had continued with them.

A more promising technique, and one that establishes itself in Graves's repertoire, makes its first appearance in 'Rocky Acres'. Here a special landscape ('country of my choice') is made to embody the poet's generalized moral response to his (unspecified) experi- ences. It happens that in this case the response is morally repellent, gloating and complacent ('tenderness and pity the land will deny', 'terror for fat burghers in far plains below'), but the handling of this new form is confident. A symbol for his neurasthenic condition and by analogy for the condition of society in post-war Britain, which also established itself and had its implications extended in Graves's later work, was that of the haunted house. 'Ghost Raddled', for example (it was later renamed 'A Haunted House' and appears in the *Collected Poems* under that title), makes use of the folk lore of hauntings to represent his 'haunted' mind. It tells of 'honest men' terrified out of sleep by guilt-laden dreams—'Of lust frightful, past belief, Lurking unforgotten', of 'spirits in the web hung room' and 'demons in the dry well'. The symbolism does not attempt to dis- guise the poet's real distress; in fact the contents of his nightmares are fairly precisely summarized. Neither are the supernatural phen- omena introduced gratuitously: the 'web hung room' and the 'dry well' where they take place are accurate images for the ordinarily unused, unvisited areas of consciousness responsible for our dream- life; and that it is 'honest men' who suffer from guilt feelings is the crucial fact in Graves's neurasthenic experiences. At the same time this is a controlled rendering, and is made so by an interesting device, the dramatic frame. The poem is a dialogue between the poet, represented perhaps as a minstrel, and an ungracious audience, on whom presumably he depends for his livelihood. They demand entertainment—'Come surly fellow, come! A song!'—which the poet is indisposed to give them; he compels them, instead, to choose from the 'tales of wrong and terror' that are all he has, and follows this with examples of his haunted condition already mentioned. By casting himself in the role of 'surly fellow' (a sort of licensed cynic like Shakespeare's Fools) pitted against a normally insensitive and uncomprehending audience he dramatizes and thus explains the bitter tone of the ensuing narrative of horrors endured—explains it, that is, as a suitable expression of the character's surliness. I do not mean that he dissociates himself completely, or even much, from his persona but that by adopting it he sets his feelings in a context which makes sense of them. For the bitterness is directed outwards at the audience; the poem ends:

> A song? What laughter or what song
> Can this house remember?
> Do flowers and butterflies belong
> To a blind December?

The suggestion is that Graves's public would like undisturbed and undisturbing poems but that he considers this is not the time for them; his war neurosis is not an unrelated phenomenon but parallels a neurosis in humanity at large—'this house' is one in which both he and they live. Consequently the tone of the poem implies, and in the last stanza throws down, a challenge—to the sentimental complacency and superficiality of a society that has forgotten (as the poet has not) the horrors of war. This is an interesting anticipation of the militantly unsentimental poetry that Graves began to write in 1926, in which a more forthright baiting of his readers also played a part.

A personal theme is what the poems of *Over the Brazier* and *Fairies and Fusiliers* notably lacked. 'Romantic love in a country setting' supplied it in *Country Sentiment*. He has been more consistently a love poet than any other twentieth-century English poet, and certainly there are examples of love poems in his latest collection which are unsurpassed by anything written since Hardy's *Poems of 1912–1913*. Yet at this stage, with perhaps one exception, the impulse behind them is defensive. 'A Frosty Night' is the only one honestly to reflect the insecurity that Graves apparently felt, and this unease and bewilderment come through powerfully in the juxtaposition of conflicting images—a cold wintry moon and the birds in summer trees, frost and starlight—to represent the two faces of love. The imagery is romantic and transforms the experience, but without falsifying it. It is admitted in 'Loving Henry' that his 'love's a pain', and the radical uncertainty of his feelings which obviously caused this pain is hinted at in Mary's insistent questioning —she doubts the permanence of his vows and anxiously demands reassurance—and yet to her question, 'why do you love me?', Henry can only reply with a repetition of his hyperbolic protestations of fidelity, never quite answering her question in the sober spirit that alone would content her. The motive of the poem is, evidently, more the desire to appease than to tell the objective truth. Playfulness is a common mood in these poems and is in keeping with the evasiveness of Graves's tactics in dealing with the emotional difficulties of his marriage. His purpose was to smooth out the difficulties rather than confront them. 'One Hard Look' (still retained in the *Collected Poems*, though cut and rearranged) is a series of emblematic illustrations of the proverbial 'little things have large consequences'. Each emblem—for instance, the gnat's whine terrifying the sleeper with its 'trumpet's din', or the mouse arousing more fears at night than the lion at midday—is an analogy for the disproportionate effect that small insignificant gestures have on lovers' feelings:

> One smile relieves
> A heart that grieves
> Though deadly sad it be,
> And one hard look
> Can close the book
> That lovers love to see.

What seems, at first, decoration of a simple statement reveals itself on second reading as a tactfully cushioned warning from the poet that if she continues to treat him badly she will destroy their love, and a tacit plea for more smiles and fewer hard looks. Again, as in 'Loving Henry', the poem's intention is impure; in this case it is the rhetorical one of persuasion.

The other theme which made its first appearance in this volume was Graves's neurasthenia. The war, which had made little positive impact on his war-time verse, in its aftermath of nightmares and hallucinations had a permanent effect on his development as a poet. As mere subject-matter it informed his poetry for only a few years, though the occasional nightmare poem has appeared from time to time since then; but morally its effect went deeper, arousing in him a latent capacity for endurance, a perseverance and resilience that ensured his eventual triumph over a tendency towards sentimentality and evasion of his emotions. But these qualities are hardly yet evident in *Country Sentiment*. With the exception of 'Ghost Raddled', the poems that exclusively deal with his neurasthenic experiences all supply false resolutions to the emotional disturbance. In order to turn this material to account Graves needed before anything else to discover ways of accepting the mere existence of what seemed to be a second, autonomous self, a nightly visitor apparently unrelated to and unknown by his waking self. This he tries to do in the dialogue poem 'Dicky', but his method is to simplify the problem. On the one hand, Dicky's description of his eerie encounter with an old man in the churchyard converts nightmare into a literary ghost-horror, a bogey to frighten children (though recalling his earlier description of the dead German in 'A Dead Boche'):

> I grew afeared
> At his lean lolling jaw,
> His spreading beard.

On the other, the advice his mother offers to allay his fears is of the kind that comforts after the event but would not give a victim strength to face the experience again: the day and the 'glorious sunshine', she says, belong to us, then 'grudge not the dead their moonshine/When abroad they ride'—in other words, be grateful for being alive and pity the dead; which is a trite response to the situation, for an irrational, physical terror cannot be met by sweetly reasonable moralizings. Moreover, for Graves to envisage neurosis as nothing but an arbitrary, meaningless torment from which one can seek protection but which is basically incomprehensible is to deny a half of his experience.

Both 'Outlaws' and 'Ghost Raddled' are better poems because they explore possible interpretations in an effort to absorb this half as a significant part of the poet's experience. 'Ghost Raddled' does this, as I have explained, by seeking a parallel between his own condition and the condition of society. 'Outlaws' attempts a larger interpretation but is not completely successful. The forces that irrupt from the poet's unconscious at night are symbolized as the pagan gods now no longer worshipped, banished from consciousness, but still leading a subterranean existence. This is an interesting conception, which links the findings of psychoanalysis and anthropology, but the poem fails to make clear the nature of the poet's attitude towards these gods. They are de la Mare's bogies, 'shrunk to shadows', but they are also descendants of the 'proud gods' 'Who spoke with thunder once at noon/To prostrate kings'. They are 'malign', 'Greedy of human stuff to snare/In webs of murk', and once commanded the reverence of an 'unclean muse', yet 'these aged gods of fright and lust' continue to impress if only by their sheer longevity, having outlived many creeds and faiths. Graves is uncertain whether to fear, be disgusted by, or respect these 'outlaws'. The title suggests an attempt on the poet's part to give recognition to, even to identify himself with, the rebellious nature of these primitive forces, whose arrogance though now defeated obviously appeals to something in Graves's personality. But he has not quite been able to overcome his fear and resentment of their cruel, capriciously exercised power.

Interestingly, in the version revised for *Collected Poems 1959*, signs of this reluctance have been removed. Thus the old gods are no longer 'shrunk to shadows', which implies a contemptible diminution of their original status, but 'tamed to silence', which carries just a hint of a dignified biding of their time; the moral loathing conveyed by 'an unclean muse' has disappeared in the new phrase, 'a drumming muse', where the epithet is not merely neutral but suggests a different kind of muse, the Muse-goddess of the later poetry to whose capricious rule Graves now submits without complaint. This suggestion is enlarged in another emendation: the pagan gods who in their prime spoke 'With thunder from an open sky/To peasant, tyrant, priest' are now represented as speaking 'To warrior, virgin, priest'. The first grouping is merely one of social rank and expresses (with emphasis on 'tyrant') a sour view of ancient societies; the second grouping, however, is by vocation, and by being silent on the subject assumes a respectful attitude towards the ancient social hierarchy. The important new character is the virgin, whose vocation was to be the servant and mouthpiece of the oracular demi-god and originally, as at Delphi, of the mother-goddess; she and the 'drumming muse' introduce elements from the later mythological poems and imply a very different view of paganism from the one Graves held at the time of writing this poem. What is interesting is that Graves should see a connection between the 'old gods' of this poem and with the White Goddess of the later poetry; it allows one to infer that there is also a connection between his early neurasthenia and the experiences symbolized in the mythology of the White Goddess, who, he claims in 'The Personal Muse'—an essay included in *Oxford Addresses on Poetry* (1962), appears to poets 'in dreams and paranoiac visions' (p. 60). In the same essay (borrowing the phrase 'wet woods' from 'Outlaws'), he points out that the White Goddess no longer receives public worship but has been 'banished to *wet woods* and bramble-bound ruins' (p. 58); the borrowing establishes the connection, and suggests that similar experiences (which Graves has merely reinterpreted) underly the two symbolisms.

The poem which, in providing an objective correlative, most completely transforms the neurasthenic experiences is 'Rocky Acres'. In fact, except for one or two betraying phrases, this grounding is almost invisible. But the relationship is a significant one, and the clue to what is unsatisfactory in the poem lies, I think, in the *way* they have been transformed. The poem describes a landscape which is the equivalent of a certain moral landscape favoured by the poet.

44

The perceptible links with Graves's personal situation are, firstly, that living in this 'wild land' is 'A hardy adventure, full of fear and shock' and, secondly, that its hilltops are 'strongholds for the proud gods': the nightmares were 'full of fear and shock' and, as is apparent in 'Outlaws', he conceives of the 'proud gods' as reigning over this submerged area of his consciousness. The landscape with its 'harsh craggy mountains, moor ample and bare' is the one near Harlech also celebrated in his war-time volumes. However, it has acquired characteristics not noted at that time—chiefly, brutality. The poet celebrates it for its freedom from not only human but animal life; mice and birds are never safe from the hovering vulture who 'scans his wide parish with a sharp eye' and if he sees any small creatures 'tears them in pieces'. It is hard to avoid the impression that Graves identifies himself with the cruelty, the absence of 'tenderness and pity', which is the chief characteristic of this country, and with the 'proud gods' who terrorize 'fat burghers on far plains below'—in other words, with the forces which are the instruments of 'fear and shock' in his nightmares. Evidently he is trying to overcome the terror of being a victim by identifying himself with the ruling powers that are responsible for this cruelty; and the psychological dishonesty of such a course accounts for the moral unpleasantness of the position he has adopted and for the implausibility of the triumphant tone. I have already referred to this tone as declamatory; I would further characterize it as strident and in parts bullying and gloating. The description of the vulture's hovering flight and ruthless destruction of 'small hidden things' is certainly gloating; the following lines illustrate the other qualities:

> Yet this is my country beloved by me best,
> The first land that rose from Chaos and the Flood,
> Nursing no fat valleys for comfort and rest,
> Trampled by no hard hooves, stained with no blood.

In eschewing the sentimental solution to the painfulness of his experiences which several poems in this volume provide, in refusing to look for it in 'comfort and rest', Graves has reacted too far in the other direction. 'Outlaws' in its original version is an uneasy experiment with the same strategy. 'Ghost Raddled' is the most satisfactory of these three poems, because there is no pretence in it that the emotions it presents are anything other than painful; it succeeds in embodying the poet's acceptance of them without denying or ignoring this fact.

Graves explains in the Author's Note introducing *Whipperginny* (1923) that the mood of the *Country Sentiment* poems originated in 'the desire to escape from a painful war-neurosis into an Arcadia of amatory fancy'. A considerable change takes place in the general mood of *The Pier-Glass*, published only a year after *Country Sentiment* in 1921. One poem in *The Pier-Glass*, however, embodies the escapist impulse more fully, but more explicitly, than any in the previous volume. One might have guessed that this was the motive behind the pastoralism of many of the earlier poems but 'The Finding of Love' is the first to state it. To that extent it is a better because more honest poem. It begins with a description of the 'nightmare mood' which preceded 'this generous time/Of love' and an admission of his longing to be released from it. The rest of the poem is an ecstatic celebration of Love in magical, de la Mare-ish imagery, drawn chiefly from fairy story. There is no attempt to disguise the purpose of such imagery or of the rhythms:

> With o, for Sun to blaze
> Drying the cobweb-maze
> Dew-sagged upon the corn,
> With o, for flowering thorn;

it is a magical incantation to induce relief, culminating in the intense, desperate gratitude of this:

> Here's Love a drench of light,
> A Sun dazzling the sight.

This is a self-aware exercise in romanticism, confessing its origin in insecurity. But by comparison with these lines it is possible to measure the amount of self-deception in the falsely triumphant conclusion, in which the poet assures himself that desire has become actuality—an *achieved* 'love in steadfastness'. At this point romantic longing and honesty are in the balance and the scales have been tipped in favour of the former. But even apart from the bluffed ending the limitations of this poem from *The Pier-Glass* epitomize the limitations, in general, of the *Country Sentiment* poems: neither of the themes, war-neurosis and love, is explored; the former is regarded merely as an appalling and apparently causeless fact, the latter is hailed simply as a panacea for all ills. The interpretations of the war-neurosis offered by 'Ghost Raddled' or 'Outlaws' point not to causes but to parallels in society and in pagan religion, respectively. The development in *The Pier-Glass* is towards self-exploration and self-discipline—in the love poems as well as in the poems concerning his neurasthenia.

The moral and psychological discovery on which several of these poems centre is of the close relationship between the poet's 'pride' and the persistence of his neurasthenic sufferings. A reference to this pride has been noted in the love-poem, 'Vain and Careless', but a more direct anticipation is to be found in 'Nebuchadnezzar's Fall'; in this poem, as I have also explained, Graves links the punishment to which the king is subjected for his pride—changed into animal form and compelled to grovel in the mud with the beasts of the field —with his own experience of trench-warfare, and he equates Nebuchadnezzar's state of mind, 'webbed with a grey shroud vapour-spun', with the melancholy which accompanies his neurotic condition. This suggests that the neurotic symptoms are the direct result of some kind of pride. Yet the analogy is relatively fanciful and not entirely clear; the poet's moral attitude is uncertain, hovering between horror at the king's fate and the desire to see it as having a salutary effect ('Mist drew off from his mind').

There is still moral confusion in the original version of 'The Pier-Glass' and in some ways the allegory is puzzling. Even so it is a much more impressive poem, chiefly because it gives a closer and terrifying rendering of the nightmare experience while at the same time probing and attempting a more thoughtful attitude towards the guilt feelings at the centre of it. The blank verse, as handled here sensitively and with control, is an improvement on the pounding rhythms of 'Rocky Acres' as a medium for closely organized narrative and compact thought.

The speaker in the poem is a woman who is apparently condemned, for an at-first unnamed sin committed in the past, to
haunt the house in which it took place and in particular a room con-
taining 'a huge bed of state'. The poem is an allegory for his neurasthenic state of mind:

> Lost manor where I walk continually
> A ghost, while yet in woman's flesh and blood.
> Up your broad stairs mounting with outspread fingers
> And gliding steadfast down your corridors
> I come by nightly custom to this room,
> And even on sultry afternoons I come
> Drawn by a thread of time-sunk memory.

The 'lost manor' is reminiscent of the haunted house in 'Ghost
Raddled' and the 'lost land' in 'Rocky Acres', both of which are
images for the poet's shell-shocked mind; here it is the place of the
woman's dream. While the dreamer is still 'flesh and blood' her
dream-self is 'a ghost'; accordingly she visits the manor at night or
during the troubled slumbers of 'sultry afternoons'; it is in dreams,
too, that repressed ('time-sunk') memories come to life again. Here
in this room, is the bed ('A puppet theatre where malignant fancy/
Peoples the wings with fear') and 'A sullen pier-glass cracked from
side to side' which, proudly,

> Scorns to present the face as do new mirrors
> With a lying flush, but shows it melancholy
> And pale, as faces grow that look in mirrors.

The woman asks if there is no life here; she can find none, not even
a rat, a fly or a spider, and outside is a picture of elemental chaos.
There is nothing, in fact, to distract her from a consideration of
herself.

> Face about,
> Peer rather in the glass once more, take note
> Of self, the grey lips and long hair dishevelled,
> Sleep-staring eyes.

She prays to the mirror, however, to be released from her mental
suffering, to be allowed some hope that true, natural life exists

somewhere. 'Sleep-staring eyes' confirms, I think, that this is a dream; primarily it is an image of the dreamer's hopeless melancholy, but physically it represents a sleepwalker.

In the recent collections the poem ends here—with the woman's plea to be delivered from this state of death-in-life. As such it makes a powerful effect but leaves one or two loose threads. What part does the 'bed of state' play in the 'island mystery', what is the woman guilty of that she should be punished with these obsessive memories? In its original form the poem continues with another twenty-five lines which are meant to provide both an answer to these questions and the token of 'true life', the promise of deliverance from the grey chaotic world of neurosis, implored by the woman. She feels the token and the promise in her pulse as she views the ordered, disciplined activity of a swarm of bees. And then we learn what the problem was: she had, it seems, been wronged in love and had been faced with a choice between two courses of action—'Kill or forgive' her lover? She chose to kill and the bed was the scene of the murder. Surprisingly, since we have been prepared for a new development by the bees and a 'new mood of judgment' which they imply, when faced again with the old question she obstinately and proudly remains true to her original choice, the 'strong solution': 'Kill, strike the blow again, spite what shall come'.

What the poem is most successful in doing is in making an image of Graves's neurasthenia, conveying the exact quality of his feelings—the hopelessness, the sense of meaningless unreality. In the cut version of the poem he keeps close to the actual experience of it: there is a hint of the underlying sense of guilt (and that this is retribution for some evil act committed in the past) but no identification of a known crime to account for it—it is an arbitrary, capricious 'malignant' fancy that makes the bed an object of fear. The mood, in reaction from that of *Country Sentiment*, is 'aggressive and disciplinary' (Foreword to *Whipperginny*); true, the desire for release from this state is intense but it is balanced against a proud refusal of the escapist solution—'Face about...take note/Of self' makes this point clearly. It is this pride which gives the poet the moral strength to 'face' the truth about himself—that the neurosis is not accidental but an essential part of his personality. The '*sullen* pier-glass' mediates this view of the situation when it, proudly, 'scorns to present' a 'lying' reflection 'as do new mirrors' but shows the woman's face to be 'melancholy/And pale, as faces grow that look in mirrors'. This truth about himself is also a general truth, again symbolized by the pier-glass: that evil is a part of every condition, and that being inextricably involved in his past actions man cannot disown his inheritance of past evil; the glass is old and cracked and refuses to present a flattering picture, as do new mirrors that take no account of the past. Specifically, therefore, these lines express Graves's acceptance of the guilt feelings and the suffering they entail but also, generally, they reveal a more responsible, courageous view of experience than he has shown before. Despite the loose threads already mentioned the poem as now printed is an impressive achievement.

The reason for the additional section in the original version, which reads like an afterthought, was, probably, the need to make a more aggressive gesture against the tyranny of neurasthenia, and a general dissatisfaction with the poem's inconclusiveness. But it is chiefly responsible for the confusion in the poem. Insomuch as the guilt feelings are of unknown origin a moral attitude towards them is inappropriate. Yet Graves is a moral poet—one for whom judgement plays a necessary part in the poetic resolution of his personal problems; it is essential that he take up a moral position. Hence he invents a past murder as the cause (the origin of his neurasthenia in his war experiences presumably helped him to this explanation) to remove this difficulty; the moral choice is now a fictitious one—between murder and forgiveness. The fact that the woman chooses murder, however, discloses Graves's dissatisfaction with this strategy. The choice reflects Graves's protest against a sense of guilt when he has committed no crime rather than considered diabolism. There is a conflict between the poet's awareness that his neurasthenic state is inexplicable in terms of origins, and is therefore not susceptible to moral comment in such terms, and the desire nevertheless to explain it in order to make moral decision possible. By throwing the emphasis on to origins Graves has concealed from himself the real moral insight buried in the poem; which is that pride, if not the cause, is at least partly responsible for the continuance, of the neurasthenia. Even in the shortened version of the poem, however, the poet has somewhat perversely given all his moral support to pride. Pride not only enables him to endure the evil that he glimpses through his neurosis but compels him, obscurely, to endorse it. This is a flaw in the poem as it now stands.

The same moral perversity disfigures another poem in this volume, 'Distant Smoke'; which presents the murderer Cain, an outlaw—'Man, yet outside the tents'—in a romantically favourable light, an object of wonder to the sons of his brother Seth. In 'The Gnat', however, a strange allegory which fails to embody the poet's personal emotions, the blame for neurasthenia is allotted unambiguously, divided between an original sin done in past years, for which mental suffering is 'due earnings of transgression', and pride, which has 'outlawed his heart' by stifling 'repentance' and is responsible for the persistence of this suffering. As in the complete version of 'The Pier-Glass', some form of release, of unexplained provenance (in 'The Pier-Glass' imperfectly explained), is envisaged, although the poet is not satisfied that it is the perfect solution. During an analysis of the poem in *The Meaning of Dreams* (1924) Graves informs us that the concluding lines of 'The Gnat' refer to his fears at the time of writing that a psychoanalytic cure of his neurosis would kill his poetic inspiration (pp. 164–5).

The best of the neurasthenic poems is 'Return'. The poem is an address by the poet to his alter-ego. It begins with the poet proclaiming the end of a 'seven years' curse' and of his exile from the 'kind land' of mulberry and apple trees. The alter-ego has been responsible for this punishment: it is for *his* 'pride' that he, the poet, has been made the 'scapegoat' victim. At first, in return, he plans revenge to make the alter-ego suffer as he has suffered, but relents; this will not serve his present purpose: he needs 'a wider peace… More ample than my own release', and he concludes, 'Go with forgiveness and no hate'. The idea of an original crime has been abandoned; by attributing all the blame to a present cause known to the poet, his pride, Graves has produced a much clearer moral situation. Pride no longer means a refusal to repent some fictitious sin but is equated with the 'cold, malicious brain/And most uncharitable, cold heart' of the alter-ego, which recalls the 'malignant fancy' that terrifies the woman in 'The Pier-Glass'.

But most important is the different attitude towards his neurosis that Graves has adopted. 'Release', implored by the woman and then rejected, desired and feared by the poet in 'The Gnat', is no longer his chief aspiration; he seeks 'a wider peace' (in recent collections, 'a surer peace'). The last stanza, in which this phrase occurs, is vague; in the revised version the tone has been sharpened and the logic tightened up but no attempt has been made to make this idea of 'peace' more precise. But obviously it is meant to express something of Graves's new self-disciplinary mood, which is reflected in the imagery and texture of this poem much more surely than it is in 'The Pier-Glass':

> Here, Robin on a tussock sits,
> And Cuckoo with his call of hope
> Cuckoos awhile, then off he flits,
> While peals of dingle-dongle keep
> Troop discipline among the sheep
> That graze across the slope.
>
> A brook from fields of gentle sun,
> Through the glade his water heaves...

Hope of release, symbolized by the robin, herald of the New Year, and the cuckoo, herald of Spring, is tempered with the readiness to work for it (as the brook *heaves* water through the glade and the bells keep troop *discipline* among the sheep). The imagery of effort and discipline is supported by a density of 'k' and 'p' sounds in the words, which compels the reader to enact a difficult but determined progress. To some extent the conceit of the ego and the alter-ego, representing on the one hand the waking self and on the other the evil self that finds expression in neurasthenic nightmares, helps to clarify the poet's moral position; for it is a dramatic conception which focuses one's attention on the conflict between the good and the bad and on the moment of moral choice between them. The

choice between 'forgiveness' and 'hate', another version of the alter-
natives proposed in 'The Pier-Glass', here has implications more
germane to the actual situation allegorized than it has in the other
poem: the poet must decide between a course of action which will
perpetuate the conflict and 'forgiveness', which will take him
beyond the conflict. He chooses forgiveness—'Here let the story end'
is the last line—and in so doing is only naming a decision the effect
of which it is possible to feel in the disciplined progress of the whole
poem. As a symbol for the divided self the ego and alter-ego idea
was an important discovery for Graves; it was extended and discussed considerably in the next three years, and after a period of
disuse was revived during the 'forties and has been ever since an
integral part of the White Goddess mythology.

Each of these four poems in its exploration of Graves's war-
neurosis suffers from a certain incoherence. This is even true of
'Return', where the working out of the 'divided self' allegory is
flawed at one or two points: what meaning for instance, can the
idea of the ego's revenge on the alter-ego have in actual experience?
The most completely realized poem treating this material, but setting
it at a much greater distance from the poet, is 'The Stake':

> Naseboro' held him guilty,
>   Crowther took his part,
> Who lies at the cross-roads,
>   A stake through his heart.
>
> Spring calls, and the stake answers
>   Throwing out shoots;
> The towns debate what life is this
>   Sprung from such roots.
>
> Naseboro' says 'A Upas Tree';
>   'A Rose,' says Crowther;
> But April's here to declare it
>   Neither one nor other.
>
> Neither ill nor very fair,
>   Rose nor Upas,
> But an honest oak-tree,
>   As its parent was.

A green-tufted oak-tree
On the green wold,
Careless as the dead heart
That the roots enfold.

The poem begins with Graves's conflict. The pain of his divided
state is expressed vividly but with emblematic compactness in the
image of the heart split by the stake. The impact of the image is the
stronger for the quiet restraint with which the conflict is stated. The
poet represents it as an argument as to whether the dead man had
been guilty or not, thus pinpointing the crucial symptoms of
Graves's neurasthenia, his irrational sense of guilt. There is nothing
elsewhere in this volume to match the quiet, matter-of-fact confidence with which release from conflict is acclaimed—'Spring calls'
and 'April's here'; the question of guilt or innocence is gently set
aside as now irrelevant, for death has been succeeded by new life—
he is 'Neither ill nor very fair', nothing more nor less than 'an honest
oak-tree', untroubled by the old heart-searchings. The allegory
works out exactly; every word and every rhythm tells. The fourth
stanza is a good example of the style: the syntax as bare as it can be,
the movement skilfully irregular following the inflections of the
speaking voice, the tone plain, sturdy, almost but not quite abrupt
(it might be called soldierly, for it matches the attitudes of the two
characters, Naseboro' and Crowther). Against this matter-of-fact
background the full effect of the symbol, the 'honest oak-tree', is
felt. The values to which this phrase appeals—those of a rich, durable
common life—derive from balladry, but they are not evoked un-
thinkingly: they are defined by contrast with the legendary baleful-
ness of the Upas tree and the perfection of ideal love, symbolized by
the rose, and sensitively expressed in the tone and rhythms of the
verse. The poem shows a mastery of ballad rhythms while remaining
completely an independent achievement. Surprisingly, it has not
appeared in any of the collections since *Poems 1914-1926*.

The love poetry since *Country Sentiment* has become more intense. The theme is still 'the pains of love', but it is presented now
without charm or coyness. The poet's problems have forced themselves uncompromisingly into the centre of the picture, and he can no

longer assume that they can be wished or flattered away. It is indicative of this intensity that revised versions of two of these poems,
'Morning Phoenix' and 'The Kiss', have found a place in the recent
three-book sequence of poems, beginning with *More Poems 1961*,
which contains some of Graves's most powerful love poetry. In
'Morning Phoenix' the poet is 'Scorched by love' and longs for
'Minnow-peopled country brooks...Sunless valley-nooks' of cool
thought where he might escape the torments of passion and restore
'calcined heart and shrivelled skin', and become 'A morning
phoenix'. The longed-for rebirth is not fact, as it is in 'The Stake'.
'Lost Love' also fails to provide a solution. The lover

> wanders god-like and like thief
> Inside and out, below, above
> Without relief seeking lost love.

Love, as in 'A Frosty Night', is a matter of extremes, either of
ecstasy, when the lover is accepted, or extreme humiliation, when he
is rejected. Yet the despair of the rejected lover has its compensa-
tions; it is represented as stimulating the preternatural alertness and
insight necessary to the poet:

> he can
> Clearly through a flint wall see,
> Or watch the startled spirit flee
> From the throat of a dead man.

These talents are ones attributed in Celtic and Greek myth to seers
and heroes. This is the first occasion on which Graves has identified
the triumphs and pains of lover and poet ('god-like and like thief')
with those of the mythological heroes; it is an isolated occasion but
this impersonation, interestingly, anticipates the role he assigns to
the poet-lover in the White Goddess poems.

In 'The Kiss', again, the poet is unable to imagine a resolution
of his problem. The position presented is a deadlock between romantic emotion and an unacceptable reality; for the first time, however,
the theme is not the general 'love is a pain' but a specific difficulty.
The same development is taking place in the love poems, then,
as in the poems of neurasthenia: with the growth in insight goes a

determined attempt to write a more self-exploratory poetry. The poem distinguishes between two phases of love. In the first stanza (which reprinted in *New Poems 1962* has become a poem in its own right) is described the ecstasy and fear of anticipatory desire and the concentration of the whole self into a single all-absorbing moment:

> Spellbound to a word
> Does Time cease to move,
> Till her calm grey eye
> Expands to a sky
> And the clouds of her hair
> Like storms go by?

Compared with this, the imagery of the last two stanzas is a little facile and the rhythms perfunctory, and for those reasons, presumably, Graves decided they were not worth rescuing. They describe the second phase of love, consummation (I take the kiss to stand for the sexual act), which only 'obscured desire' and returns the lover to his separate, scattered elements, the original 'void and dearth'. The same image is used for this state of despairing disillusion in the man-woman relationship as for the grey hopelessness that is the result of neurasthenia in 'The Pier-Glass'. It is the first sign that Graves has discovered a pattern in his experience which brings together the two hitherto discrete themes—the beginning of a steady progress towards the self-understanding on which his mature poetry is based.

Similarly, there is a connection between the moment of desire here and the unchanging landscape of 'Rocky Acres': each presents a state of being in which all sense of time is lost. Images of timelessness recur frequently in Graves's poetry; they evoke a world of unchanging values to set against the flux of life lived in time. Here the range of suggestion is narrowly romantic; later, in such poems as 'Time', 'On Portents', 'Worms of History', and 'Through Nightmare' the ideas of time and timelessness will imply a deeply felt, carefully thought-out moral scheme and will not involve outright rejection of physical reality.

The personal development brought about in Graves's poetry between 1918 and 1920, during which time the poems of *Country*

Sentiment and *The Pier-Glass* were written, was the gradual coales-
cence of the two halves of his divided self. The process was not yet
completed. The division lay between his awareness of irruptive
forces bringing disaster, confusion and a sense of meaninglessness to
his emotional life, and his longing for release from disaster, for the
restoration of order, and ultimately for positive values which might
rescue him from uncertainty and give some moral centre to his
mental world; a helpless awareness because he did not know how
release could be effected or what sort of order and values would
give him strength to accept his condition, and a fruitless longing
because it was essentially romantic and impractical in form. At first
he saw the two sides more simply than this: the two-headed Janus,
the emblem by which he represents poetry in 'The God called
Poetry' (*Country Sentiment*), has one head of comfort and one of
terror—'He brings down sunshine after shower,/Thunder and hate
are his also'. Moreover he identified them respectively with the two
kinds of experience that were dominant themes in his poetry at this
time, love and neurasthenia; his neurosis was to him merely something terrifying, and in love he saw merely a source of comfort. This
was an unexploratory view of both kinds of experience. As he
explored more deeply he came to realize that each elicited from him
the same conflicting responses—on the one hand a realistic awareness
of 'evil', and on the other an impulse towards order and some faith
permanently available as a source of spiritual strength. For instance,
in the neurasthenic poems the mere registering of pain and fear of,
say, 'Ghost Raddled' was soon replaced, in 'The Pier-Glass' and
'Return', by a deeper insight into the evil responsible for the pain;
in the later love poems the intensity with which pain is realized and,
specifically, the image of chaos in 'The Kiss' reveal a parallel awareness there. Again, as the love poems gained in the recognition of evil
so the later neurasthenia poems carry intimations within themselves
of a source of strength beyond the evil imaged from which a solution
might come. In 'Ghost Raddled', from the earlier volume, a poem
which ends on a note of impotent protest, a protest by one half
against the other half of the poet's divided self, no such source is
evident; whereas in 'Return' it can be located in the imagery of

57

effort and self-discipline, and 'The Stake' records a state beyond struggle, an achieved victory of good over evil. The love poems in *The Pier-Glass*, however, do not display the same resourcefulness. They show honesty—the painful situation is admitted—and 'The Kiss', in particular, is perceptive about the discrepancy between desire and possibility, but the impulse towards good is still an ineffectual longing rather than a resolve to work towards a moral position which would enable him to accept this discrepancy. In the love poems, in short, Graves was still committed to a disabling, unmodified romanticism, the belief in a good to be won without struggle.

3
'Love's Defeat'

IN OCTOBER 1919 Graves went up to Oxford, where he read for a degree in English. The poems that appeared in *The Pier-Glass* (1921) were written between 1919 and 1920. He failed to sit his Finals examination but was given permission to proceed to the higher degree of Bachelor of Letters. The subject he offered was *The Illogical Element in English Poetry* and the result of his researches was, in fact, published four years later as *Poetic Unreason* (1925); this was accepted in place of a formal thesis.

In 1921 Graves and Nancy moved away from Oxford to a cottage in Islip, where they lived until 1925. This began a new phase in his writing. Neither of his postwar volumes had had much success and after *The Pier-Glass* he ceased to expect it; he made no more attempts to write for the ordinary reading public. One other volume of poems, *Whipperginny* (1923), was published commercially, but it was followed by four volumes in limited or virtually limited editions. His next public venture was the first collection of his poems, *Poems 1914–1926* (1927), which brought this period in his poetic development to an end.

Whipperginny was in several ways a surprising volume. Neurasthenia as a theme had almost entirely disappeared and the situation in the love poems had changed considerably. These now recorded the loss of the poet's initial romantic emotion and the waning of desire.

In 'Sullen Moods' he attributes his sullenness, his ungentleness in love, rather to self-dissatisfaction—'indignation at my own/ Shortcomings, plagues, uncertainties'—than to dissatisfaction with the relationship. He asks the woman to

> Be once again the distant light,
> Promise of glory, not yet known
> In full perfection—wasted quite
> When on my imperfection thrown.

59

The poem is an attempted evasion of the seriousness of his situation. Rather than admit and accept his present loss of desire the poet must make it a reason for self-accusation and an idealization of the initial romantic love. He is indignant that he cannot have love in 'full perfection' because he will not recognize that the 'uncertainties' that beset him as a consequence of his neurosis are an inevitable part, too, of his experience of the man-woman relationship.

Another strategy to which Graves has recourse to escape despair is the creation of ideal images of love. In 'The Red Ribbon Dream' the poet dreams that 'Dazed for the memory of a lost desire', he stands alone in the upper hall of a house unable to enter any of the rooms, which are locked against him. Without warning, however, a door opens and a voice says 'Easily', and another voice says 'Come', and at once he is able to proceed unhindered to a place 'past all hope', a place where more than anything he longs to be. He finds there a girl 'Whose beauty I knew to be fate and all/By the thin red ribbon on her calm brow';

> Then I was a hero and a bold boy
> Kissing the hand I had never yet kissed;
> I felt red ribbon like a snake twist
> In my own thick hair, so I laughed for joy.

Suddenly the dream ends, and he is once more outside the rooms;

> Once I found entrance, but now never more,
> And Time leans forward with his glassy wall.

The poet is well aware of the status of this kind of image. He is explicit about its origin in his despair at the loss of desire. It is a dream of impossible perfection, 'past all hope', based on memories of romantic falling-in-love ('Kissing the hand I had never yet kissed'), and of being released from the bonds of Time, which reasserts its power when the dream ends. Without being openly self-critical Graves allows himself a certain irony: 'Then I was a hero and a bold boy' is cruelly contemptuous of his own innocence as a lover. For the girl's snake-like ribbon twisting in his hair symbolizes the inevitable betrayal that follows the ecstasy of romantic love and heralds the return of the poet's despair.

The poem is not, however, successful as a whole and has not appeared in recent collections: the self-contempt is a little too near self-pity, and the place symbolic of love contains some embarrassing allegorical objects—'The cushions were friendship and the chairs were love,/Shaggy with love was the great wolf skin'. But in some respects the conception of love approaches the one which informs the later, mythological poems, that first appeared in the 'forties. The notion of timelessness is here escapist but it came to be used with greater seriousness; in particular, in the White Goddess poems it has become a criterion for evaluating experience. The girl with the 'calm brow' whose beauty is the poet's 'fate', benevolent and malignant, in joy or despair, is related to the Fatal Women of late nineteenth-century literature, but in a general way anticipates the Goddess herself. The idea of love which the White Goddess Myth dramatizes is that it is a cycle in which periods of reciprocal love and periods of estrangement or betrayal succeed each other in regular rotation like the seasons; the same idea can be seen here in embryo. The snake is a traditional emblem of betrayal—noted by Graves in *Poetic Unreason* (p. 35)—but also appears in the mythological poetry with this meaning.

A better poem is 'The Ridge-Top'. The subject is again loss of love, but its title in the collections, 'Love in Barrenness', points to the same cyclic conception of love as an underlying assumption in the poem. The bleak landscape described—snow-topped mountains, fields of boulders, plains covered with heath, and moors—stands as symbol for the lover's desolation: he and the loved woman 'heard the lost curlew/Mourning out of sight below'. Then the North Wind, pressing against her body so that her dress and her hair were swept back behind her, moulded her into an image of inaccessibility, of love withdrawn:

> So now no longer flesh and blood,
> But poised in marble thought you stood,
> O wingless Victory, loved of men,
> Who could withstand your triumph them?

Her stance is that of the Greek sculptures of Winged and Wingless Victories, embodiments of joyous triumph. For Graves she is a *wingless* Victory because hers is a triumph of barrenness not fulfilment. In this bleak reversal of the usual associations of these sculptures lies the only hint of the poet's pain in accepting this phase of love. Yet the image remains an embodiment of some kind of victory —if not of the warm reality of felt love, then of the cold ideal of love, denied but still longed for and still revered.

But this kind of acceptance of experience—more the conversion of defeat into affirmation—was not characteristic of Graves's writing during this period. The strategy was romantic, though without the sentimentality of 'The Red Ribbon Dream', and the tendency now was antiromantic. 'Song of Contrariety' is more representative of the new mood making its first appearance in this volume. The same problem, the waning of desire, confronts the poet. But it is the paradox of the situation which engages his attention: when the woman denied him her favours he could still enjoy her in dreams that compensated for his despair; but now that her 'flesh and blood consent.../Joy and passion both are spent'. The poem conducts neatly and drily a methodical argument—logical yet paradoxical, as in Metaphysical poetry:

> Far away is close at hand,
> Close joined is far away,
> Love might come at your command
> Yet will not stay.

In 'The Ridge-Top' Graves distances himself from his emotions by the use of symbol, in 'Song of Contrariety' by formulating them intellectually. But, as with the best Metaphysical verse, it is not so much a matter of abandoning emotional tension as of finding its equivalent in the abstract or argumentative mode. The personal impact of his experience is still there—to be felt in the tautness of the argument and the pervasive presence of self-mockery. The poem is an implicit moral criticism of the kind of dreaming that appears in such poems as 'The Red Ribbon Dream'. This tone and this strategy were new to Graves but after a short time of experiment soon came to play an important part in his verse, notably in the period that began with the publication of his first collection in 1926 and ended with the appearance of his second collection in 1938.

In *Country Sentiment* love was the one certainty in Graves's experience, a place of sanctuary, as it were, from neurasthenic disturbance. In *The Pier-Glass* the love poems were beginning to reveal a core of disturbance. Even so, though love might be painful, it was undeniably there, and apparently proof against time and change. But with the new theme in *Whipperginny*, the almost exclusive preoccupation with the problem of 'lost love', went the recognition that now there was no value, not even love, that was unchallengeable. Confronted with this situation he adopted regressive tactics in 'Sullen Moods', and in poems like 'The Red Ribbon Dream' set out to create compensatory ideal images of love. 'The Ridge-Top' and 'Song of Contrariety', however, in their opposite ways, contrived satisfactory resolutions and they have kept their places in recent collections: both admit and accept that in love the emotions are unpredictable, not to be counted on, are beyond the individual person's control.

This reluctant discovery is the more intensely explored theme of 'Children of Darkness': that freely given love between two people necessarily creates uncertainty; anxiety and discontent are, in a sense, the penalties for such freedom. The poem contrasts the 'certitude' which informs the acts of darkness with the painful 'freedom' of daylight love. The blind satisfactions of physical love enclosed the lovers in a charmed circle of apparent safety, and the 'night-seed' that engendered the children of darkness 'knew no discontent,/In certitude his changings went'. Day restores powers of reflection; the poet asks why it is

> That in this freedom, by faith won,
> Only acts of doubt are done?

The question answers itself: for 'by faith won' means that freely given love is an act of faith between two people ('the union of two prayers by faith' is its definition in *The Feather Bed*, a long poem published in the same year as *Whipperginny*) and as such, depending on no external assurances, is by its very nature a precarious achievement. During my examination of the wartime volumes, in Chapter 1, I argued that the attitude most suited to Graves's poetic temperament is one of studied detachment from the (invariably strong) emotions that give rise to his poems. It was an attitude that in the next two volumes he rarely succeeded in fully establishing. As Graves explains in the Author's Note introducing *Whipperginny*, these were years in which he was suffering from a painful war neurosis and the 'increasing emotional stress' was reflected in his poetry. He announces that in most of the poems in this new volume 'will be found evidences of greater detachment in the poet and the appearance of a new series of problems in religion, psychology and philosophy, no less exacting than their predecessors, but, it may be said, of less emotional intensity'. There is, certainly, greater detachment in the two love poems, 'The Ridge-Top' and 'Song of Contrariety', than in most of his previous love poetry. The symbolic method of the former and the intellectual austerity of the latter—comprising a verbal plainness, clipped unemotive rhythms, and a tone of mockery—are, in fact, recognizably the principal strategies for impersonality adopted by Graves in his mature poetry. Roughly speaking the latter method predominated during the next phase, from 1926 to 1938; the former has predominated since then; though, to be more precise, one would have to say that since 1938 something like a fusion of the two modes has taken place.

But Graves in his Note is probably not referring to these poems when he mentions detachment; he has in mind two kinds of poems which, apart from some immature instances in *Fairies and Fusiliers*, are a new departure for him. These are firstly cynical poems, the themes of which range from love to religion; secondly theoretical poems which take religious, psychological and philosophical ideas and wittily argue them through to the point where they can be confirmed or refuted. Evidently both kinds were the result of a conscious plan for renewing his poetry and were a reaction against the incoherence that seemed to be threatening it in *The Pier-Glass*. He continued resolutely with this plan until about 1925. Of the poems written during this period very few have remained in his collections. In the Foreword to *Collected Poems 1938* (p. xxi) he notes that anything worth preserving from these years was written in spite of rather than by help of his new theories. Basically his opinion does not seem to have altered since, but there is perhaps evidence of greater leniency toward them now in the fact that ten of the eighteen previously discarded poems revived as *The More Deserving Cases* (1962), and published in a limited edition, first appeared during these years.

The aim of the cynical poems was, by treating his problems with unromantic flippancy, to lessen the emotional tension in himself. The purely cynical approach is not usually a fruitful one in poetry; but these poems are often unconvincing simply because they were written with a preconceived purpose—as psychotherapy for the poet rather than as truthful and coherent responses to the mental situations in which they originated. They are unconvincing largely for the same reasons that many of the poems in *Country Sentiment*, written to help Graves forget his war neurosis, are unconvincing. The *Country Sentiment* poems are often sentimental, these in *Whipperginny* are militantly unsentimental. They may, therefore, appeal more to contemporary taste, but the motives underlying both groups of poems are equally escapist.

'The Lands of Whipperginny' ('The Land of Whipperginny' in the amended version which appears in the collections) is as it were a rewriting in the cynical, antiromantic mode of some of his early love poems. Its theme is the paradoxical nature of love. It was first given effective expression in 'A Frosty Night' (*Country Sentiment*), where love was imaged as a fusion of opposites, frost and starlight, representing the two faces of love, benevolent and baleful. The subject has been the central, often painful preoccupation of Graves's love poetry. Here he makes a bid to dismiss the problem once and for all by refusing to take it seriously. The lovers are watching the sunset and the poem opens, in a parody of the pastoral style, with the man's addressing to his sweetheart a series of nonsensical endearments—'sweet honeysuckle, my coney' (the parody technique seems to be influenced by Dunbar's 'The Man of Valour to his Fair Lady'). The sun diffuses a glow of uncertain meaning, symbolizing their love, over the wood, and the first stanza ends with a challenging gesture of indifference:

> Be this Heaven, be it Hell, or the lands of Whipperginny,
> It lies in a fairy lustre, it savours most good.

Whatever the meaning of love's ambivalence, it is of no importance to the lover, for whom all that now matters is (in a debunking phrase that denies any higher significance to romantic love) 'it savours most good'. The poem makes a virtue not only of not caring but of not knowing; it is deliberately inconclusive. In the second and final stanza the music of psalms, which the lovers hear coming from the chapel on the moor, carries two contradictory messages; at one moment it seems to be saying that love is 'a howling of whores', at the next that it is 'an airy glory too strange to be spoken'; the poet makes no attempt to decide which it is. This pose of facetious unconcern strikes the reader as an uneasy one because the anti-romanticism is expressed in romantic images—'fairy lustre', 'airy glory', 'a low sun gilding the bloom of the wood'—which betray an intense commitment to the experience that ostensibly the poet is belittling.

In recognition of this Graves has since modified these two stanzas, removing all traces of cynicism, and has added a third which provides the conclusion that the poem originally lacked. The last two lines of the first stanza now read:

> Is it Heaven, or Hell, or the land of Whipperginny
> That holds this fairy lustre, not yet understood?

It is this lack of understanding that the uncertain tone of the first version betrayed. The last stanza, as it appears in *Collected Poems 1965*, reads:

> Soon the risen Moon will peer down with pity,
> Drawing us in secret by an ivory gate
> To the fruit-plats and fountains of her silver city
> Where lovers need not argue the tokens of fate.

The imagery and two lines of this were drawn from *The Marmosite's Miscellany*, a satire on contemporary poets first published under the pseudonym of 'John Doyle' in 1925. It is a resolution which offers, not a new understanding of love's elements, but an image of an ideal state of being: moonlight smoothes out the unevenness of an intractable reality. The moon with its 'ivory gate' and its 'silver city' is a symbol for the poet's release from the normal fate of lovers, the perpetual alternation of joy and despair: it is a place, therefore, 'Where lovers need not argue the tokens of fate'. This strikingly anticipates the moon symbolism in some of the White Goddess poems. Here, however, the feeling is escapist (in *The Marmosite's Miscellany* passage the Moon is 'the Mistress of escape and pity'); in the later poems the romanticism is at the service of a complex and positive conception of love.

'Richard Roe and John Doe', a development of the ironic anecdotal style that had first appeared in *Fairies and Fusiliers*, is a more successful exercise in cynicism. It records how Richard Roe, who had been cuckolded and cheated by his enemy, one John Doe, longed for the qualities and the fortunes that would enable him to bear his wrongs. He wished in turn for the wisdom and strength of mind of Solomon, for the power of Alexander, and for the patience and religious belief of Job. The cynical 'twist' comes in the last stanza (I quote from the more carefully written revised version):

> He wished himself Job, Solomon, Alexander,
> For patience, wisdom, power to overthrow
> Misfortune; but with spirit so unmanned
> That most of all he wished himself John Doe.

His determination to *oppose* misfortune was less strong than the unmanly, secret desire to have none to oppose.

'The Lands of Whipperginny' fails because in it the poet clumsily evades the poem's central emotional situation; whereas in 'Richard Roe and John Doe' no attempt is made to disguise the real painfulness of Richard Roe's plight. All the poet's cynical energies are concentrated in the debunking of false, high-sounding rationalizations calculated to obscure the painful truth of Richard Roe's situation. The cruelty of the poem's mockery testifies, despite the off-hand tone and the brusque rhythms in which it is conveyed, to the poet's involvement in the character's sufferings rather than the contrary. Interestingly, the abstention from straightforward moral comment—the refusal, in fact, to take the kind of moral stand that Graves tried for in some of *The Pier-Glass* poems—is largely responsible for this. The tone of 'so unmanned' in the last stanza, for instance, is not so much morally disapproving as jeering, and mixes a measure of sympathy for the poor worm Richard Roe with contempt for his weakness. Implicitly the poem is saying, 'he is weak, but then aren't we all?'

At least by the time Graves had gathered together these poems for publication in *Whipperginny* he had come to appreciate that the cynical mode was only a temporary expedient: that they were evasions of his despair rather than a solution to it. The title poem makes this point when it defines their character through an analogy with card-playing: as 'we have recourse.../To Courtly Bridge for stress of love', so these poems are 'A game to play apart/When all but crushed with care'. There is evidence of this saving self-awareness in several of the poems; in for example 'The Lord Chamberlain Tells of a Famous Meeting', a poem which has not been reprinted since its appearance in his first collection, *Poems 1914–1926*.

The poem is not cynical but belongs with that group because it is antiromantic and favours a neutral, unexcited attitude towards the poet's problems. The Lord Chamberlain of the East Kingdom tells of a chance meeting between the princes of East and West, each disguised, in the hostile camp of the Middle Kingdom. Though each knew the other neither gave any sign of recognition; they played cards together and then went their separate ways. In itself the meeting was undramatic and uneventful, and yet through the tacit understanding which grew up between East and West during the game, it proved later to be a 'turning movement in world history'. The Lord Chamberlain then warns the reader never to believe embroidered accounts of what happened, here recorded plainly and honestly, offered by credulous annalists, approved biographers, elegant essayists, vagabond dramatists and allegorical painters. This is an attractive, witty poem. It allegorizes a self-admonition—to put off the various romantic disguises in which hitherto Graves had decked out his conflicts and to state the plain truth. One's only criticism is that this scepticism is not self-denying enough; for the plain truth is that the occasion was even more heroic than the annalists, biographers, essayists, dramatists and allegorical painters had made out—an over-comfortable conclusion.

The poem offers however not only, through the Lord Chamberlain, a model viewpoint for the poet but also, in the behaviour of the two kings, a model of restrained conduct for the man. For of all the sights seen by the Lord Chamberlain

> That was the noblest, East encountering West,
> Their silent understanding and restraint,
> Meeting and parting like the Kings they were
> With plain indifference to all circumstance.

But as applied allegorically to Graves's personal conflicts 'plain indifference to all circumstance' strikes one more as an aristocratic pose deliberately assumed, perhaps ironically, for the occasion than as a genuine, viable alternative to emotional intensity. It works negatively as antiromanticism but not positively. Graves is well aware of how much gesture and how little substance there is in this attitude: the pose is consistent, for instance, with the style, direct but stately, which he has adopted from his persona, the Lord Chamberlain. That it *is* assumed ironically, is not meant as a serious alternative to what is dismissed, is made clear in an earlier passage— when East

> For an instant let the heavy soldier-mask,
> His best protection, a dull cast of face,
> Light up with joy.

Dullness like 'indifference', Graves admits, is a mask to conceal emotion not replace it.

Cynicism, as Graves almost immediately recognized, was not a serious answer to his problems; he soon abandoned this tactic. It was in what I have called the theoretical poems that the seeds of his development during the next two or three years lay. In a passage from the Author's Note already quoted, Graves announces 'a new series of problems in religion, psychology and philosophy' as the material on which these poems work. This does not make it clear that they were, in fact, despite appearances, a direct development out of his earlier poetry. The poems of *The Pier-Glass*, for example, were written in states of severe emotional conflict, brought about by the difficulties of his marriage as well as by his neurasthenia. The

theoretical poems of *Whipperginny*—the same holds for the subsequent volumes, *The Feather Bed*, *Mock Beggar Hall*, and to a large
extent for *Welchman's Hose*—were the final results of a period of
intellectual reflection upon the reasons for this psychological state;
they were attempts at abstracting some general, philosophical
lesson from the confusion of his previous experience.

Such poems as 'The Bowl and Rim' were the first in a series of
analyses of the *idea* of conflict. It might be conflict between people,
classes, groups, nations or religions, yet, since Graves still regarded
the poet as a person in whom the warring 'group-consciousnesses of
particular sects, clans, castes, types, and professions' are housed
together in the form of subpersonalities struggling for reconciliation
in his poems,[1] the implied analogy was with his inner conflicts and
the analysis was only a wider application of conclusions drawn from
his introspections.

'The Bowl and Rim' is the story of how a rabbi and a friar,
representatives of hitherto irreconcilable religious points of view,
were condemned to live together for many years in a dungeon cell.
As time passed and as by 'joint distress' they came gradually to
appreciate the need for peaceful co-existence they grew closer to
each other, until at last they had fully 'Learned each to love his
neighbour well'. They abandoned religious hostility and together
re-examined the tenets of their separate faiths, only to find that in
both there was the same inconsistency of doctrine. Love had been
the agent of their reconciliation and it was in the quality of love that
each religion was imperfect. Together they arrived at a new conception, neither Jewish nor Christian. Christ had said 'Love all men as
thyself', but then had made an exception of the Pharisees. The friar
spoke for the rabbi too when he declared:

> If they did wrong, He too did wrong,
>   (For love admits no contraries)
> In blind religion rooted strong
> Both Jesus and the Pharisees.

Only in crucifixion was Christ perfect, for

---

[1] *On English Poetry*, p. 123.

> He died forgiving on the Tree
> To make amends for earlier spite;

only then could he and did he become an image of perfect love:

> Man-like he lived, but God-like died,
> All hatred from His thought removed,
> Imperfect until crucified,
> In crucifixion well-beloved.

This parallels Graves's own psychological history in that it was the persistence of 'distress' that forced him to his present conviction that the conflicting elements within himself must learn to tolerate each other. The important conclusion he comes to in this and other poems is that conflict cannot be solved by fighting; fighting only perpetuates conflict. For instance, to love the good man and hate the sinner is incompatible with the kind of love that Graves envisages— a love which reigns only in the absence of conflict and righteous hatred, a perfect tolerance. Both 'The Pier-Glass' and 'Return' dramatized this struggle for dominance between the two halves of the poet's divided self, the one thought of as good and the other as evil. The last stanza of 'Return' already had the germ of the new attitude: the poet tells his alter-ego, in terms which we recall when reading 'The Bowl and Rim', to 'Go with forgiveness and no hate', and the 'wider peace' in the interests of which forgiveness is granted vaguely anticipates the perfect love of the later poem. Yet at that time Graves still thought in the conventional moral mode and identified good with the favoured self and evil with the self currently out of favour, and so 'Return' ends with the faint suggestion that hatred, though rejected in name, is only dormant and peace only temporary. In 'The Bowl and Rim' the idea of good and evil has changed: now it is conflict itself—whether between principles *called* good and evil or not—that is the evil to be combated, and good is the peace or love that is both the consequence and the instrument of reconciliation.

This aspiration towards a state of emotional tranquillity is the nearest to a general motive in *Whipperginny*, which is a heterogeneous collection of poems in a variety of moods and styles. It reveals itself sometimes in the poet's cynical determination merely to withdraw from the area of conflict; on other occasions, for example in 'The Lord Chamberlain Tells of a Famous Meeting', in his partial adoption of the classical approach to experience and his practice of the classical virtues of soberness and restraint. In several poems like 'The Bowl and Rim' it is expressed philosophically, as a state beyond conflict; these poems, like many of Blake's, express paradox in simple stanza-forms and regular metres to stress the idea-content and use allegory no longer as a means of tidying dream-images but as a medium for clear, unambiguous thought. This assertion of the mind's control in the planning of his poems and the introduction of classical attitudes are the important events in Graves's development during this period. But the examples in *Whipperginny* of this change as yet lack the personal tone—the wit and irony that appear, for instance, in *Welchman's Hose* (1925)—that will make theoretical argument the convincing expression of recognizably personal experience.

Yet at least half the poems included in *Whipperginny* are written in the earlier modes. 'A False Report'—especially the technically more polished version of it which now appears in the *Collected Poems* under the title of 'Angry Samson'—is sufficient reminder that the emotionally committed poem can achieve impersonality without the loss of personal tone.

Are they blind, the lords of Gaza
  In their strong towers,
Who declare Samson pillow-smothered
  And stripped of his powers?

O stolid Philistines,
  Stare now in amaze
At my foxes running in your cornfields
  With their tails ablaze,

At swung jaw-bone, at bees swarming
  In the stark lion's hide,
At these, the gates of well-walled Gaza
  A-clank to my stride.

This is a proud, aggressive assertion of the poet's ability to recover from the torments of despair in love and to confound those ('Philistines' in the Arnoldian as well as the biblical sense) who perhaps doubted that his poetic powers would survive the struggle. The tone is not modest but neither is it boastful for, by assuming the persona of Samson, Graves has borrowed the right to take his (God-given) strength for granted. The terse contempt of the first stanza expresses the confidence of a person who has never paused to question the sufficiency of his powers, and who therefore has no desire to waste words in proving it. As part of Samson's story the blazing foxes, the ass's jaw-bone and the swarm of bees are extraordinary but inevitable symbols of poetic renewal—of energy, richness and, in the dead lion swarming with bees, a kind of death and resurrection. The poem has been separated from the poet, impersonalized in the manner of 'The Ridge-Top' rather than 'Song of Contrariety', by this use of symbolism—in conjunction on this occasion with the related device of impersonation.

But the speculative trend was now the main one; there was a direct line of development from such poems as 'The Bowl and Rim' through *The Feather Bed* (1923), which was being composed between 1921 and 1922 at about the same time as the later poems in *Whipperginny*, to *Mock Beggar Hall* (1924) and *Welchman's Hose* (1925).

The Feather Bed consists of an Introductory Letter addressed to John Crowe Ransom; a Prologue, which symbolically sets the scene for the poem; the title-poem itself, which is an angry but inconclusive interior monologue—passages of conscious reflection alternating with dream-sequences—by a man whose lover had deserted him to enter a convent; and an Epilogue, which offers a symbolic resolution of the man's conflicting attitudes to his situation that in the poem he has failed to work out for himself. The poem combines a psychological study of the frustrated lover with speculations about love, secular and religious, and the nature of Jesus Christ. Without the help of the Introductory Letter it would be hard to extract a consistent theory from these deliberately disorganized reflections, intended as they are to mirror the confusion of the man's motives. The Letter throws light on the obscurities of the Prologue and

Epilogue too, explaining the sequence of thought by reference to which sense can be made both of *their* symbolism and of the poem's psychological action.

Graves writes to Ransom that he has been reading the Old and New Testaments 'as a record of the progressive understanding of God throughout the ages by a single representative race, the Jews', and has come to the conclusion that the idea of God has 'three degrees at least'. There is, firstly, the primitive idea of God, the creator of man but of man still animal of the animals, the God, in other words, of the self-seeking animal instincts. Then there is Jehovah or Jove, the God of 'the new experimental period called civilization'. The conflict between the repressed, latent animal instincts and the 'new principle of social order…split the primitive idea of God into two, the ideas of Good and Evil, Good being the approval by the social mind of those non-conscious workings of the body which further its aims, Evil being the condemnation of the old Adam inclinations which run counter to it'. This is 'the God of the present, predominantly male, violent, blundering, deceitful'. Finally there is Lucifer, the Morning Star, 'the hope of eventual adjustment between ancient habits and present needs'. He is the spirit of reconciliation who 'puts out of date the negative virtues of Good fighting with Evil, and proposes an Absolute Good which we can now conceive of as Peace'. This is 'the doctrine of tolerance', and 'the doctrine of mutual responsibility for error, and of mutual respect between individuals, sexes, classes, groups and nations'. This is the aspect of God that was glimpsed by Jesus Christ but was soon forgotten by his followers, who have fallen under the renewed tyranny of Jehovah.

The idea of God is, in this outline, man's developing moral consciousness. One may conjecture that Graves arrived at this particular account of it as much through introspection as through his study of the Bible. For it is easy to see that the three degrees in the idea of God can be paralleled by the three stages in the development in Graves of a moral conception of his neurasthenia and the changing symbolisms with which he represented it in his poems; they also correspond to roughly three different attitudes in the love poems towards the man–woman relationship.

His first idea of his neurosis was like the Jew's primitive idea of God. It seemed to reveal a world in which the usually repressed instincts prevail, but according to no moral law: a world belonging to the 'old gods…malign' of 'Outlaws', in which the spirit of animal cruelty that, for example, pervades the land of 'Rocky Acres' rules. These are the forces which Graves discovered in his nightmares. But the fear and horror of them that he expressed in 'Ghost Raddled' and 'Outlaws' suggest that his point of view was that of the 'civilized' person of the second stage in man's moral development. This 'civilized' idea of neurosis got its fullest and most characteristic expression in 'The Pier-Glass'. Just as the single, undifferentiated idea of God split into two, so Graves discovered that his psyche was divided between two selves, the self that belonged to the 'old gods' and a self hostile to them; and he conceived of one side as representing Evil and the other as representing Good. At this stage he saw the moral life as a matter of inevitable conflict—Good pitted against Evil. He was undecided, however, about which were the Good and which the Evil elements in his psyche. In 'The Pier-Glass' the poet's pride is the Good, but in 'Return' it is the Evil responsible for all his sufferings. The final stage in the development of this idea is about to take place. Graves is not sure how much, in his own case, it is a psychological idea—'the hope of eventual adjustment'—and how much a fact. There were *hints* of a new attitude in *The Pier-Glass*: I have already instanced the last stanza of 'Return'; a more revealing example is 'The Stake'. There the poet refuses to choose between the guilt or innocence of the dead man; he is 'Neither ill nor very fair' but 'an honest oak-tree', not discussable in terms of Good and Evil. This bypassing of the ethical question and the acceptance of the whole man is the psychological equivalent of the social 'doctrine of tolerance'.

The three degrees in the Jewish idea of God also correspond to three kinds of response that Graves has had towards the uncertainties of the man-woman relationship. Instead of marking stages in a developing point of view they make up a composite idea of love; they may appear separately in different poems, or together in the same poem. The first kind of response was that of bewilderment or numbed despair at the sufferings which as a lover he must undergo; it is implied in such poems as 'The Kiss' that lovers are the victims of some cosmic joke. The perpetrators of this joke might well be the lurking gods of the unconscious described in 'Outlaws'. 'Old Wives' Tales' (*Whipperginny*), which now appears in the *Collected Poems* revised and retitled 'Mermaid, Dragon, Fiend', argues that these creatures of fable have not a literal but a metaphorical existence—as representations of the unaccountable, irruptive forces in man's psyche, 'bound by natural laws', that ultimately control our lives, and that the mermaid symbolizes the malign force which destroys the hopes of lovers and betrays the ideal of love: 'Mermaids will not be denied/Of our last enduring shame'. In *The Feather Bed* the Prologue, the poem, and the Epilogue stand, respectively, for the three aspects of love, which are also the three aspects of God since love is given both its religious and its secular senses. The Prologue describes how a traveller lost his way in a bleak, hilly country; all his attempts to find a path down were circlings round the same place, a 'sedged pool of steaming desolation' know as the 'Witches' Cauldron'. He tried once again, but after six miles of walking he came upon a finger post which read, 'The Witches' Cauldron One Mile';

> There was a dead snake by some humorous hand
> Twined on the pointing finger; far away
> A bull roared hoarsely, but all else was mist.

Suddenly a 'graceful hare' with 'innocent eyes' came leaping down towards him out of the mist. In general anger and resentment he gave chase, hurling stones and shouting at her until she screamed with fear. This traveller is the lover, 'leg-chafed and footsore' after his day's walking, whose interior monologue makes up the title-poem. The Witches' Cauldron, the pool of desolation, symbolizes the lover's despair, and the whole episode the inescapable frustra-tions of his love-affair; the hare is the woman, cruelly made scape-goat for his wretchedness. But the significant lines for my argument, those that illustrate most pointedly the first aspect of love, are the ones quoted. The 'dead snake' is symbolic of a dead desire in the lover (the theme of the love-poems in *Whipperginny*) and the 'hoarse bull' perhaps of a baffled love; once again there is some apparently vindictive power at work, for the snake was twined 'by some humorous hand' round the finger pointing to the desolate pool, as if it were jeering at him, assuring him that he is trapped. In the Epilogue Graves identifies the finger post with Nehushtan, a pagan god rejected by the worshippers of Jehovah, and the bull with Aaron's idol of a golden calf. Though arbitrary, this identification makes his intention plain, which is to attribute the sudden disasters that overtake lovers to the agency of an amoral primitive life-force resembling the primitive conception of God. The irony of love is that underlying the ideal which each man and woman tries to realize is this unappeasable chaos waiting to engulf them. In the poem the man, reflecting on the violence of his emotions, concludes:

> Break the ideal, and the animal's left
> Which this ideal stood as mask to hide.

Graves's second kind of response to love answered by his account to the Jews' idea of Jehovah, a typically 'male, violent, blundering, deceitful' God. The lover in 'The Feather Bed', whose response is of the bullying sort, favours a conception of Christ as a proud and violent man rather than the bringer of peace and the teacher of the doctrine of tolerance: his is the Christ who whipped the money-changers from the temple, the scourge of sinners. His own pride will not let him submit to the uncertainties of love: he must have a scapegoat, and Rachel, his beloved, evidently suffered for his frustration and resentment as the hare did. He wonders whether the best way to escape from the unbearable deadlock of his emotions would be 'To beat Love down with ridicule'; which is the course that Graves took in the cynical poems in *Whipperginny*.

His third kind of response to the man-woman relationship was, again in *Whipperginny*, the creating of ideal images of love, love that is exempted from ordinary fluctuations, uncertainties and treacheries —the equivalent in fact, of the new God, Lucifer. The Epilogue to *The Feather Bed* contains a poem which symbolizes this anticipated state of being as the Morning Star: a state beyond the righteous conflict of the sexes, of Good with Evil; neither night nor day but 'the star of morning poised between/The dead of night and the coming of the sun', whose light is a 'mild light, a relief, a pity'. The moon takes on the same symbolic attributes in *Marmosite's Miscellany*—'mistress of escape and pity' (p. 13)—and in the stanza added to the revised 'Land of Whipperginny'—'Where lovers need not argue the tokens of fate'.

The Feather Bed was at least a lively attempt to write a dramatic poem within a frame of symbolism; where it falls down is in its failure to contain some of the larger ideas intended for it and in the laboriousness of the symbolism. *Mock Beggar Hall* is the opposite: most of the poems are lucid expositions of ideas but, with a few exceptions, they are poetically pedestrian. They are, largely, allegorical investigations into the idea of conflict, frequently in a flat, tired, loosely iambic blank verse; the title-poem is a combination of this and prose, and 'Interchange of Selves: an Actionless Drama...' is entirely in prose. The latter was jointly written with Basanta Mallik, an Indian student of philosophy, who became a close friend of Graves at this time. The influence of his views is at its strongest in this volume. In *Goodbye To All That* Graves describes Mallik's philosophy as

a development of formal metaphysics, but with characteristically Indian insistence on ethics. He believed in no hierarchy of ultimate values or the possibility of any unifying religion or ideology. But at the same time he insisted on the necessity of strict self-discipline in the individual in meeting every possible demand made upon him from whatever quarter, and he recommended constant self-watchfulness against either dominating or being dominated by any other individuals. This view of strict personal morality consistent with scepticism of social morality agreed very well with my practice. (pp. 405-6)

The idea of conflict is explored at greatest length in the title-poem, 'Mock Beggar Hall: A Progression'. It is a dialogue in prose between a philosopher and a poet, who meet to discuss the allegorical implications of a narrative poem which the latter is in process of writing; as a result of these discussions the poem goes through successive versions, each of which is quoted. The narrative, however, is simple: it tells of a house haunted by the ghosts of its previous tenants whose interminable quarrelling, each claiming the rights of sole occupation for himself and his generation, makes the life of the present inhabitants unbearable. Refusing to 'practise tolerance' and learn to co-exist with the others, each tenant must seek to dominate his neighbour and be prepared to hold the property by force. The present landlord has other troubles too: there are three other claimants to the estate. His lawyer, spokesman of the *status quo*, urges him to assert his authority with the tenants, put an end to their conflicts by force, and immediately to take legal steps to confirm his ownership. But the landlord stays away from the house, refusing either to assert his authority or to press his claims to ownership.

At one level the haunted house symbolizes, as it does in 'Ghost Raddled', the divided mind of the poet. But with each revision of the poem the allegory extends its range: the ghostly disputants come to represent other conflicts—between the Individual and Society, between the flesh and the spirit, between irreconcilable traditions in the European heritage, and between different religious beliefs, codes of ethics and modes of behaviour. The absentee landlord represents 'the hope of reintegration' between the conflicting points of view. By refusing to exercise authority he is rejecting the dominative-submissive mode of behaviour by which civilization was established and is maintained; and by abstaining from asserting that his is the only rightful claim to ownership of the house, he is denying that his is the only solution to conflict, that any solution is more than temporary and provisional, or, in the most general formulation of the idea, that any truth is absolute and eternal.

The mixed form of the whole piece has three functions. Critically, the whole 'progression' is a kind of practical illustration of interaction between philosophical and poetic thought; for the new ideas that grow out of each of these discussions, though undoubtedly responsible for the subsequent revision of the poem, are not consciously worked into the poem but, more or less without premeditation on the part of the author, find appropriate poetic expression—each occasion, that is, contributing an additional layer of meaning to the allegory. Secondly, it is an example of how a true exchange of ideas, one in which neither side merely argues for victory, will result not in compromise but in the emergence of an entirely new idea. But, primarily, the piece is meant to demonstrate that no one version of the poem is more 'true' than another; each has its relative 'truth', which cannot be compromised by the different 'truths' embodied in other versions, because each revision responds to a fresh set of ideas illuminating a 'truth' or an approach to Truth, but not *the* Truth. That truth is relative is what we deduce, therefore, from the form of the whole piece as well as from the contents of the poem. Each philosophic scheme, religious or political creed, tradition, moral code, or preferred mode of behaviour is true only for the precise circumstances of the culture and the time that are responsible for its existence.

'Mock Beggar Hall' continues the theme begun in *Whipperginny* and *The Feather Bed*, broadening its range of application, examining more closely some of its consequences, for instance the consequences of dominativeness in relationships, and seeing it through to its logical conclusion—relativity of standards. It is more cautious than *The Feather Bed*, however, in its references to the mode of feeling and behaviour that will supersede conflict: there is no romantic invocation, as in the Morning Star poem, of the longed-for state of peace. Though the landlord stands for 'the hope of reintegration' the poem makes no attempt to give this dramatic or symbolic reality. Graves's attitude is more negative, more stoical: it goes no further than a theoretical conviction that, in the concluding words of the philosopher, 'the very act of abstention [from conflict] and endurance will introduce a new element to solve existing differences'. In the poem the landlord's behaviour exemplifies this faith: he refrains from imposing his will on others and prefers to wait passively for the conflicts to die out. But the expectation of a time of peace to follow is hedged with irony now. He refers to his policy of waiting, deprecatingly, as 'the hopeful feats of sloth'.

'Abstention and endurance' summarizes the trend of these poems: refusal to co-operate with evil when choice is possible, endurance when it is not. It is an attitude of stoical realism made more explicit in 'Interchange of Selves', the joint work of Graves and Mallik. This is an 'actionless drama' in which the characters are three philosophers—a mystic, a practical man, and a man with a 'genius for compromise'. They all agree that 'the disease of the human society is conflict', but have different points of view concerning causes and possible cures. They, along with a large body of people, are travelling through a wild mountainous country towards a lake bordered by a forest, beyond which can be seen towns and villages and above which there is a hill-city. Suddenly they are overtaken by a violent, terrifying storm; everyone rushes for shelter and in the confusion squabbles about sites for bivouacking soon develop into serious disputes, which gradually spread over the whole camp. Hitherto the philosophers have remained aloof from the main body but now, having found that they must either give up their own site or fight for it, they are forced to engage in the human conflict which they were deploring and so far had successfully evaded. Losing his philosophic detachment, each in the heat of action betrays his avowed view of life, so fervently upheld a moment before. It is the practical man, the man of facts, who is allowed to speak for the authors in the final summing-up. He concludes that 'we are at the mercy of whims and passions': 'not one of us carried his profession into practice, not one of us kept his true colour to the end'. 'It is a fact', he generalizes—and it is the purpose of the drama to compel recognition of it—'the most gruesome and insistent fact, that caprice turns the wheel of life as much as reason does'. But the authors are propounding not a philosophy of pessimism but a common sense point of view; for it is also true that 'the caprice-laden moment must live only to die; its mission is fulfilled when all the evils have been overcome'.

The facing of facts, undistracted by either romantic or speculative aspirations beyond the facts, is the austere literary programme that Graves has set himself to follow. This is to bring within the circle of his scepticism the latest panacea for his emotional problems, the practice of a philosophical, aloof 'detachment', the first examples of which are to be found in *Whipperginny*. But even in *Whipperginny* in some of the poems, for instance 'The Lord Chamberlain Tells of a Famous Meeting', the proposed solution is put forward with ironic reservations; in the persons of the three 'aloof' philosophers it is directly satirized in 'Interchange of Selves'. In 'Attercop: The All-Wise Spider', Graves's two previous poetic selves, Walter the romantic and James the philosopher, confront each other with their separate solutions to his plight, which is to be caught in the web of the 'All-Wise, omnivorous/Attercop', a 'capricious Beast' whose whims are the poet's destiny. James attempts by paradoxical 'argument and synthesis' to prove that the Web is Liberty; Walter believes he can nullify Attercop's power with the 'natural-magic charm' of his fanciful verses. Both are, in the poet's present view, equally ineffectual: Attercop still rules and they are

> Like trapped and weakening flies
> In toils of the same hoary net;

he (implausibly it is a male spider) will always demand, and they will continue to render, their 'blood and bones and sweat'.

The spider is evidently a sardonic symbol for the force of Caprice referred to in 'Interchange of Selves'; but, more interestingly, he, the All-Wise, tyrant, controller of the poet's destiny, anticipates one aspect of the White Goddess. The Goddess in the cruel exercise of her powers represents for Graves now the cruel side to woman's nature, but also those elements in his own temperament which make being-in-love at times an 'almost insufferable ordeal'.[1] These elements are perhaps traceable to the fact that his first experience of woman's love coincided with the worst stages of his war neurosis. The imagery of his mythological poetry, as I have pointed out, is to some extent drawn from his early poetry—from the poems having their source in his neurasthenia, like 'Outlaws' and 'Return', as well as from the love poems. In *Mock Beggar Hall* Graves's particular experiences have been replaced by theories inferred from them; but it is clear from the similarities between Attercop and, say, the old gods in 'Outlaws' that for the idea of the former Graves has at the least drawn on his neurasthenic experiences, and perhaps also on his experience of the vicissitudes of love. It may be said that either the tyrannical, bloodthirsty spider symbolizes, more crudely, the same aspect of love as is represented by the Goddess in her most male-

---

[1] 'Intimations of the Black Goddess' in *Mammon and the Black Goddess* (1965), p. 154.

volent aspect, or the White Goddess myth draws on other areas of Graves's experience than love for its imagery of apparently causeless suffering.

The position taken up by Graves in 'Mock Beggar Hall'—that values are relative—is matched by the formulation in several poems of an agnostic point of view. The conclusion of 'The Rainbow and the Sceptic' is that man cannot know, he can only hope; he may set up ideas and follow them but may not expect the revelation of any certain truth:

> Knowledge of changing lock and key,
>   So much the FINITE is;
> Let the bow beckon 'Follow me,
>   Whose hopes are certainties',
>
> Yet beyond all this rest content
>   In dumbness to revere
> INFINITE GOD without event,
>   Causeless, not there, not here.

One of the few poems in *Mock Beggar Hall* not to be in the prevailing discursive style, the medium most suited to the exposition of Graves's theories, is also the best—'Full Moon'. (It is the only poem from this volume to keep its place in the *Collected Poems*.) The poem symbolizes the loss of romantic emotion, the failure of love, as a landscape emptied of its colours by pallid moonlight:

> She exorcised the ghostly wheat
> To mute assent in Love's defeat...

'The fields lay sick', an 'owlet cried', and the nightingale's song was like the 'inconsequent debate' which man and wife keep up even in their dreams. It was the lovers' phantoms who kept this tryst, for each 'wore the moon's cold mask'. Two images from earlier poems are reused with greater distinction: they gather from the moon symbolism a greater force of suggestion than they had in their original context. The first occurs when the phantoms watch in each others' eyes 'a grey distraction rise/To cloud the eager flame' like the 'white-steaming mist' that 'obscures desire' in 'The Kiss'; the second when frozen in the moonlight,

They glared as marble statues glare
Across the tessellated stair...

as did the wingless Victory, set in 'marble thought', in 'The Ridge-Top'. 'Full Moon', indeed, is the most complete expression of the theme which dominated the love poems in *Whipperginny* that Graves has yet made. The poem concludes with another echo—reminder of a symbol discussed in 'Old Wives Tales' (*Whipperginny*). Their love was frozen like the Arctic Sea; they were two bays of ice divided by the moon's cruel power; and

> There swam the mermaids, tailed and finned,
> And Love went by upon the wind
> As though it had not been.

The mermaids, symbolizing the flaw inherent in the jewel of romantic love—the inevitable betrayal of what it seems to promise, are no longer a mere intellectual token; here, by absorbing the associations of the preceding images, they become the felt *embodiments* of cold, pitiless indifference.

'Full Moon' holds an important position among the poems of this period not only because it is, so to speak, the definitive treatment of the theme that makes its first appearance in 'The Kiss' (*The Pier-Glass*) and is at the heart of *The Feather Bed* and several poems in *Whipperginny*; it is also the symbolic counterpart, and the finest expression, of the morality presented exclusively in intellectual terms and laboriously argued in the majority of the *Mock Beggar Hall* poems: it embodies, in rhythm and symbolism, the attitude of mind merely recommended and discussed as ideas in those poems. The practical man's resolve in 'Interchange of Selves' to face the fact that evil and caprice form a radical part of experience, and the philosopher's conviction in 'Mock Beggar Hall' that to abstain from conflict and to endure evil are the only sane courses of action—both the resolve and the conviction are reflected in the mood of this poem: there is no protest against 'Love's defeat', just a plain recognition of the fact, and no anguish of conflicting emotions, only a 'mute assent', a numbed acceptance of the inevitable suffering. The metre is unusually regular; the rhymes being firmly stressed and succeeding each other with smooth inevitability, the rhyme-scheme sets up a strong pattern of expectation which is never disappointed; and the syntax submits without protest to the restrictions of the verse pattern—that is, the stanza sub-divisions, in two couplets and a final triplet, are allowed to dictate what shall be the units of sense, and within these subdivisions the lines are end-stopped. It is by these means chiefly that Graves creates a feeling of the poet's stunned, almost hypnotized submission to his fate.

'Full Moon' is also the most important yet of the poems to anticipate Graves's use of moon symbolism in the later mythological love poetry. Earlier examples include 'I hate the Moon', one of a group of three poems in *Over the Brazier* entitled 'Nursery Memories'. The poet in his childish persona declares his fear of the moon, which according to Nurse can drive people mad, and his hatred of its cruel, round, bright face and its 'horrible stony stare'— he knows that 'one day it'll do me some dreadful thing'. In 'The Cruel Moon' (*Fairies and Fusiliers*), as the title implies, the soldier's feelings are not unlike the child's; the only difference is that the soldier tries to laugh away his irrational fears. It is by moonlight, according to another poem in that volume, 'Finland', that pagan rites were performed; the Finnish bard 'Hurls his rough rune/At the wintry moon/And stamps to mark the time'. These early poems record an obscure unease of the poet's, attributing it to the moon's influence, and a vague sense that the emotion and the symbol are integral to his poetry. In one remarkable poem, 'Reproach' (*The Pier-Glass*), the moon seen through bramble-thorns is an image for the grieving reproachful face that the poet sees in a guilt-dream; it powerfully symbolizes emotions of inexplicable horror, shame and bewilderment. 'A Frosty Night' from *Country Sentiment* I have already commented on: there, as in 'Finland', it is a wintry scene— frost is on the ground and 'Coldly gaped the moon', but the images refer, more specifically, to a menacing, ominous quality in romantic love. 'Full Moon' completes the definition of this quality: felt no longer as merely an unrevealed menace but as active oppression, it leads to the death of desire. The moon shows her most malevolent aspect. It is the aspect which in 'A Love Story', a poem that precedes by three or four years the first White Goddess poems and has many of their characteristics, is called 'Queen Famine'. In the earlier poem she is 'the tyrannous queen above/Sole mover of their [the lovers'] fate'. In the later poem signs of Queen Famine's presence are a full moon rising in a winter sky, 'hedges high in snow, and owls raving': 'Solemnities not easy to withstand'. He encountered this scene first, he says, in boyhood and 'suffered horror'. 'A Love Story' traces three successive responses to love: at first horror at what the scene might portend, then an optimistic romanticism, and finally chastened submission to Queen Famine. The final attitude is very like the attitude that informs 'Full Moon', and, if it is recalled that an 'owlet cried' also in that poem, then the connection between these 'solemnities' and certain images not only in 'Full Moon' but also in 'Finland' and 'A Frosty Night' will be plain.

The Marmosite's Miscellany (1925) is the first poem in which the moon is represented as a Goddess and as exercising a benign rather than baleful influence; she is portrayed as the patroness of *successful* love:

> Her regions are portalled by an ivory gate.
> There are fruit-plats and fountains in her silver city.
> With honeysuckle hedges where true lovers mate.
> ...
> She is the happy Venus of the hushed wood,
> So artless Actaeon may banquet his eyes
> At the crisp hair curling on her naked thighs.   (p. 13)

These lines, in spirit though not in their details, are evidently inspired by a passage describing a vision of the Goddess Isis in *The Golden Ass* of Apuleius, a book which contains, in Graves's opinion, as recorded in *The White Goddess*, 'the most comprehensive and inspired account of the Goddess in all literature' (p. 69). Fittingly, therefore, the last of the lines in a recast and improved version appears again in the poem entitled 'The White Goddess': 'With hair curled honey-coloured to white hips'. Thus by 1925 the moon has come to symbolize the polar extremities of the lover's experience—both the ecstasy of a promised glory and the despair of lost or rejected love. This idea of love's duality and the rendering of it in

86

mythical terms as a queen or Goddess, cruel and kind guardian of the poet's destiny, are the conceptual and technical origins of the White Goddess poems.

Mock Beggar Hall is on the whole a cumbersome volume, a collection of theoretical structures rather than poems; but in it were worked out the attitudes and values that are assumed without self-consciousness in Graves's next volume, *Welchman's Hose*. The poems in *Welchman's Hose* do not, however, follow the path of symbolism and the almost religious attitude indicated in 'Full Moon', but move, rather, in the direction of greater sophistication. More than anything else the reader is conscious of the mask of urbanity which these poems wear. Generally, the verse is 'classical'—the tone polished and glinting with irony, and most of the poems are either wittily presented allegories or lightly mocking discussions of ideas.

'Ovid in Defeat' is representative. In it Graves neatly summarizes the cynical 'grammar of Love's Art' as taught by Ovid:

> Let man be ploughshare,
>   Woman his field;
> Flatter, beguile, assault,
>   And she must yield.

Other Ovids, he continues, either advocated celibacy or merely reversed the roles—representing 'Woman as the ploughshare/Man, her field'. Neither of these conceptions if acted upon will release us from the ever-recurring cycle of 'Conflict, domination/Due defeat'. This conclusion is exactly that of the poems in Graves's previous volume, but he now makes the point more succinctly, without lengthy preamble. Moreover, Ovid's arguments are ridiculed and dismissed with a wit and elegance equal to those of the Roman poet. The poem thus does more than reaffirm the intellectual position of *Mock Beggar Hall*. It demonstrates the poet's personal aloofness now from the dominative-submissive mode of behaviour. It is typical of this new trend that Ovid's cynicism should be treated with polished contempt and rejected in the name of a greater not a lesser urbanity: the poet, engaging him with his own weapons, defeats him not with hot invective but on a point of logic—convicting him 'Of false analogy,/Offending both philosophy/And psychology'. The Roman is made to look in comparison clumsy and uncivilized—'Grotesque in Pontic snow/And bearskin breeches'. To the idea that in love 'Where two ride together,/One rides behind' Graves opposes the idea of equality but not sameness, offering it in the spirit of one who states the obvious to expose an absurdity. Woman is neither inferior nor superior to man, but different; their thought, deeds, and art are just not comparable.

This is closely connected with the relativist theme of *Mock Beggar Hall*, which is taken up again in 'Alice'. Alice is hailed as the 'prime heroine of our nation' because she discovered behind the sober Victorian façade a reality not ruled by the laws of reason—in fact, the reality of what Graves would now call 'poetic thought'. By accepting 'with proper British phlegm' life through the looking glass for what it was—not doubting, or seeking metaphysical justification for, its existence but proceeding practically to learn its rules and customs—she became an adept in this kind of living and thinking. She refused to take the world of dream as merely a nonsensical imitation of the logical world of waking life, but accepted it

> As queer but true, not merely in the main
> True, but as true as anything you'd swear to,
> Not worse or better than the Life we are heir to

—the life ruled by Reason, Time and three-dimensional Space. Like man and woman, the worlds of waking and dream, prose and poetic thought, reason and unreason are of equal validity, neither superior nor inferior to each other but different:

> neither did this chance-discovered land
> Make nohow or contrariwise the clean
> Dull round of mid-Victorian routine,
> Nor did Victoria's golden rule extend
> Beyond the glass: it came to the dead end
> Where formal logic also comes...

Nevertheless, although the argument is for relativist impartiality, the poem betrays a preference for the intuitive truth of the unconscious mind to the rational truth of the conscious mind:

thereafter
Begins that lubberland of dream and laughter,
The red and white flower spangled hedge, the grass
Where Apuleius pastured his Gold Ass...

The relativist position, in fact, is argued with a gay insouciance
which belies its apparent seriousness, the poet's real aim being a
light-hearted mockery of his dull, pedestrian, logical readers and the
'normal' way of looking at things. Making Alice the focus of the
poem's argument is the central impudence. Her unquestionably
pragmatic approach to life gives Graves the excuse for blandly
assuming as typically British attitudes which would be unacceptable
to the ordinary member of the British public. He baits the reader
with the monstrous claims that he makes for Alice's intellect—that
she was, for instance, an earlier Einstein and the possessor of a
'philosophic bent'—and he uses her gay confident tone and her
childlike earnestness ('queer but true...as true as anything you'd
swear to') to parody logic and solemn formality. The same humour
lights up the mock-logical 'nohow or contrariwise'; it is a succinct
way of saying 'neither unreal, non-existent, nor an opposite reality',
but its oddity is that it suggests the language of the nursery: it has
the brisk dismissive effect of a child's reasoning.

'Alice' throws light on the change that had taken place in Graves's
poetry since 1921. He had escaped from the emotional stress of *The
Pier-Glass* poems by the path of abstraction—the making of ideas out
of specific conflicts. But this involved the exclusion from his poetry
of all personal emotion. 'Alice' has retained the intellectual framework but has admitted a personal tone—gay, impudent, mildly de-
risive—to replace null neutrality with a self-confident, witty kind of
detachment. Graves apparently feels himself capable of accepting
the life of unreason—in the past the life of terrifying nightmares and
inexplicable torments in love—lightheartedly and without evident
struggle. (At about this time, in some stanzas of *The Marmosite's
Miscellany*, pp. 16–17, he was forswearing allegiance to Apollonian
poetry, which he defines as poetry of the unconscious divided self,
and announcing a new kind—'In grammar of unreason marching
close and free': this seems to mean a poetry that obeys the rules of

poetic—symbolic—not philosophical thought but, like 'Alice', leaves the mind in control.) In some respects this marks a return of Graves's natural optimism, which had almost entirely disappeared from his verse since the publication of *Country Sentiment*. In 'Alice' the gaiety makes for an attractive but limited poem, as it paints a picture of the life of unreason—as a land of laughter and fulfilment—which is only partially true; not only is it untrue to Graves's experience, a fact that the reader unacquainted with his earlier verse has no means of knowing, but it gives the poem a slightly irresponsible air.

This mood of good-humoured self-confidence produces another attractive poem in 'The Figure-Head'. It is the agnostic's cool, ironic 'placing' of supernatural religion, avoiding on the one hand the apostate's bitterness and on the other the brash knowingness of the atheist. Its theme is 'the death of the Christian God as typified by a farmer' (Foreword to *Collected Poems 1938*). The Ox and the Ass, whose forbears had 'at his birth/Proclaimed the reign of Heaven on Earth', are quite clear now that they had been deluded, and that gods are subject to the laws of nature, growth and slow decay; like all the others this one was better in his rise than in his fall. Disillusion had come slowly, but now, the Ass concludes disrespectfully,

> I doubt there's one can dare pretend
> Grief at this dodderer's end.

Despite the Stallion's alarm at 'A farm-yard moving masterless', the animals' tone on the whole mirrors an imperturbable composure. Things will go on much as they did before his birth—that is until a new master comes, as they are now confident one will. Theirs is a historical, sophisticated approach to religion: the cow, for instance, declares in a characteristically bland, off-hand way that

> Though interregna, history shows,
> Are fruitful of alarms and blows,
> New masters always seem supplied
> In place of those who have died.

But their sophistication extends to a little politic cunning, and they have taught the poor simple-minded poultry to believe the farmer immortal. In the sweetly reassuring accents used by an authoritarian régime when pressed and with arguments perhaps parodying those of Christian apologists, they have lectured them thus:

> 'Granted', we've said, 'he's no more seen
> Tending fat sheep in pastures green,
> Or scattering at the break of morn
> Largesse, profuse, of corn.
>
> 'Master must be assumed to know
> Where best his favours to bestow.
> He has left us (caring for us still)
> To cultivate free-will.'

The attitude is delightfully urbane—sceptical but open-minded. The last two lines of the poem strike a balance between genuine uncertainty about the future of religion and a mock-reverence at the passing of the last one:

> But if this next reign too starts well...
> Hush, now! the passing bell!

It is the quality of resilience in Graves's attitude that causes one to regret the absence of this poem from his recent collections. Fear of the terrible insecurity inherent in the *free* exchange of love was the specific theme of 'Children of Darkness'; this was generalized to include the element of uncertainty in all experience, named 'Caprice' in 'Interchange of Selves' and the 'capricious beast' in 'Attercop...'. Now Graves is devoting himself, without illusions but hopeful, with grace and wit to the task of cultivating 'free-will' whether God is 'caring for us still' or not.

In *Welchman's Hose* we see the freakish humour of Graves's juvenilia now fully matured into a cool, well-judged impudence and an ironic detachment. Appropriately this development coincides with a revival of the ironic anecdote, the first, callow examples of which are to be found in *Fairies and Fusiliers*. There were examples of this form in *Whipperginny*, notably 'The Lord Chamberlain Tells of a Famous Meeting'; 'The Clipped Stater' in the later volume is of the same kind. It is the story of how Alexander—invincible conqueror of the known world, 'deified/By loud applause of the Macedonian phalanx' and, it seems, the possessor of 'Infinite power, infinite thought and knowledge'—seeks a final test of his Godhead. He decides that, since

> Omnipotence by its very nature
> Is infinite possibility and purpose,
> Which must embrace, *that it can be confined*,[1]

this will have to be the voluntary assumption of man's flesh and anonymity. Thought to have died of a fever, in fact he is magically translated to the borders of the Chinese Empire, where he is found and forcibly 'enlisted for the frontier-guard/With gaol-rogues and the press-gang's easy captures'. He endures without complaint the hardships and cruelties of a soldier's life, carrying self-denial so far as to banish memory of his divinity even from his dreams. One day, however, he is disturbingly reminded of his former life; going up to receive his pay, he is given a silver coin, which though clipped and defaced he immediately recognizes as a stater, a Silver Alexander, minted during the time of his divine rule and still bearing the impression of his head. He is much troubled by the problem this presents: 'how does the stater, though defaced, owe service/To a God that is as if he had never been?' His doubts force him to the conclusion that he is not God. The only powers remaining to him are human ones; all he knows, therefore, is that he must continue as he began and endure the fate he has chosen. This is a fable illustrating Graves's new viewpoint, agnostic and relativist: that a God lives only in the faith of his worshippers, 'deified by their loud applause'; and—the lesson of the clipped stater—that he is a God only for one particular time and in one particular place. Alexander's argument for embracing the human condition parodies theological arguments for the Incarnation; and the man-god's career is, in intention, a non-heroic version of Jesus Christ's (or possibly any religious hero's), in which self-sacrifice leads not to transcendence in martyrdom but to a life affirming the 'manly' virtues and concluding in an obscure and unremarkable death.

---

[1] My italics.

The main achievement of the poem is the suave, amused tone, friendly yet all the time insinuating ridicule of the bland conceit implicit in the heroic pose, and, by analogy, in the absolute pretensions of Gods; for example

> He would not take a Goddess to his Throne
> In the elder style, remembering those disasters
> That Juno's jealous eye brought on her Consort.
> Thaïs was fair; but he must hold his own.

The indulgent good humour that characterizes the style of narration is presumably influenced by Graves's attitude towards the man whose career this anecdote allegorizes, his friend T. E. Lawrence. Lawrence, like the Alexander of this tale, had in a process not unlike apotheosis become the object of awe and veneration for a large following of people, and subsequently had sought anonymity and apparently self-mortification by joining the R.A.F. under the assumed name of T. E. Shaw. The poem imputes to him a certain romantic vanity in taking this course, stemming perhaps from an unadmitted belief in his own 'divinity'—a self-opinion which it is part of the narrative's purpose to deflate. But Alexander in the poem learns his lesson, accepting his fate with genuine humility and stoicism, and Lawrence was not offended; Graves reports that 'he laughed and laughed and laughed'. (Graves's judgement on such man-gods, as on the whole masculine ethos, was to become increasingly severe in the succeeding years.)

But in pointing to something unsatisfactory in the ending we are uncovering a weakness of the whole poem: Alexander asks himself—

> Is he still God? No, truly. Then all he knows
> Is, he must keep the course he had resolved on;
> He spends the coin on a feast of fish and almonds
> And back to the ramparts briskly enough he goes.

This stanza, with its idealization of suffering silently and 'briskly' borne—of keeping face, in fact—reveals a flaw in the poet's urbanity hardly perceptible but occasionally present in other parts of the poem too. There is a tendency for the tone of tolerant amusement, which indicates not acquiescence in but detachment from the case, to take on romantic accents of its own; the result is the creation out of Graves's new found stoicism of a new kind of heroic ideal—as it were, the heroic antihero. The last stanza can be matched by an earlier one:

> And he grows grey and eats his frugal rice;
> Endures his watch on the fort's icy ramparts,
> Staring across the uncouth wildernesses,
> And cleans his leather and steel; and shakes the dice.

The succession of 'and's', of course, evokes the monotony of the routine; but it also creates a cadence faintly suggesting a mood of ritual celebration—in honour of the hero's stern endurance of such daily monotony.

This kind of lapse indicates a flimsiness in the confident mood—by turns gay, polished, bland, ironic, witty, urbane—that informs these poems. It is as though the poet has won his position of detachment from the personal content of his themes too easily: the stance assumed is one demonstrating effortless superiority rather than hard-won victory, or a steadily maintained control, over strong emotions. The return of an expressive, individual tone to Graves's verse has not on the whole meant a new confrontation of his emotional problems.

The only poem in *Welchman's Hose* to do this—at the same time not failing to apply the lessons in a sceptical approach to experience learned in the years since the publication of *The Pier-Glass*—is 'Essay on Knowledge'. This is better known in the considerably revised version retitled 'Vanity'. I am using the later version as it appears in *Collected Poems 1965*, because, remaining in essentials unchanged, in form and style the poem is vastly improved.

> Be assured, the Dragon is not dead
> But once more from the pools of peace
> Shall rear his fabulous green head.
>
> The flowers of innocence shall cease
> And like a harp the wind shall roar
> And the clouds shake an angry fleece.

'Here, here is certitude', you swore,
'Below this lightning-blasted tree.
Where once it struck, it strikes no more.

'Two lovers in one house agree.
The roof is tight, the walls unshaken.
As now, so must it always be.'

Such prophecies of joy awaken
The toad who dreams away the past
Under your hearth-stone, light forsaken,

Who knows that certitude at last
Must melt away in vanity—
No gate is fast, no door is fast—

That thunder bursts from the blue sky,
That gardens of the mind fall waste,
That fountains of the heart run dry.

The theme once again is the insecurity that lies at the core of what is most valued by the poet, especially the poet as lover: the absence, one might say, of a fixed centre to the world of his values. This condition is accepted much more firmly than it was, for example, in 'Children of Darkness', where it gave rise to a mood of anguished nostalgia for the darkness in which alone acts of 'certitude' might be performed:

> Was Day prime error, that regret
> For darkness roars unstifled yet?

On the other hand, Graves's awareness of uncertainty has become something more than a sanction for intellectual scepticism, its function in *Mock Beggar Hall*, or an opportunity for the exercise of a light urbanity, as it is in the majority of the poems in *Welchman's Hose*—the forms that his antiromantic sentiment has taken so far. In this poem it is the basis of a positive realistic attitude towards romantic love. To the innocence of lovers who imagine the perfect happiness of their desires accomplished in a temporary peace between them the poem opposes the toad's wisdom, 'who knows that

95

certitude at last/Must melt away in vanity'. At first the imagery is made to stress the unexpectedness and the apparently conscious hostility of the elements, but the last four lines, by recapitulating the images used in a variant form, change the emphasis: 'No gate is fast, no door is fast' is the sensible answer to 'The roof is tight, the walls unshaken'; 'That thunder bursts from the blue sky' is to be set against the superstitious assurances of the third stanza; 'That gardens of the mind fall waste' makes it clear that 'the flowers of innocence' are the victims not of a supernatural but a natural force. Graves's object, in fact, in using his images twice over is to show that the destructive elements, though seemingly acting with the evil purposes of sentient beings are actually the passive agents of natural processes. All this is applied to the situation of the lovers. The simple answer to the lovers' illusion is there in the last line, 'That fountains of the heart run dry'; disaster though it is, this too dies a natural death. In some ways this is the first fully realistic poem that Graves has written—a poem, that is, whose chief aim is to embody some aspect of truth, to represent things as they actually are, rather than to express—or exorcise—some state of conflict in the poet. In the *Mock Beggar Hall* poems, whose ideas prepared the way for this poem, what was there called 'caprice' was still thought of as a kind of metaphysical power operating in the physical realm.

'Vanity' differs from its neighbouring poems in *Welchman's Hose* in that its impersonality is tense rather than relaxed: it is still stamped with the pain of the emotions that have been curbed and impersonalized in the writing of the poem. The strength of emotional resistance to this process, of the poet's bitterness and angry disillusion resisting his struggle for command, is clearly intimated in the toughness of the poem's controlling attitude—in, for example, the curt tone and clipped rhythms of the first stanza and in the aggressively logical pattern of the argument throughout the poem (which when stripped of its images has an almost propositional simplicity). Control is exercised similarly through the kind of imagery used. This is, characteristically, emblematic: 'pools of peace', 'flowers of innocence', 'gardens of the mind', and 'fountains of the heart' are examples. Emblems have a limited range of association, and aim to be fully explicit in meaning, where symbols do not. They are more easily manageable units in the sort of poem that argues and makes statements, as distinct from the poem that presents a complex state of mind; they belong to a distancing art. Yet, like the tone and the rhythms, here they also convey a sense of emotional disturbance fiercely restrained. In the last stanza, for example, the precision of meaning in the images, their neat disposal, the repetitive movement and the dry tone, when set against the brief but sharp impact of each, separate image and the cumulative force of the succession of images, have the same kind of effect as understatement. There is a similar balance in the poem's use of folk lore. The toad, for instance, is a richly evocative symbol, the associations of which, however, are precisely relevant to the part he plays in the poem. He is the spokesman for disillusioned experience on the naïveties of innocence, and is qualified for this function by representing at least three similarly circumstanced creatures of literature and fable. Primarily, he is the toad of fairy-tale who has once been a prince and has been transformed by witchcraft, but he recalls also both Milton's Satan, a *fallen* angel, whispering in Eve's ear, and then another creature exiled from the realm of light, Grendel (described frequently in *Beowulf* as 'light-forsaken'). Again, the dragon suddenly breaking the pool's surface is a powerful emblem for unreason or caprice irrupting through the smooth crust of everyday life; yet the poet's horror is immediately placed, with an effect of sour wit, by the dragon's epithet 'fabulous'. The poet both makes us feel his emotion and then, by pointing to the dragon's origin in the folk imagination, makes us aware of the romantic excess in his presentment of it. 'Vanity', in fact does what the other poems in this volume fail to do—it *dramatizes* the poet's struggle for detachment. The realistic attitude is shown as emerging painfully out of the stubbornly innocent emotions of a passionately romantic temperament. The sceptic and the realist in Graves win, but their victory is not allowed to appear an easy one; in this the poem is truer, one feels, to the balance of forces within the poet, and certainly it reads as a more committed product of his imagination. It ranks with the best poems in any period of Graves's writing and like many of them its success consists in maintaining a tension between the romantic and realist elements in his personality.

The last poems to be written in this period that had not already appeared in *Welchman's Hose* were grouped together in the fifth section of *Poems 1914-1926* (1927). They include 'Pure Death', generally accepted as one of Graves's most impressive poems, and 'The Cool Web', another very good poem though not quite as well known; both have kept their places in the *Collected Poems*.

'The Cool Web' presents Graves's more mature conclusions concerning the problems first set forth in the Author's Note in *Whipperginny*: whether poetry should be written out of an 'unceasing emotional stress' or from a standpoint of intellectual detachment. In reaction from the hectic character of his early poetry and the romantic critical theories by which he justified that sort of poetry (in *On English Poetry*), he had swung to the opposite extreme. But by the end of this period a new equilibrium had established itself— it is there most securely in 'Vanity'—and a more balanced theory of poetry. At the same time as it illustrates this personal equilibrium, 'The Cool Web' states the theory: that either extreme will result in a kind of death. Children are taken as the types of those whose senses are shockingly exposed to the direct impact of experience— on the one hand the agonizing ecstasy of the summer rose's scent (love), on the other the terrors of 'the tall soldiers drumming by' (war). 'We' adults, and poets in particular, have language to 'spell away' the power of such unbearable emotions (the intention of the pun in 'spell' is sardonic—pointing to the degree of mere conjuring in language so used).

> There's a cool web of language winds us in,
> Retreat from too much gladness, too much fear.

This is the first kind of death: the use of language as a mask, or an armour against pain so successful that it anaesthetizes the emotions. The other kind of death takes place when we refuse the impersonality made possible by the poetic use of language—acting, as it does as a mediator between ourselves and our emotions. Not availing ourselves of its protective qualities we 'lose self-possession' and

> Facing the brightness of the children's day,
> Facing the rose, the dark sky and the drums,
> We shall go mad no doubt and die that way.

Poetry, it is to be inferred, must be written between these two extremes—weighing the *poet*'s need for detachment against the pressure of intense emotions out of which the poem originates.

Realism—to represent impartially the full force of reality—is not the only impulse behind the writing of 'Vanity' and 'The Cool Web'; there is also the desire to correct a previous unbalance. They strike the attitude of one who fiercely eschews the self-deceptions of idealism, scorns to believe in the search for 'solutions' through poetry, and confines himself to the ascetic practice of 'self-humbling honesties' (a phrase used by Graves in his Foreword to *Collected Poems 1938*, p. xiii, to describe a group of poems written mainly between 1926 and 1933, but equally applicable here). In both poems there is an asperity of feeling. Just as it is the difficulty of maintaining an equilibrium that is revealed in the taut, spare rhythms and acid tones of 'Vanity', so it is the near impossibility of reconciling such contrary demands on the poet as detachment from and truth to his emotions that informs the tone of 'The Cool Web'.

It is, then, in a self-chastening spirit that Graves has forced himself to face unpleasant facts; both in these two poems and in another, 'Pure Death', he confronts the most unpleasant fact of all—death. As we have seen, he evaded the challenge of this subject in his war-poems, and it led only a subterranean existence in the volumes published immediately after the war, fear being the only response. 'Vanity' was the first poem to accept death as an inevitable part of existence; there it is the death of love that is recorded. In 'The Cool Web' he turned to two kinds of emotional death—caused, respectively, by overexposure and underexposure to one's own emotions. In 'Pure Death' the theme is, unmetaphorically, physical death.

> This I admit, Death is terrible to me,
> To no man more so, naturally,
> And I have disenthralled my natural terror
> Of every comfortable philosopher

Or tall doctor of divinity:
Death stands again in his true rank and order.

Therefore it was, when between you and me
Giving presents became a malady,
The exchange increasing surplus on each side
Till there was nothing but ungivable pride
That was not over-given, and this degree
Called a conclusion not to be denied,

That we at last bethought ourselves, made shift
And simultaneously this final gift
Gave. Each with shaking hands unlocks
The sinister, long, brass-bound coffin-box,
Unwraps pure Death, with such bewilderment
As greeted our love's first accomplishment.

It is notable that the final gift in the lovers' progressive giving of
themselves in love is 'pride'. The pride referred to is probably
Lucifer's—belief in one's self-sufficiency, the refusal or inability to
give oneself finally to another person. In 'The Pier-Glass' and 'Return' the poet's attitude was partisan—arguing for or against this
aspect of his personality. But as in 'The Cool Web' and 'Vanity', in
'Pure Death' he has ceased to take sides. There is no means of
knowing whether he thinks it a good thing or a bad thing to surrender one's pride and throw oneself completely on the mercies of
love. The poem is saying no more than—'these are the facts, this is
the nature of love'. Love demands such surrender, and the natural
sequel of this action is the discovery of pure death: it exposes the
lovers for the first time to a naked awareness of death—the fact of
death, that is, separated from its aura of what, in a discussion of the
modernist poet's attitude towards this theme, the authors, Graves
and Laura Riding, call 'bourgeois convictions' the consolations of
philosophy and religion.[1] This is both a terrible and, by restoring
Death to 'his true rank and order', a salutary necessity. The exchange
of gifts in love—the gradual giving of oneself to another person—is
judged a 'malady' and yet was apparently incurable; and, though
the gift of the last remnant of the lovers' self-dependence and self-

[1] *A Survey of Modernist Poetry*, 1927, p. 256.

sufficiency seemed at first 'ungivable', nevertheless the sacrifice was made. It was 'a conclusion not to be denied', the inevitable final stage in the progression of their love.

Since the late 'thirties this kind of neutrality has ceased to be common in Graves's poetry; in fact, in the revised versions of 'Pure Death' the poem expresses a more active acceptance of the consequences of such a sacrifice; for example, in the emendation of lines 7 to 9:

> It happened soon, so wild of heart were we,
> Exchange of gifts grew to a malady:
> There worth rose always higher on each side.

This version suggests more than does the original that the exchange of gifts was a matter of choice, a sign of courage, a generous refusal on the part of the lovers to count the cost. In place of the bald, matter-of-fact tone, the deliberately awkward rhythms and syntax and harsh sound we have the rapt cadences of romantic emotion; in such a phrase as 'wild of heart', in the smooth flow of the verse and the mellifluousness of sound the poet celebrates the unreasonable virtues of excess.

As Douglas Day has pointed out, the verse of 'Pure Death' is a blend of usually incompatible elements that characterizes much of Graves's mature work. The impression conveyed by the rhythms and diction of the poem as a whole is of abruptness and plainness in the utterance of unembellished truth. Yet even at its most uncompromisingly downright—as in the first stanza with its staccato movement and its casually off-beat rhymes—the style keeps a certain formality. In the proud gesture of the first lines for example, with the inversion and the uncolloquially precise use of 'terrible', there is a literary and dramatic quality. Throughout the poem the diction and phrasing alternate between the awkwardly plain, usually Anglo-Saxon, and the literary, formal and archaic, usually medieval French in origin. Thus the second stanza is poised between the effects of harsh directness—the result of a rough and broken verse movement, the hard 'g' and 'k' sounds, and the baldness of such phrases as 'giving presents', 'ungivable pride' and 'over-given'—and of urbane elegance in words like 'malady', 'exchange', 'degree' and 'conclusion'. Note particularly how 'exchange' repeats on the urbane level the sense of 'giving presents'—the French word muffling the physical impact of the preceding phrase and smoothing out the incipient hints of emotional distress in the poet. In the next stanza the relationship works the other way; by juxtaposing the almost ponderous decorum of the archaic 'bethought ourselves' with the blunt archaic-dialectal 'made shift' (of course, the contrast of sounds plays an important part in the effect), Graves has given the latter phrase a brutality to match the shockingness of what is revealed. An elegant distance, however, is resumed in the ceremonious tone of the last line and especially of the last word, 'accomplishment'.

Graves's language is rarely sensuous. Its associative tendency is frequently literary—that is, it taps the reader's memory of previous usages in English literature. The balance of the concrete and the abstract in the most general way owes something, it seems to me, to Shakespeare's example (as does, more blatantly, the early verse of Hardy, a poet admired by Graves), or perhaps to the whole corpus of Elizabethan and Stuart poetry; certainly in some of his verse the tone is reminiscent of the Cavalier poets. In this poem the doubling of nouns—'rank and order'—is a typically Shakespearean trick of rhetoric. Its function is in the first noun to make Death concretely present by personification, and in the second to relate it to a kind of world-view. The style of the line—its rhetoric, one might say—parallels the deliberately antique nature of the sentiment expressed: it is flavoured with an archaic philosophical gravity. This is a functional use of archaism. But, in a less specialized sense, Graves uses words with an unusual sensitiveness to their past semantic histories and literary contexts—more than is usual, that is, among modern poets. (This literary sensitivity extends even to rhythms and syntactical forms.) Examples are 'malady' and 'accomplishment', whose romance associations delicately echo something here in the poet's attitude towards love. The same element comes through, more forcefully, in the Gothic images of the 'tall, dark doctor of divinity' and the 'sinister, long, brass-bound coffin box'. Yet—to summarize the total effect—through the literary, the elegant, the formal and the archaic the note most clearly heard is that sounded in the opening lines, sharp and brusque to the point of seeming uncouth. The other elements are there for specific, contextual reasons, but generally to lend authority and impersonality to the expression of painful feeling.

The achievement of these three poems, 'Vanity', 'The Cool Web', and 'Pure Death', is to restrain without extinguishing the poet's romanticism. In this they are the final stage in the main line of Graves's development during this period, and prepare the way for the more aggressive antiromanticism of *Poems 1926–1930*. Yet during this period also there were occasional romantic poems, or poems which in some respects anticipated the romantic poetry that Graves has been writing since 1938. These poems were, of course, closely linked in mood and theme with the realistic poems written at the same time—the themes, for example, of 'The Ridge-Top' and 'Attercop' with those treated elsewhere in *Whipperginny* and *Mock Beggar Hall*, and the mood of 'Full Moon' with the general mood of *Mock Beggar Hall*. Their romanticism is tempered with the same resolve to face facts. It is this that distinguishes them from the poems of *Country Sentiment* while making them a development towards Graves's later poetry. But their likeness to the White Goddess poems is more startling still. 'The Ridge-Top', 'Attercop', 'Full Moon' and two stanzas of *The Marmosite's Miscellany* together outline a picture of love as a power for good *and* evil—on the one hand presiding like the moon over an ideal realm where 'lovers need not argue the tokens of fate', on the other responsible for periods of spiritual barrenness and unaccountable reversals, a primitive deity that must be appeased with 'blood and bones and sweat'. In this and in the poet's attitude of 'mute assent' these poems resemble the White Goddess poems; the myth has only filled out and complicated the picture.

One important element of the mythological poetry that was missing, however, was the deification of poetry itself, or rather of the 'poetic state' (the title and subject of a poem in *Welchman's Hose*). This element is supplied in two poems, 'Virgil the Sorcerer' and 'The Corner Knot', first published in *Poems 1914–1926*, though both were written in 1924. In late poems like 'Through Nightmare',

'The Secret Land' and 'The Green Castle' the 'promise of glory' shadowed forth in love is identified with the similar promise of perfection, imaged as various kinds of paradise, implied in the 'un-looked for moments' ('The Poetic State') of inspiration that pre-cedes the poetic trance. Muse and Moon-Goddess are indivisible. This identification is not explicitly made in the two earlier poems but a comparison of them with, say, the contemporary passage in praise of the Moon Goddess in *The Marmosite's Miscellany* (p. 13) reveals an obvious similarity in the fantasies.

'The Corner Knot' describes how as a boy, listening to Mozart, the poet, was snatched away to a 'green land of wonder' where he found shallow brooks, rough mountains, and 'fields yellow with small vetch'. Now, twenty years later, he realizes that Mozart him-self, 'estranged and wild at heart', had been carried by inspiration to the same green land, but like the poet had been unable to retain in art more than a 'remembrancer' of the perfection of that moment. In 'Virgil the Sorcerer' Graves tells the story of the other Virgil, the sorcerer of Toledo who, confined by his enemies in a filthy and verminous dungeon, made use of his skill in magic to secure his freedom. With a piece of charcoal he drew a galley on the dungeon wall and then challenged his fellow prisoners to launch with him 'on midnight air/A ship of hope'. They brought him sticks for oars, 'stepped from solid ground,/Climbed into phantasy' and rowed themselves out of prison. They landed like Noah on a mountain top and there, 'without disillusion, all were free'. This, says the poet, is an allegory for poetry: 'Poetry is a spell of furious power', and there are many poets who hope by devoting themselves to the perfecting of their art rather than to the gods of worldly success (the contrast is with the Roman Virgil) to reach Mount Ararat before they die. The tale, in other words, is a romantic image not so much of an escape from reality but of a freedom, achieved by effort and faith, from the yoke of worldliness and mere moment by moment existence: 'Time the limiter wears us to rags/Aided by Doubt and Sloth'. Life is fre-quently for Graves a prison of despair from which poetry alone can liberate him into a world of free moral choice.

But even more than in 'The Corner-Knot' the poet's outlook in

'Virgil the Sorcerer' is pessimistic. 'We are not Virgils'; 'Art is most rare though boasts of art are plenty': defeated by Time, Doubt and Sloth,

> we condone
> The unmoving present: on a mound of mud
> We loll red-eyed and wan, whittling a bone,
> Vermined, the low gaol-fever in our blood.

The poem lacks the poise and tension of 'Vanity'. The desire for release and the nauseating reality are confronted in clumsy contrast, the conflict between them unresolved. In a very interesting revision of this poem (included in *The More Deserving Cases*, 1962, where also 'The Corner-Knot' has reappeared), the excision of nine stanzas and a minimum of alteration to the last stanza has changed the whole bias of the poet's attitude. The last stanza now reads:

> Ah, fellow-captives, must you still condone
> The stench of evil? On a mound of mud
> You loll red-eyed and wan, whittling a bone,
> Vermined, the low gaol-fever in your blood.

The attitude is confident without being complacent. By dissociating himself from those who submit to evil—'we' has become 'you'—Graves turns self-pitying despair into a firm contempt for their (originally his own) moral terror. On the other hand he is careful not to make overweening claims for himself and his art. The assumption behind the question is not that evil can be easily dismissed, or dismissed at all, but that no man has any moral worth who does not *attempt* to resist evil or struggle to escape the prison of himself. We must take the magician Virgil morally as our example but not expect his miraculous success. The very question-form, as is the case with many of Graves's later poems, combines romantic protest against the conditions of life with a shrewd appraisal of the difficulties involved in eluding them. The original poem frames a conception of poetry which in essentials is the same as that of the Muse in the White Goddess poems; the difference, neatly pinpointed by the revision, is all in the quality of the romanticism. In the first version it is generated out of a sense of defeat, a despairing nostalgia for the impossible (the best poems written at this time and in the succeeding period are self-critical, self-limiting, negative). In the later version the romanticism exemplifies and celebrates resilience in the face of difficulty, is indicative of a moral assurance in Graves (behind all the poems written since, say, 1938, there is the poet's unwavering loyalty to a certain scheme of values).

Two other poems in the last section of *Poems 1914–1926* are remarkable for their closeness to Graves's later poetry; both of them have recently been revived—'Pygmalion to Galatea' in *The More Deserving Cases* and 'This is Noon', retitled 'In Single Syllables', in *More Poems 1961*. The first is the sculptor Pygmalion's speech to Galatea, originally a statue in marble which in answer to his prayers has been given life. He lists the womanly qualities which he would have her possess: she should be lovely, merciful, constant and various. The epithets are conventional in love poetry, but the ideal of a woman which they are made to fit is precise and individual. Thus one of the attributes of loveliness is a 'fearless carriage'; mercy in woman is both in being true to herself and, equally, honouring man's truth:

> As you are lovely, so be merciful:
> Yet must your mercy abstain from pity:
> Prize your self-honour, leaving me with mine:
> Love if you will: or stay stone-frozen.
> So be merciful!

and constancy means to keep the love they share 'aloof and strange'. Summarizing, Pygmalion asks her to be 'witty, kind, enduring, unsubjected'. The image of woman so presented is one we meet frequently in the White Goddess poems. The most admired feature of her character is her independence and her pride in being independent—she is to be fearless, self-honouring, unsubjected—the quality most stressed by Graves in his portrait of the Muse-woman, the name he now gives to the woman, an incarnation of the Goddess, who inspires his poetry. 'Royalty' is the word he has used for it in recent essays: it suggests not only independence but command, and Galatea is enjoined to take the dominant role ('Love if you will: or stay stone-frozen') that according to Graves's present convictions

belong to all real women by right, real carrying here also its ety-
mological sense of 'royal'. Again, the love that is 'aloof and strange',
something mysterious, apart from and alien to ordinary experience,
is what he now calls 'poetic love'. But the most startling anticipation
of his late love poetry comes in Galatea's reply:

> Pygmalion, as you woke me from the stone,
> So shall I you from bonds of sullen flesh.

Like the Muse-woman her function is to release man from some of
the bonds of mortality. Man is imprisoned in himself, tied there by
the tyranny of his own emotions—despair, doubt, pride—and by a
failure of will. Only woman can free him to an unhampered spiritual
and moral life, a life of choice. And yet, in a sense, this conception of
woman is a creation of the poet's as Galatea is of the sculptor's, so
that it is as much poetry as woman that is the medium of his liberation. These lines make explicit the identification (already noted in
relation to 'Virgil the Sorcerer' and *The Marmosite's Miscellany*
passage) that had been latent in several of Graves's recent poems,
and there has been no clearer subsequent expression of this paradox
or complex of ideas central to much of the White Goddess poetry.

At the same time, Graves has compressed into the one vivid
phrase, 'bonds of sullen flesh', several years' thought concerning his
conflicts. It fuses two contrary implications: that unregenerate flesh
stubbornly and apathetically refuses to be awakened (we recall
'Sullen Moods', where the poet's mood is inward-turned indignation
at his own 'Shortcomings, plagues, uncertainties'), and that it is
helplessly subject to the limitations of its nature (which is nearer to
the original version of 'Virgil the Sorcerer'). The phrase thus epitomizes a more complete view of the poet's condition than had previously been available to him, to set against his romantic search for
an alternative condition. Compared with 'Vanity', 'Pygmalion to
Galatea' is romantic, but it shares 'Vanity's realistic self-knowledge. This strengthens rather than destroys the poem's romantic
structure, and in so doing brings it nearer to the kind of poem that
Graves has been writing since 1938. It is not a matter merely of
anticipatory themes and images, as it is with 'Full Moon', the lines

in *The Marmosite's Miscellany*, and 'Virgil the Sorcerer', but of tone; romantic in aspiration though the poem is, yet the tone is a blend of fervour with plainness and restraint.

'This is Noon', too, has a theme often treated in the later poetry, but is perhaps even closer in style to that poetry than 'Pygmalion to Galatea', especially to a certain kind of poem more common in the volumes published since *Collected Poems 1959*. In fact, in this respect, the revised version—and revision is slight—has nothing to distinguish it from its neighbours in *More Poems 1961*. The theme is the lover's central uncertainty and the alternation of doubt and hope in his relationship with woman. At night 'love rose up in wrath to make us blind', its reality was unquestionable; but now, at noon, the woman's smile is equivocal and he cannot tell whether she loves him still or not.

> Now I too smile, for doubt, and own the doubt,
> And wait in fear for night to root it out
> And doubt the more; but take heart to be true,
> Each time of change, to a fresh hope of you.

The manner of treating this theme distinguishes 'This is Noon' from near-contemporary poems like 'Children of Darkness' or even 'Vanity'. The writing is spare but not anguished or 'self-humbling'. Rather, the hesitantly careful movement and the monosyllabic diction embody an attitude of submissive humility, of patience in waiting, in the midst of anxious uncertainty. At the centre of the poem there is a persistent faith in love and an acceptance of its changing phases. This faith and this acceptance inform almost all the later love poetry, and the White Goddess is the *incarnation* of love's changeableness. It is the repeating cycle of doubt and hope in the lover's experience that is symbolized and dramatized in the Myth as the death and resurrection of the Demigod of the Waxing Year. But the poem's affinities are with Graves's most recent work—to be found in the three-book sequence comprising *More Poems 1961*, *New Poems 1962* and *Man Does Woman Is*—rather than with the mythological poetry. It resembles the poems of this sequence in that it narrows its focus to a view of the strictly human experience, the psychological moment, out of which the Myth grew; in this too, therefore, it is an anticipation of the later poetry. Here, for the first time then, we have the presentation of the 'uncertainty' theme from a point of view still central to Graves's poetry twelve and even thirty-four years later.

4

'Self-humbling Honesties'

THE PUBLICATION of the first collected edition of his poems, *Poems 1914–1926*, in 1927 was, presumably, intended by Graves as a formal indication that a period in his poetic development had come to a close. Certainly the poems he now began to write revealed a decisive change of direction in his poetic aims; they seemed startlingly different from those of his previous volumes both in style and thematic preoccupations. This was due, Graves makes it clear, to the personal influence of the American poet, Laura Riding. The influence was partly technical: the example of her poetry and her personal criticisms were evidently largely responsible for a new terseness, sharpness of attack and a surer intellectual control of his material. On this level she performed for Graves the sort of service that Pound performed for Yeats in the middle of his career. Similarly Graves's verse, though indebted to hers, maintained its independence; a few poems only read like imitations.

But the influence went deeper than that. He had first become acquainted with her writings in 1925. His interest aroused, he and Nancy invited her to visit them in England. She accepted and arrived in 1926. Very soon they agreed to join in a literary partnership, which lasted until 1938. They first collaborated in the writing of two critical works, *A Survey of Modernist Poetry* (1927) and *A Pamphlet against Anthologies* (1928). Laura Riding's voice seems to be the dominant one in these collaborations and her name appears first on the title-page, but obviously Graves gave his convinced support to the arguments advanced in them. It was not only his attitude towards poetry and his critical opinions, however, that underwent a change, but his whole moral outlook. Slowly during the four years from 1926 to 1929 he absorbed Laura Riding's ideas concerning the nature and function of poetry, the nature of the poetic self, life in society and human existence; he acquired in the process a new set of poetic and moral values (identical, as we shall see), a much clearer sense of purpose, and something like a *Weltanschauung*.

In a preface to her *Collected Poems* (1938) Laura Riding states her belief that poetry is 'an uncovering of truth', and 'Truth is the result when reality as a whole is uncovered by those poetic faculties which apprehend in terms of entirety, rather than in terms merely of parts' (p. xviii). The activity of mind required in the reading and, even more, in the writing of poems is the instrument of the good existence: 'To live in, by, for the reasons of, poems is to habituate oneself to the good existence'. This had always been the basic tenet of her faith. The living through and for poetry was put forward as the only alternative to living in time and serving the purposes of a purely physical existence. Summarizing her achievement in 1940, Graves states that the chief premise of her thought was 'that historic Time had effectively come to an end'. He quotes from her 'Preliminaries' to *Epilogue I* (1935): 'all the artificial excitement in events which no one really regards as either very important or very interesting has been exhausted. All the historical events have happened'; and this left the poets with the task of reporting 'the single event possible after everything has happened: the determination of values'.[1]

This point of view Graves quickly accepted as his own. In 1925 he was unable to claim for poetry more than that it 'is for the poet a means of informing himself...of the relation in his mind of certain hitherto inharmonious interests...sub-personalities or other selves' (*Poetic Unreason*, p. 1). By 1929 he was 'now declaring his intention of becoming a poet in a more responsible sense: considering the intrinsic truth of his statements rather than their probable appeal to anthology readers' (*The Long Week-end*, p. 217). His judgement in the same book on the poems published in *New Verse* during the 'thirties also reflected Laura Riding's critical standards: 'The work that appeared in it, though designed to represent actuality, made no evaluation of good and bad elements in actuality' (p. 300). The title of his autobiography, *Goodbye To All That*, published in 1929, indi-

[1] *The Long Week-end: A Social History of Great Britain 1918–1939*, by Robert Graves and Alan Hodge, pp. 200–1.

cated the transformation of his moral and intellectual outlook. It was
intended, though studiously neutral in tone, as an indictment of the
society which had educated him, for which he had fought, and whose
patronage for his poetry and critical works he had attempted to win;
more radically, it was a dismissal of the self that had participated in
the purposes and shared the values of that society—'This is a story
of what I was, not what I am' (p. 442). Finally, the book was a fare-
well to autobiography itself—to the world of events, of things
happening to him, to life in historic time—and a pledge of his
release from the prison of that world and that life. In the *Dedicatory
Epilogue to Laura Riding* appended to the first edition he affirms her
responsibility for the fact that instead of 'arguing morals, literature,
politics, suffering violent physical experiences, falling in and out of
love, making and losing friends, *enduring blindly in time*' (my italics)
he is now living outside time and ordinary human nature, 'against
kind—indeed, rather against myself' (p. 445). In Laura Riding's
sense, he was living in, by, for the reasons of poetry. The last
sentence in *Goodbye To All That* is a summary list of unusual facts
concerning the author's life; the last item in the list is the most
startling one—that he has 'learned to tell the truth—nearly' (p.443).

The poetry he wrote during the early years of his association with
Laura Riding reflected more precisely than this, however, her ideas
and attitudes. It is possible to form some idea of her thought at this
time from the opinions expressed in *A Pamphlet against Anthologies*
and *A Survey of Modernist Poetry*, but it can best be studied in a
collection of essays entitled *Anarchism Is Not Enough* which was published in 1928. It starts by questioning the conception of reality by
which the great majority of people live—'the Myth' that there is a
collective meaning and purpose in life, a pattern or system, a universal significance in the 'irregular succession and grouping of
moments' in the individual. As individuals we gradually learn that
this is a pretence to keep us happy, but as members of a social group
we unite in upholding the fiction. 'It becomes the universal sense of
duty...It is the repository for whatever one does without knowing
why; it makes itself the why.' Society is indifferent to what form or
system is given to it, 'so long as it be given *a* form and *a* system by

which it may absorb and digest every possible activity'. It is the guarantee of social unity. 'Poetry is essentially not of the Myth...It has no system, harmony, form, public significance or sense of duty' (pp. 9–11). 'Poetry is consciousness...of what is self'—the final untranslatable reality of self (p. 79). By contrast with the other arts it is 'an art of individualization' not communication (p. 114). It is antisocial. In writing, the poet's aim should be to disentangle the original self from all that is not self—from what the author calls history (that is, the pattern seen in events), synthesis and systematized reality. The chief characteristic of poetry, therefore, is its compression; for its purpose is destructive or analytic, to eliminate all that is inessential and 'leave everything as pure and bare as possible after its operation' (p. 117). In their *Survey of Modernist Poetry* the authors make the same point with greater particularity when they commend the assumption underlying Marianne Moore's poetry: that the reader 'is willing to part with the decayed flesh of poetry, the deteriorated sentimental part, and to confine himself to the *hard, matter-of-fact skeleton of poetic logic*' (p. 112; my italics). The stress in *Anarchism Is Not Enough* is on the part played by the intellect in poetry. Mind is the instrument of individualization, 'the analytic intensification of personality' (p. 118). 'If every one began systematically treating himself as mind, we should all quickly become separate individuals and know ourselves' (p. 108).

This summary should make it clear that *Anarchism Is Not Enough* sets out the basic principles of a scheme of ethics, in which the qualities required of a man to create poetry provide the moral criteria for living: in other words, poetry is conduct. What is at once an ethic and an aesthetic for the poet is a system of personal morality for everyone. In identifying himself with this view Graves was committing himself to a remaking of both his poetry and himself. Some poems in *Poems 1914–1926* were already showing signs of this double process, but it is to be seen most clearly in the next three volumes, all published in limited editions: *Poems 1914–1927* (published in the same year as *Poems 1914–1926*, it included nine new poems), *Poems 1929* (1929), and *Ten Poems More* (1930). These poems were brought together in *Poems 1926–1930* (1931), and it is from this volume that I shall quote. It was followed in 1933 by *Poems 1930–1933*.

It is not surprising that the effort of remaking himself and his poetry and affirming a new set of values should express itself in largely belligerent terms, as was the case in *Poems 1926–1930*. A new faith implies rejection of the old faith or lack of faith. Moreover in Graves's new personal morality and conception of poetry analysis, elimination of the inessential, destruction, played an important part in the uncovering of truth. In *A Survey of Modernist Poetry* Graves scrapped most of his previous critical opinions. *A Pamphlet against Anthologies* was an attack on the literary world and the reading public. In *Goodbye To All That* he finally took leave of his old self: it was a repudiation of the life he had lived and the society to which he had belonged and a disavowal of all that he had believed in. Concurrently he was writing poems motivated by the same furious need to liberate himself from what he hated in himself and his society.

'To the Reader Over My Shoulder' (*Poems 1926–1930*) strikes a characteristically antisocial note. It is a truculent dismissal of the reader's claims to criticize or in any way influence the form of a poem:

> All the saying of things against myself
> And for myself I have well done myself,
> What now, old enemy, shall you do
> But quote and underline...

Once Graves had paid conscious attention to the problems of communication and to the needs and capacities of his audience; he had acknowledged it as 'judge and patron' of his work. But now for him, as for Laura Riding, poetry is 'not concentrated on an audience but on itself'. The reader's role is to be attentive, to 'quote and underline', to accept poetry on its own terms. Poetry is an act of purification; by isolating self from the impurity of contact with what is notself the poet releases himself from the determinations of the flesh and existence in time. This is the idea that lies behind the claim made in the last two lines (addressed to the reader): 'I am a clean spirit/ And you for ever flesh'.

But in this form the claim does not prove itself, the poet's superiority is not obvious. In each of the passages quoted the gesture is merely self-applauding. Equally the poet's opinion of his reader is only a matter of arrogant assertion; he abuses him but does not demonstrate his reasons for doing so. The faintly archaic manner affected in the last lines is histrionic, an attempt to hide the feelings of personal resentment, revealed in the strident tone of the whole poem, behind the assumed persona of *grand seigneur*. (This lack of control is more extreme in another antisocial poem, 'Pavement', an attack on anthologies; retitled 'Wm. Brazier' in the *Collected Poems*. This is a typical sentimentally nostalgic anthology piece into which Graves has inserted bracketed passages, intended as debunking comments on its cloying unrealities but turning out to be in fact hysterically abusive of the reader:

> It's an old story—f's for s's—
> But good enough for them, the suckers.)

The failure of 'To the Reader Over My Shoulder', as Donald Davie points out, is a failure to be impersonal, and he attributes this to the fact that Graves is here speaking directly to the reader and not, as he usually does, through the depersonalizing medium of emblem. He contrasts the use of emblematic fable in 'The Legs' (*Poems 1930–1933*). This treats the same subject, the poet's attitude to his public, though attacking its mindless conformism rather than its critical pretence. It describes a road on which 'the traffic was legs,/Legs from the knees down', 'unstoppable/Legs', impelled by no purpose but their own momentum 'Resolutely nowhere in both directions'. At first, arrogantly, the poet assured himself that 'he was not a walker/From the knees down', a creature, that is to say, ruled by the body's automatisms, that his legs were safe from this madness. But the consequence of a moment's doubt proved his confidence misplaced:

> They had run in twenty puddles
> Before I regained them.

Instead of directly abusing a society not represented in the poem Graves has, in this image of 'legs from the knees down', given us an emblem of that society (as it seems to him), and thus an explanatory dramatic context for his attitude towards it. The reasons for his attitude are implied in the picture he presents:

> What drew the legs along
> Was the never-stopping,
> And the senseless frightening
> Fate of being legs.

The horror that the poet feels for this unceasing traffic of legs enacts and explains itself in the suggestion of the senseless flow of movement in the participial endings and the *frighteningly* relentless, pounding rhythms of the last two lines. It is a horror of life going on under its own momentum, uncontrolled by mind. A further impersonalizing agent is the humour. The extravagance of the fantasy renders the mindlessness of society at once horrifying and absurd and creates an atmosphere of *mock*-horror, in which not only society but the extravagance of the poet's (that is, his persona's) reaction to it, oscillating between fear and a blustering confidence engendered by fear, is ridiculed. The poem thereby criticizes the poet for being disturbed by what is only absurd and comes to rest on an attitude of urbane detachment.

In being directed against his literary public and an actual society, the objectives of Graves's campaign waged in these poems were the same as those of the critical books and *Goodbye To All That*. Other poems in *Poems 1926–1930* are closer to *Anarchism Is Not Enough* and to Laura Riding's poetry in rejecting, more generally, the intellectual and emotional foundations of society—the social Myth. 'Philatelist-Royal' is an elegantly mocking dismissal of absolutes, scientific certainties, panaceas of all sorts, and abstractions. The title of another poem declares Graves's resolution 'To be Less Philosophical'. 'Sandhills' (revised and retitled 'Sea Side' in the *Collected Poems*) sees the pairing of lovers as the beginning of the socializing process, whereby individuals are changed into replicas of each other. Lovers seek to lose their single selves in a common identity and then to reproduce this

> With two-four-eight-sixteenish single same
> Re-registration of the duple name.

The process is identified—the metaphor is more explicitly worked out in the revised version—with the related process of bringing 'symmetry', in rows of identical houses, to the

> gentle wildness and confusion,
> Of here and there, of one and everyone,
> Of windy sandhills by an unkempt sea.

It is the imposition of an abstract, ideal pattern on a reality made up of dissimilar particulars—'here and there', 'one and everyone'—that is ultimately responsible for turning individuals into social beings indistinguishable from each other. These ideas are recognizably Laura Riding's but have been successfully absorbed in the poem. The imagery of the three lines just quoted, for instance, relates the poem's point of view to emotional preoccupations revealed in earlier poems—to 'Rocky Acres', in which, however, the wildness and chaos were cruel not gentle (the point of view has changed and the poet is no longer afraid of them), and more closely to some of the recent love-poems, like 'Pygmalion to Galatea', where wildness was, as it still is for Graves, a quality associated with (boldly individual) romantic as opposed to married love.

The substitution by society of a systematized reality for the direct experience of reality is a process paralleled in the world of words. Poetic truth is truth apprehended directly and therefore in its entirety, reality as an individual whole; for the poetic faculties are those that 'apprehend in terms of entirety'.[1] 'History of the Word' is an attack on the users of words, in the name of poetic truth. The poem lists the stages in the gradual deterioration of words; it describes how the level of reality that they originally contained has progressively drained away. By a process of analysis and abstraction the primal Word, Truth in its entirety, has been divided into parts and further subdivided into smaller parts, moving steadily away from the original precision and wholeness of poetic truth. At first the Word was 'The Word/For two of three, but elsewhere spoke unheard', then for purposes of interpretation it was translated into other words, and from these in turn were deduced abstract rules

---

[1] Laura Riding in the preface to her *Collected Poems*, p. xviii.

and dogmas. The already tenuous connection with reality was finally cut when people came to think in terms of these concepts rather than of the reality from which they were derived. The time is nearing, he concludes,

> When every ear shall lose his sense of hearing
> And every mind by deafness be close shuttered—
> But two or three, where first the Word uttered.

The poets are still the only guardians of Truth in its entirety.

Not only the themes were new in these poems; Graves's style of writing also changed considerably. Two characteristics are chiefly remarkable—an austerely intellectual approach and a certain bizarre quality, in both of which they are representative of this collection as a whole. The impression of the bizarre or the incongruous is caused by a disparity between the exclusively logical, analytic character of the allegories now employed by Graves and the nature of his subject-matter—society, love, the abuse of language and the misrepresentation of reality. The reduction of these themes to the status, as it were, of problems in formal logic is a contemptuous manoeuvre which has the effect of dismissing them from further consideration. Society becomes a logical absurdity—legs detached from their heads and bodies; lovers are no more than 'two in search of symmetry'; the process by which language deteriorates as a vehicle of meaning is the merely logical one of division and subdivision. In each case the vision offered is horrifying as well as absurd: in 'Sandhills' 'the sea parts in horror at the view' of rows of houses back to back, as the poet recoiled in horror from the view of legs in 'unstoppable', mindless movement; and the syntactical structure of 'History of the Word' is a nightmarish imitation of the continuous process of word-multiplication. But the final impression that these poems leave *is* of the absurdity of the reality they image; the poet is not implicated in it. Their message is the same as that of *Goodbye To All That*: 'there is a pattern here, but *I* am no longer within the pattern'.

In eliminating inessentials from his verse—discarding for the time being personal emotion and with it the temptation of self-dramatization—Graves was reacting against more than the sentimental or feverish character of his early poetry. These poems eschew even the gestures of aloof, philosophical detachment with which he had experimented in *Mock Beggar Hall* and the elegantly ironic detachment of *Welchman's Hose*. In them Graves has succeeded in reducing poetry to a 'hard, matter-of-fact skeleton of poetic logic'.[1] But other poems in *Poems 1926–1930* are even further from the polished wit of *Welchman's Hose*, and more closely approximate Laura Riding's conception of poetry as 'properly harsh, bare, matter-of-fact'. 'Hell' is an example. It describes a world ruled, on the one hand, by people whose lives are empty, wasted, unfulfilled and, on the other, by words similarly exhausted and meaningless, the meaning in them deadened by constant repetition. The fantasy of the poem is that these people and these words have been deprived of their souls by 'the great-devil'.

> Husks, rags and bones, waste-paper, excrement,
>   Denied a soul whether for good or evil,
> So casually consigned to unfulfilment
>   Are pronged into his bag by the great-devil.
>
> And words repeated, over and over and over,
>   Until their soul sickens and all but dies...

Here the sound is harsh, the rhythms are broken and staccato—as in the opening lines of 'Pure Death', one of the first poems to show Laura Riding's influence. In this dissonance, in the half-rhymes and off-beat rhymes and the ejaculatory, impatient rhythms—adding up to a total effect of perfunctoriness—the poet, more than in the poems so far examined, reveals his intention to dissociate himself from his subject-matter. The fantasy of the great-devil who collects waste matter and forms out of it 'the pavement-feet and the lift-faces' is even more perfunctory—fails to take itself seriously. The poet shows himself disgusted, but then with an offhand gesture that matches the casual contempt of the great-devil dismisses the subject.

[1] A process he commends in Marianne Moore's poems in *A Survey of Modernist Poetry*, p. 112.

In these poems Graves attacks the socializing process—the sacrifice of personal identity in the interests of the group—and the substitution, in the life that social man makes for himself and the language he uses, of an artificial, abstract reality for personal truth. Underlying the immorality of this process is, according to Laura Riding, a deeper immorality. Social man accepts unquestioningly that the conditions of physical existence—ruled by time, space and the body—constitute the whole of reality, and thus denies the moral and spiritual existence of the self.

Two poems, 'It Was All Very Tidy' (*Poems 1926–1930*) and 'The Cell' (*Poems 1930–1933*) satirize this acceptance. The former creates a grotesque, dream-like image of the deathly existence led by social man. In his house

> Music was not playing,
> There were no sudden noises,
> The sun shone blandly,
> The clock ticked.
> It was all very tidy.

Where time reigns comfortably and life is so neatly explained according to the Myth of an all-inclusive purpose no room is left for unpredictable disturbances. Here, as in 'Sandhills', all is symmetrical: 'It was all very tidy'. System has replaced the unorganized, uninterpretable, the untidy reality of self; persons are no more than a 'row of figures' in the abstract sum of life. The poet asks:

> 'Apart from and above all this',
> I reassured myself,
> 'Am I not myself?'
> It was all very tidy.

The answer is not in doubt but the question is put (as in 'The Legs') with a show of diffidence. Once again the poet's response is one of mock-horror. The absurdity of the fable is a guarantee that he does consider himself immune from this death-in-life, but on the other hand its nightmarishness is a powerful reminder that he may not remain so. The structure of the poem—divided into sections of diminishing length, dwindling from seven lines at first to two lines, the last line of each section being the catchphrase, 'It was all very tidy'—enforces this suggestion. The gathering frequency of the repetitions conveys the hypnotic power that this clockwork dream-life exercises over the narrator. In a quite literal manner it also performs what is according to Laura Riding the prime function of poetry: the stripping down of reality to a hard core of truth.

The assumption embodied in the allegory of 'The Cell' (retitled 'The Philosopher' in the *Collected Poems*) is that time, space and the body constitute a prison for the self, the prison-cell of the title. The philosopher does not question these conditions but attempts to reconcile himself to the limitations they impose by 'ruling out distractions of the body...Thoughts of escape...memory and fantasy', and to evade the pain of living by constructing a substitute reality based on logic: one

> In which the emancipated reason might
> Learn in due time to walk more accurately
> And neatly than at home.

A contrast between the philosophic and the poetic points of view is implied. Historic time may have stopped being of importance in Laura Riding's and Graves's scheme of values—to have 'come effectively to an end' in that sense—but, for Graves certainly, the rescue of self from its circumscription was an arduous, recurrent task. On the one hand 'memory' does not allow the poet to rule out the pains of bodily existence or the restrictions of a purely material universe, on the other 'fantasy' is unceasingly active in its search for ways of escape and of expressing protest against his imprisonment. The poet does not accept but neither does he ignore the conditions of life in time.

There is evidence here of a deep continuity between these poems and Graves's previous work. This balance of memory and fantasy in perfect opposition repeats the balance of the realistic and the romantic principles in some of the later poems of *Poems 1914–1926*, notably 'Vanity', 'Pure Death' and 'The Cool Web'. Laura Riding was responsible for much that was different in *Poems 1926–1930*, in his style and in the terms of his thought, but his inspiration was rooted in the same conflicts as before. The growth of self-knowledge and the development of a tighter moral self-discipline had also begun before he had come under her influence. The evidence of continuity is plainer to see in one of Graves's best known poems, 'O Love in Me' (*Poems 1926–1930*),[1] which in mood and tone as well as in theme is closer to 'Vanity' than to the other poems in this volume. It expresses pregnantly with what is now uncharacteristic emotion the poet's sense of love's 'momentariness'; but it maintains a painful tension between affirmation of romantic love, the 'smiling innocent on the heavenly causeway', and the awareness of its limited, physical expression—of the 'dumb blind beast' which is both lust and death (because the physical implies mortality);

> Be warm, enjoy the season, lift your head,
> Exquisite in the pulse of tainted blood,
> That shivering glory not to be despised.

Love is both 'exquisite' and 'tainted', a 'glory' and a lustful fever.

There are signs in 'It Was All Very Tidy' and 'The Cell' of a continuity even in thought with Graves's previous poetry: that his picture of reality has been not so much transformed as given intellectual stiffening. The portrait of the philosopher is in direct descent from that of James in 'Attercop: The All-Wise Spider'. As the philosopher seeks through logic to reconcile himself to his imprisonment, 'Threading connexion between wall and wall', so James sought an illusory freedom from the entangling spider's web in the discovery, through 'argument and synthesis', of a necessary pattern in its strands. The 'sudden noises' and the 'distractions of the body' are only more precise, matter-of-fact references to those 'violent physical experiences'[2] in which Graves has identified the principle of uncertainty or caprice or evil than such symbols as the spider in 'Attercop' and the dragon in 'Vanity'. In 'Saint', *Poems 1926–1930*, another poem more closely connected in style and allegory with the recent work in *Poems 1914–1926* than with its neighbouring poems,

---

[1] Retitled 'Sick Love' in the *Collected Poems*. It takes its new title and the image of apples in the first stanza from The Song of Solomon 11.5.

[2] *Goodbye To All That*, p. 445.

the thematic link is more obvious. In an ironic retelling of Spenser's story of the Red Cross Knight and the Blatant Beast the Beast, symbolizing evil, proves indestructible and accompanies the Knight, to the secret relief of the populace, for the rest of his life. It is, the poem shows, a necessary evil that must be lived with, a kind of shadow or alter-ego, the unconscious self perhaps to the conscious self symbolized by the Knight.

The aggressively antisocial nature of many of these poems cannot be attributed solely to Laura Riding's influence either. It was the culmination of a gradual process of estrangement from his public and society in general that first showed itself in *Whipperginny*. As the public lost interest in his poetry so Graves wrote less and less *for* them. For several years his work appeared in limited or virtually limited editions. *The Marmosite's Miscellany* (1925) was a Skeltonic satire on the literary world which though pseudonymous made no attempt to disguise its authorship and appeared in *Poems 1914–1926*. *Goodbye To All That* mentions his loneliness and growing dissatisfaction with society during these years, and it is the subject of an introductory poem to *The Marmosite's Miscellany* addressed to Basanta Mallik: 'In India you/Exiled at your own home as I at mine'. His relationship with Laura Riding enabled him to pass from unhappy withdrawal to militant rejection of society, from involuntary to voluntary exile. Exile became the moral standpoint of his poetry. Only three years later in 1929 metaphor was to change to fact when Graves left England to make his permanent home in Majorca.

But his radical scepticism concerning society was also turned upon himself. *Goodbye To All That* makes it clear that in rejecting his society he was rejecting the part of himself that had lived by social values. As I have said, these poems, too, were motivated by Graves's furious need to be liberated from what he hated in himself as well as in society. Their purpose is self-reduction (that is, in Laura Riding's terms, reduction to self), their tone frequently self-punishing.

Such is the tone of 'Ship Master' (*Poems 1926–1930*; retitled 'The Furious Voyage' in the *Collected Poems*), which shows Graves as strict in self-discipline as in his attack on society. The poet harshly and grimly reproaches himself, under the figure of a ship's captain, for the grandiose expectations of life in time that he had once harboured. These were delusions: there are no romantic victories to be won, encounters neither with 'growling ice' nor 'breakers perilous' (images that ironically recall passages in two romantic poems, 'The Ancient Mariner' and the 'Ode to a Nightingale'). The mind is powerless to influence the course of events on this voyage—man is *not* the 'master' of his fate—and the voyage is without external purpose or pattern. The 'vessel' (the body) manned by a 'surly crew' of captious, unpredictable emotions—'surly' recalling the 'sullen moods' of an earlier poem—has but one goal, death. Its scope for morally meaningful action is drastically cramped:

> In ballast only due to a fetch
> The turning point of wretchedness
> On an uncoasted featureless
> And barren ocean of blue stretch;

which is no more than 'enduring blindly in time'. The poem is concerned to enforce the same lessons as 'The Cell' and 'Sandhills'; namely that purely physical existence is a prison, has neither pattern nor a moral dimension. But in presenting a case against the poet's unregenerate self it goes further. Primarily it is a repudiation of the naïve romanticism that sought its values in a temporal and physical world.

'Thief' (*Poems 1926–1930*) is the savage exposure and repudiation of that romanticism seen in another aspect. As romantic lover in his earlier verse, the poem says, Graves had played the part of thief—stealing 'rings, flowers, watches,/Oaths, jests and proverbs', and claiming as his own sentiments and words that did not truly belong to him. The real self had become encrusted with a patina of lies, self-deceptions and spurious emotions and his real poetic self hidden beneath a clutter of mannerisms and petty fancies. The time has come to strip thoughts, feelings and language clean of what is untrue, unnecessary and irrelevant. The old self is therefore sentenced for its dishonesty to the galleys where, the poet explains with a grim wit, it will be condemned to a more desperate kind of 'thiefdom':

> you shall steal
> Sleep from chain-galling, diet from soured crusts
> ...the excuse for life itself
> From the galley steered towards battles not your own.

Its punishment is to be subjected to a stricter, alien discipline. The new master will be, presumably, the mind, and the new battles those incidental to 'the determination of values'. In keeping with the poem's content the tone is cruelly self-castigating and the allegory is stripped bare of all that is not essential to the plain statement of an unpleasant truth.

The spareness and the directness—the absence of flourish—in communicating poetic thought which Graves achieved at this time have remained characteristic of his style ever since. A poem of his is usually, in the first place, an emblem or symbol, at once intellectually precise and emotionally evocative; but in the working out of the total image the mode of expression is direct, unmetaphorical statement. However, the excision from many of the poems in *Poems 1926–1930* of all but the negative emotions was an additional austerity that severely limited their scope. In this volume the negative poems predominate, and the proportion is still high in those poems written between 1930 and 1938; after 1938 they form only a small part of Graves's output.

Two of the best poems in *Poems 1926–1930*, 'Warning to Children' and 'The Terraced Valley', have this in common—that in contrast with a majority of the poems they are less puritanical in their (implied) self-criticism; the tone is more admonitory than dismissive. 'Warning to Children' warns against trying to encompass and explain the rich variety—

> All the many largeness, smallness
> Fewness of this single only
> Endless world...

—with an intellectual system. If you do, thought transforms reality into a Chinese nest of boxes, one inside the other, each promising in turn to be the single secret that explains the various whole:

Lumps of slate enclosing dappled
Red and green, enclosing tawny
Yellow nets, enclosing white
And black acres of dominoes.

In fact you thereby leave reality behind and enter into a private
world. The final box contains a parcel in which there is 'a small island'
promising complete escape. But on that island there is a tree that
bears a husky fruit, and if you open up the fruit 'In the centre you
will see/Lumps of slate enclosed by...' The secret inevitably eludes
you; the kernel of the fruit reveals the same series of logical problems
in reverse order. In imposing a pattern upon the formlessness of
reality you lose it; you substitute a private world for a real one; and
that private world of reason will become a prison of nonsense:

If you dare undo the parcel
You will find yourself inside it.

The poem's thought is, as it were, a conflation of the themes of
'Sandhills' and 'The Cell'. But the poet's admonitory tone makes
possible a more sensitive, less ruthlessly single and negative account
of the dangerous temptations inherent in the philosophical method.
In enacting the vertiginous effect of the endlessly diminishing and
expanding logical series the poet gives expression to a gathering fear
that is real, not assumed for the purpose of rendering its object
ridiculous (as in 'The Legs'). The approach is exploratory rather
than scornfully dismissive, concerned to establish degrees and kinds
of difference between the real world and the mentally constructed
one, rather than to make a simple black and white distinction. A
comparison is implied, for instance, between the two kinds of progression involved: each is equally endless, but the one in its various-
ness, the other in a frightening closed pattern of recurring cycles.
The smaller world is permitted to be attractive as well as frightening, its attractiveness differing from the larger world's as neatness
and prettiness differ from rich profusion. The poem, in short, reveals
a subtler, more flexible relationship between the poet and his subject than has been evident in the poems so far examined.

'The Terraced Valley' is also a warning against the dangers of intellectual idealism. The poet describes how in a moment of intense meditation upon the woman he loves he finds himself in a world, 'turned outside-in', of his own creation:

> Calm sea beyond the terraced valley
> Without horizon easily was spread
> As it were overhead
> Washing the mountain-spurs behind me:
> The unnecessary sky was not there,
> Therefore no heights, no deeps, no birds of the air.
>
> Neat outside-inside, neat below-above,
> Hermaphrodising love.

There is a brilliant suggestion in the womb-like image of the first six lines that, like the neat patterns of thought in 'Warning to Children', this daydream of a 'perfect' state of being, an inner world from which opposites have disappeared, has become for the poet an encircling, enclosing prison; far from liberating him, he now finds himself as before 'inside it'. It follows logically that, though thinking of his love has brought him here, there is, as he discovers, no place for her in this 'strange region'. It is only her voice close by him on the olive-terrace that, breaking the spell, restores the world suddenly (this is the last line of the poem) 'To once more inside-in and outside-out.' Man's private dream of love makes for an unnaturally 'calm', 'neat', untroubled existence; true love can exist only in the real world of opposites, conflict and disorder.

This 'trick of time', as it is called revealingly in the revised version, is one made possible by the 'relativity' theory, which according to Graves and Hodge in *The Long Week-end*, as popularly interpreted in the 'twenties to license a completely solipsistic point of view. 'The word "relativity" now came to be commonly used, out of the context of Einstein's theory, to mean that a thing was only so if you cared to assume the hypothesis that made it so. Truth likewise was not absolute: "beautiful results" could be obtained by mathematicians from consistent systems based on the hypothesis, for example, that one could slide a left hand into a rigid right-hand glove' (p. 97)—a conception used in the poem. Evidently Graves in

'The Terraced Valley' has abandoned the relativist standpoint he had held in such poems as 'Alice'. He has come to see the same idealizing tendency at play, the same evasion of reality, in the philosophical experiments of *Mock Beggar Hall* and *Welchman's Hose* as in the dreams of a perfect love in, say, 'The Red Ribbon Dream'. The 'easily' that describes the fusion of opposites in 'The Terraced Valley' was the magic word that ushered the poet of the earlier poem into his dreamworld.

'The Terraced Valley' also resembles 'Warning to Children' in embodying a more complex response to its subject. The internalized landscape manages to express both the poet's luxurious satisfaction in his imagined world ('calm', 'easily' and the sound of 'Washing the mountain-spurs behind me') and at the same time growing revulsion from its unnatural perfection. This makes itself felt as a blending of normally incompatible elements in imagery and language—of the dryly abstract-logical and the emotionally resonant, for example. The same has been shown to be true of 'Pure Death'. 'The Terraced Valley' answers to the conception, that emerges from the authors' analysis of a Hart Crane poem and subsequent general comments in *A Survey of Modernist Poetry*, of the typical modernist poem. It leaves an impression of 'well-controlled irregularity' or of a 'regularity of design more fundamental than mere verse regularity' (p. 48); the poem has been allowed to find its own natural size, form, line lengths, and movement. (One can see this as the culmination of a process that had its simple beginnings in some of the 'folk-poems' of *Country Sentiment* and *The Pier-Glass*.) Chiefly this 'naturalness' is exercised in the interests of brief, straightforward statement, sparing of adjectives—but not, this time, brief to the point of harshness or abruptness. Matter-of-factness is combined and enriched with a gravity of diction (the poem begins: 'In a deep thought of you and concentration'), and with the emotion inherent in the poem's total symbolism. This offers us a surrealistic landscape, the natural horror of which begins to accumulate imperceptibly in 'calm' and 'easily' and the sibilant smoothness of those first four lines, gathers urgency in the pressing echoes of 'there/Therefore' and 'no heights, no deeps, no birds of the air' and the biblical associations of that line, and rises to full frenzy in the obsessive repetition of the word 'neat'. At one point, in the one-word synonym for reconciliation of opposites, 'hermaphrodising', logical precision and emotional impact combine with spine-chilling effect.

'The Terraced Valley' is one of Graves best poems. Charles Tomlinson, who also thinks highly of it, is nevertheless unable to exempt it entirely from his general criticism of Graves's poetry, which tends in his opinion to simplify rather than explore the experience it treats.[1] Where I would agree *in this case* is in finding the change of mood introduced in the last line too brisk and neat. It has the effect of devaluing the poem's experience, which is made to carry for that moment no more weight of significance than a bad dream.

I have chosen to lay my main emphasis on the negative bias to this collection of poems because it is the most striking aspect, and was besides the most important single factor in the transformation of Graves's verse technique—one which affected all his poems, whether negative in attitude or not. However, the use of destructive, analytic and reductive methods is a process complemented in other poems by the direct affirmation of the values implied by them. Foremost of these is self. Assertion of the poet's self in opposition to society and convention and the refusal to restrict its field of behaviour are moral actions reflected in the manner of some of these poems.

The manner varies according to which persona Graves has assumed to dramatize this individualism, but the persona most commonly used by him for this purpose belongs to what might be called the intellectual roughneck. 'Railway Carriage' (better known by its title in the *Collected Poems*, 'Welsh Incident') is a well-judged and amusing example. It takes the form of a dialogue between two Welshmen. In response to the one's eager questions the other narrates in tones of pious horror how on Easter Tuesday last the chapel congregation witnessed the emergence from the sea-caves of Criccieth of a strange gathering of 'things'. Never having seen anything like them before, they watched in amazement as they moved across the sands, not heeding the crowd, slowly, silently and 'Not keeping time to the band'. The only sign they gave of being aware of their

[1] See Volume 7 of *The Pelican Guide to English Literature*, 2nd ed., p. 465.

observers was when, on being addressed ceremoniously if somewhat
nervously by the mayor, they emitted 'a loud belch'; in the revision
this becomes—

<blockquote>
a very loud, respectable noise
Like groaning to oneself on Sunday morning
In Chapel, close before the second psalm.
</blockquote>

The mythical creatures are evidently a disrespectful embodiment of
the poet's non-conformism. They are 'various, extravagant, utterly
peculiar/Things'—the revised version adds 'un-Welsh'; they are all
shapes and sizes, 'each perfectly unlike his neighbour'. As distinct
from the eponymous heroes of 'The Legs', these had 'Not a leg or
foot among them'. And they end by insulting—in the revision
parodying—the respectability and piety of mayor and congregation.
The revision removes from the original version the only traces of
self-indulgence in the satire.

Generally speaking, however, Graves was not successful in this
role, and he soon stopped writing in it. He was more successful with
a manner first employed in *Welchman's Hose* that went with an
urbane tone, modulating at times into well-bred arrogance. It is a
tone that has been heard frequently in his work ever since. A good
example of its use in *Poems 1926–1930* is 'Quayside' (retitled 'A
Former Attachment' in the *Collected Poems*), in which a ship moving
away from shore is an emblem for the breaking of a former attachment:

<blockquote>
And glad to find, on again looking at it,
It was not nearly so good as I had thought—
You know the ship is moving when you see
The boxes on the quayside sliding away
And growing smaller—and having real delight
When the port's cleared and the coast out of sight,
And ships are few, each on its proper course,
With no occasion for approach or discourse.
</blockquote>

This persona has the advantage of being ironic—on the principle
that the best form of defence is attack. Irony is an aggressive-
defensive weapon, and the aristocratic pose both shelters and asserts
the poet's eccentric individuality. The informality of the opening (a

device now characteristic of Graves's verse) represents elegant un-concern. The image of boxes 'growing smaller' seems innocuous but manages to be mildly and suavely insolent. 'Proper course' means here, primarily, the course that truly belongs to each particular ship, but carries also the sense of 'socially decent'; while the last line evokes the standards of upper-class decorum.

A second value affirmed in some of these poems is life as measured by a strictly human scale. 'Midway' is the fullest, if a not entirely satisfactory, exposition of this point of view. Man stands, in the poet's estimation, at a 'midway' point between the romantic's inflation and the pessimist's depreciation of his worth. He is self-sufficient and has no need of a 'system of extrinsic values'[1]. But the poem conveys its humanistic message in terms of the 'relativity' theory: 'Clocks tick with our consent to our time-tables,/Trains run to our time-tables'. Graves expresses disillusion with this fashion-able theory in 'The Terraced Valley', and confusion on this point may have contributed to the moral uncertainty of 'Midway' in its original version. Ostensibly the poet is stating his disbelief in the existence of an eternal human destiny, in infinite reality or absolute values, and presenting a conception of life as accidental, anthro-pocentric and without collective meaning or purpose. In fact the tone works for and against the stated meaning:

> Midway is man's convenience; we no longer
> Need either hang our heads or lift them high
> Unless for the weather's sake or when we dance;

and

> The scale steadies, at this point we renew
> Our fears of earthquakes, adders, floods, mad dogs
> And all such wholesomes.

Graves seems undecided whether his sarcasm is at the expense of the old order or the new world-view with which he apparently associates himself. In the first passage the sneering attitude towards extremists revealed in 'convenience' partly condemns itself by its vulgarity; certainly 'we' put themselves out of court by the triviality of their

---

[1] *Anarchism Is Not Enough*, p. 78.

interests. Yet this does not detract from the firmness with which the romantic and pessimistic positions are rejected. The poet is torn between contempt for the old idealism and resentment at the loss of its protection, and he has chosen to defend mediocrity in a paradoxical spirit of revenge. Although the second passage is making the point that it is healthy and sane to admit our natural fears and refuse to find a unifying pattern in the series of unrelated evils that beset us—in the words of 'Pure Death', to disenthrall our 'natural terror/ Of every comfortable philosopher'—nevertheless the word 'wholesomes' is, again, bitterly sarcastic. The ordinary disasters, about which we are being so *wholesomely* realistic, are rendered no less disastrous for our being so, and no more ennobling: some of the accidents that may determine our lives—the list includes 'adders' and 'mad dogs'—are trivial and without dignity. It is necessary to be human, but the human condition is both painful and ridiculous. The poem then, as printed in *Poems 1926–1930*, swings violently from one extreme to the other—between the truculent support for and shrill protest against seeing life as it is; the attitudes do not balance, as they do in 'Pure Death'. Graves has toned down the shrillness and ironed out inconsistencies in successive revisions, so that as it stands in its most recent version (*Collected Poems 1959*) it is an unambiguous vindication of the relativist viewpoint. But such a viewpoint is so distasteful to Graves now that this alone may account for its withdrawal from *Collected Poems 1965*. Another reason, however, may be that the final version was the result of misunderstanding the nature of the original poem. In removing the signs of conflicting feelings Graves had betrayed the poem's original inspiration, having abandoned the search for a proper tension between the opposing forces in favour of an easier solution.

I have already had occasion to note that underlying the assumed or stated values, the assertion of self and the self-humbling affirmation of the human norm, a number of poems appeal to a further value—the impersonal operation of the mind, in particular the probing, analytic, critical mind. It is implied in 'The Legs' and 'Thief'. It is the sole criterion of judgement in one poem not yet discussed, 'Landscape' (retitled 'Nature's Lineaments' in the *Collected Poems*), an attack on Nature, the novelty of which perhaps accounts for its undeservedly high reputation. It offers, though not without a distancing touch of self-mockery at its own vehemence, an extremely uncomplimentary account of the purely physical—insensate or animal—existence. The chance human resemblances suggested by rocks, trees or clouds are mere 'scribblings' that 'Caricature the human face'; one of them may take the shape momentarily, for example, of 'The ragged mouth in grin/Of cretin'. Again, Nature's winds move among '*empty* spaces/Ruffling the *idiot* grasses' (my italics). The only emendation in the version that appears in the *Collected Poems* makes the point explicit: 'all she has of mind/Is wind'.

But a surprising consequence of Graves's new moral sureness—surprising, that is, in a volume where it shows itself largely in sceptical, astringently realistic or self-critical verse—is the thin scattering of romantic poems. Romanticism, a new kind of unsentimental romanticism, was beginning to appear again towards the end of his first period, in the most recent work to be included in *Poems 1914–1926*. Under Laura Riding's influence the last vestiges of sentimentality disappeared and the moral quality of its aspiration was further developed. 'The Next Time' illustrates its chief qualities, restraint and impersonality. These have already been noted in 'Pygmalion to Galatea', but the dryer tone noticeable in some of the other poems in this volume has been added. 'The Next Time' begins, like 'Quayside', casually in mid-sentence—'And that inevitable accident'—and maintains through its concise but easy conversational style the air of being a random jotting.

It goes on to symbolize life as a train-journey for the duration of which we are confined to a single compartment and in which freedom of movement is accordingly restricted. The poet invites our consideration of that moment of free will—the 'inevitable accident'—in an otherwise predestined course when, the train stopping unexpectedly at 'Somewhere Nowhere', we are allowed time to 'stretch our legs and pick wild-flowers'; and finally puts this question—'Suppose that this time I elect to stay there?'. As the moment is snatched from a time-driven journey, the condition to which the poet aspires is evidently exemption from time's rule. This aspiration follows from the horrifying picture of life in time—life as dominated by time to the exclusion of all else, a purely physical existence— depicted in 'Castle', 'The Cell', 'It Was All Very Tidy', and 'Ship Master'. Laura Riding repudiated 'historic time' but images of timelessness had occurred earlier in Graves's work—in, for instance, 'Rocky Acres', and notably in more recent romantic poems like 'The Corner-Knot' and 'Virgil the Sorcerer'. Laura Riding had only added, or made clearer, a moral dimension to this deliverance from the rule of time; it has become now, precisely, the exchange of one image of life—a journey ordinarily estimated in terms of distance and price, 'miles and shillings'—for a superior one—a place, 'Somewhere Nowhere', where the values are other, presumably moral and spiritual.

Both in idea—'Suppose that this time I elect to stay there?'— and in the one image of picking wild flowers this poem is romantic. The image is reminiscent of the gathering of 'yellow vetch' in 'The Corner-Knot'. But that poem, 'Virgil the Sorcerer' and 'The Next Time' resemble each other in a more important way: they are all romantic in the sense that they express a desire for the extraordinary or the impossible. They are similar also in identifying the object of their desire with poetry, though its nature and aims are defined more specifically now. The difference lies in their emotional quality. The fantasy in 'Virgil the Sorcerer', although in the original version it was followed by a pessimistic conclusion, nevertheless expressed an urgent personal longing; it shared this emotional intensity with the earlier celebration of a timeless state in 'Rocky Acres'. By comparison the romanticism of 'The Next Time' is cooler and more tentative— and, paradoxically, more confident. It is as though Graves can afford to be cool because what he desires is now more nearly within his grasp; it only remains to convert a brief moment into a permanent condition. The tentativeness of the question-form merely enacts the mind's calm weighing of the chances.

The confidence of this new romanticism was, of course, a reflection of Graves's confidence in Laura Riding—it was she, after all, who had made a 'next time' possible—and generally it is this faith in woman, his discovering in her the source of all his values, that distinguishes the new romanticism from the old. The oddly cool, detached tone adopted by him here to express this confidence was appropriate to the kind of intelligence and the moral qualities displayed by Laura Riding. These are celebrated in 'Against Kind'. The title, it will be recalled, is a phrase also used of her in the Epilogue to *Goodbye To All That*. The poem opens:

> Become invisible by elimination
> Of kind in her, she none the less persisted
> Among kind...

By eliminating all that made her merely like other people she became purely herself. It was the impossibility of describing her in any other terms than those of her uniqueness, her simple, untranslatable individuality, that made her virtually non-existent, 'invisible', to people who were not individuals and thought in general, abstract terms.

> She went her private and eventless way...

> But soon it vexed them that her name still stood
> Plain on their registers, and over-simple,
> Not witnessed to by laundry, light or fuel,
> Or even, they wondered most, by drink and food.

What mattered to her was the inner, timeless reality of the mind rather than the external, material reality of events, or even the physical existence indicated by laundry, light, fuel, drink and food. She is, in other words, the embodiment of all the values implied or affirmed in the rest of this volume, and expounded by Laura Riding in *Anarchism Is Not Enough*.

The poem not only describes Laura Riding but describes her with the sort of vocabulary used by her and with her kind of wit. But the ideal of woman proposed here is related to both earlier and later ideals. Though presented in the specific terms of new beliefs, it agrees generally with Pygmalion's requirements as set out in 'Pygmalion to Galatea', written in 1925 before Graves had become personally acquainted with Laura Riding, that she should be fearless, self-honouring and unsubjected. In these respects, as I argued in my discussion of that poem, she anticipates the Muse-woman of the White Goddess poems. But there is more striking evidence in 'Against Kind' that Graves has drawn on this early ideal, made real in Laura Riding, for his portrait of the Muse-woman: he has since borrowed from this poem. In 'The Portrait' (*Poems and Satires 1951*) he reuses an important image to define her kind of difference ('She can walk invisibly at noon') and the title of another poem in the same volume, 'Your Private Way', actually echoes a phrase in the earlier poem, 'her private and eventless way'. As late as *Man Does, Woman Is* (1964) he is expressing individuality in the same way: 'she gave herself to herself' ('Deed of Gift') is recognizably the same kind of individuality as that depicted in the opening stanza of 'Against Kind'. More generally his conception here of the good life —living 'among kind' but at the same time 'against kind'—is remarkably like his most recent brief formulation of it—'to be in the world but not of it'.[1]

Another romantic poem, 'The Age of Certainty' (retitled 'New Legends' in the *Collected Poems*) is also notable for having interesting connections both with Graves's previous work and the White Goddess poetry while remaining a product of its period, bearing in theme and style the impression of Laura Riding's personality. The structure of the poem mirrors in the same literal way as 'It Was All Very Tidy' her idea of the poetic function: to strip down reality to a hard core of truth. It is divided into five sections of diminishing length with a repeated *first* line but this time the keyphrase, 'content in you', that begins each section, states a positive not a negative truth. For the poet once more proclaims his confidence in woman, naming her, however, in some of her mythological guises—Andromeda, Atalanta, Niobe, and Helen (while himself assuming the appropriate male part)—but altering the main event of the legend in which each figures so as to give her the dominant role. Thus Andromeda, 'Chained to no cliff', does not need to be rescued by him, and Atalanta wins her race:

[1] See his introduction to *The Sufis* by Idries Shah. Actually it is, he says, the Sufi ideal but one to which Graves gives his assent.

> Content in you
> Mad Atalanta
> Stooping unpausing
> Ever ahead
> Acquitting me of rivalry.

Here she shows her supremacy to consist in an unwavering sureness, which contradicts the opinion of woman's character revealed in the classical story. Other qualities mentioned in the poem are her serene independence, singleness of purpose, and the moral strength to transcend disaster.

Where the likeness with the White Goddess poems is most striking is in the method: here, as of course later, Graves uses mythology to impersonalize his feelings. The extremely laconic manner, indeed, gives 'The Age of Certainty' a particular resemblance to many of the poems that have been written during the 'sixties. Moreover the drive to interpret his sources was there apparently from the start. But, again, in the poet's conception of woman as morally superior it most importantly anticipates the later poetry. According to the earlier poems the poet's contentment in the woman he loves, his dependence on her natural 'certainty', is the only certainty he can ever possess—and over thirty years later Graves's attitude remains unchanged: in 'The Personal Muse', an essay included in the *Oxford Addresses on Poetry* (1962), he declares that the poet must 'learn from his Muse how to cultivate an intuitive certitude' (p. 77). But Graves's experience of her involves uncertainty as well as certainty. The Goddess personifies the principle of uncertainty in romantic love; similarly in 'The Age of Certainty' woman in one of her forms is the 'Invariable she-Proteus', eternally changing and unpredictable yet ultimately possessing (in the clearer logic of the revised version) 'singleness/Past all variety'. The poet's faith in woman countervails against the continuing vicissitudes of a relationship with her. This was the first poem to introduce this new element into a theme that had preoccupied Graves for most of his first period; which he had treated in a large number of poems, but notably in 'Sullen Moods', 'Song of Contrariety', 'Children of Darkness', 'Vanity' and 'This is Noon'.

Poems 1926–1930 is a remarkable volume and contains a large proportion of good poems. Graves wrote them during a period of high general literary productivity, other publications including criticism, essays, a story, a biography and an autobiography. In retrospect the separate works can be seen each to be the expression of a single activity: a process of tidying up and setting his own house morally and intellectually in order, in preparation for a final severance of ties with society and his own past. In 1929 he separated from Nancy, wrote *Goodbye To All That*, and left with Laura Riding for Majorca, where except in times of war he has lived ever since. In 1927 they had begun learning to print by hand and founded the Seizin Press; they set up the press again at Deyá, Majorca, and continued to issue limited editions—their own work and that of their friends. Seizin 6 was Graves's *To Whom Else?* (1931), a collection of twelve poems and a group of prose-poems, which, revised and supplemented by another thirteen poems, were made available to the general public in *Poems 1930–1933* (1933).

Basically Graves's moral and intellectual position in this volume is that of *Poems 1926–1930*. The main changes are in emphasis and in a slightly different approach to his themes. In the first place, there are fewer poems—the best examples, 'The Legs' and 'The Cell', have already been cited—occupied solely in denouncing a world living by false values; in the majority critical attention is focused on the poet's own moral limitations. Secondly, his relationship with the refractory, unregenerate part of himself has altered. Where in the previous volume his practice was to disown it with an icy or impatient contempt, most of the poems here have dropped this mask of clinical detachment. The tone confesses the poet's involvement: it is committed in its anger ('Trudge, Body'), in its scorn ('Ogres and Pygmies') and its disgust ('The Succubus'); or self-criticism is associated more openly with its complement, the romantic acclamation of love and woman as the only means of liberating the poet from himself.

One theme, referred to briefly in *Poems 1926–1930* and infrequently before that—the conflict between the discrepant purposes of lust and love, or between man's carnal nature and the nature of the moral and spiritual gifts that woman has to bestow—recurs obsessively in this volume. Lustful fantasies were the partial contents of the nightmares allegorized in 'Outlaws' and 'Ghost Raddled', but they received only a passing, horrified mention. 'The Succubus', in this collection, is a far bolder, unevasive rendering of the same experience:

> Thus will despair
> In ecstasy of nightmare
> Fetch you that devil-woman through the air,
> To slide below the sweated sheet.

The incompatibility of romantic aspiration with the horrors and limitations of its physical expression was the subject of a few other poems—'The Kiss', 'Children of Darkness' and 'O Love in Me'. In *Poems 1930–1933* the theme is similar but is presented within a new framework of thought and handled with greater poise and sureness. It is on the one hand a more specific version—that is, more personal in reference than in *Poems 1926–1930*—of the body-mind dichotomy; on the other, while the tone indicates the presence of personal emotion, Graves yet avoids the feverishness of his earlier treatments of the theme.

'Down, Wanton, Down!' explores the moral aspect of the conflict with wit and with preciser distinctions than before. As the title suggests, it takes the form of an address by the poet to his sexual organ. Firstly, he says, he is an automaton: mockingly he reproaches him for being so easily and promptly aroused, 'presto!', by the mere 'whisper of Love's name'. Secondly, he laments such lack of discrimination when he chooses: indifferent 'So be that in the breach you die'. He refers to him with familiar, smiling disdain in this connection as 'poor bombard-captain', and later with more contempt as 'my witless'. There follows in imperious tones a contrast between lust, as so defined, and love:

> Love may be blind, but Love at least
> Knows what is man and what mere beast:
> Or beauty, wayward, but requires
> More delicacy from her squires.

The tone turns to jeering at his fine pretensions and, lastly, at the absurdity of his believing that Love or 'many-gifted Beauty' should be answerable to *his* requirements.

The dominativeness that Graves diagnosed and repudiated in the behaviour of the lovers in *The Feather Bed*, and elsewhere at that time, has been discovered in this poem to be inseparable from the sexual act itself, the very nature of man's physical demands. The ideal set against the dominative, indiscriminative, mindless function of the animal part of man is, even more than love, woman—'many-gifted' (more richly endowed and with more to give than man) and 'wayward'. Her whims, rather than his physical compulsions, are the laws that now rule their relationship. This conception, it is clear from the term used, 'squires', as G. S. Fraser points out, is derived ultimately from the mediaeval poetry of Courtly Love. It is needless to stress at this stage that it is also, of course, central to the White Goddess mythology.

We have had mockery, ridicule and the aristocratic manner before; what is new in this poem is the relaxed demeanour. The poem is self-critical, but not in the self-humbling spirit of 'Thief' or 'Ship Master': the primary intention is affirmative not destructive. It has a playful, bantering rather than a tense detachment, and implies reserves of strength. These are drawn, evidently, from his pride in the woman he loves; for in order to establish his right to this standpoint of detachment from his conflict the poet has assumed the cadences of her voice, so that in effect it is her mockery, her ridicule and her aristocratic manner speaking in the poem.

'Ulysses', another rendering of the theme, shows the same firmness in tone and the same moral certainty; but here we feel more urgently the poet's personal presence. Out of the adventures of Homer's hero Graves has constructed an allegory of his own conflict. The length of Ulysses' absence from his wife and the extremity of his physical desires had finally blinded him to the difference between love, which he had felt for his wife, and the lust he felt for every woman he encountered; so confused were Penelope and Circe in his mind that it was thoughts of his wife Penelope that aroused 'lewd fancies' in him and the whore Circe who bore him a son. The 'counter-changings' of these two images of woman were symbolically represented time and again during his journeyings: in one episode they appeared as the clashing rocks, in another as Scylla and Charybdis; or

> Now they were storms frosting the sea with spray
> And now the Lotus Orchard's filthy ease;

and again, 'They multiplied into the Siren's throng'. The poet's verdict on his case is this:

> One, two and many: flesh had made him blind.
>   Flesh had one pleasure only in the act,
> Flesh set one purpose only in the mind—
>   Triumph of flesh...

Here, in this exposure of lust's 'filthy ease' (later modified to 'drunken ease') and narrow, mindless drive to dominate its object, the poet's emotions, though well under control, are patently more engaged than in 'Down, Wanton, Down!' There is an unwonted use of rhetoric. In the last passage the repetition of the word 'flesh' and the repeated, relentless rhythms convey his personal horror at the 'triumph of flesh'. This is balanced by an equal intensity of positive emotion; the poem rides with ease the swell of lyrical feeling in the romantic 'storms frosting the sea with spray'. An emblem for sexual abstinence, the phrase idealizes, and expresses the poet's acceptance of, the difficult tasks imposed upon the romantic lover. 'Ulysses' more than 'Down, Wanton, Down!' embodies, at the same time as it transcends, Graves's conflict.

The purely romantic poems in this volume share with some of their neighbouring poems, like 'Ulysses', an atmosphere of emotional release, and get a stage nearer to the mythological poetry of the 'forties. Both these statements can find their justification in 'To Whom Else?'. The title-poem of the first collection of his poems to be issued by the Seizin Press in Majorca, this is Graves's dedication of himself, presumably, to Laura Riding. For she it was who, in the words of the poem, 'mercilessly' yet 'lovingly' 'Plucked out the lie'. The relative characterization of man and woman which it offers is expressed however with unacceptable extravagance: its acclamation of woman is too breathless in its rapture and in the end not credible. Its chief fault lies, perhaps, in its uncertainty of genre. The poet is undecided whether he is celebrating a real woman or a mythological figure symbolizing certain aspects of woman's power.

There is no such confusion in 'On Portents'. Douglas Day reports that Graves was reading Plutarch's 'On Isis and Osiris' at this time; Apuleius's description of the Goddess in *The Golden Ass* was, of course, already well known to him. We may safely assume that it is therefore Isis whose presence causes the supernatural events recorded in the poem.

> If strange things happen where she is,
> So that men say that graves open
> And the dead walk, or that futurity
> Becomes a womb and the unborn are shed,
> Such portents are not to be wondered at,
> Being tourbillions in Time made
> By the strong pulling of her bladed mind
> Through that ever-reluctant element.

One is tempted to say that this is the first fully-fledged White Goddess poem—written (between 1929 and 1931) well over a decade before her official advent. The only signs of its period, of its partial origin in the poet's veneration for Laura Riding, are in the references to the dangerous ('bladed') clarity and acuity of her mind and her unenslavement by time. But in all other respects this is identical with many of the later mythological poems. It has the same tone of wonder and awe combined with intellectual precision and compactness in the imagery, and the same skilful manipulation of sound—where, for example, the criss-cross of assonances in the phrases 'Time made' and 'bladed mind' enacts the interpenetration of mind and time described in those lines. In 1938 Graves placed 'On Portents' in the last section of his *Collected Poems* among a small group of poems which, he noted in the Foreword, display 'a more immediate sense of poetic liberation'.

Even more outstanding than the development of a new authority in his romantic poems is the achievement in two poems, 'The

Felloe'd Year' and 'Time', of a kind of tension that has often since been characteristic of Graves's poetry at its best. They are related to poems like 'Vanity' and 'O Love in Me' in being balanced presentations of romantic and realistic motives operating simultaneously, but lack the touch of asperity or bitterness in those poems. 'The Felloe'd Year' (unaccountably never reprinted) moves with a calm, steady and firm decorum, merely hinting in a barely perceptible shift in rhythm or an unostentatious but carefully placed word at the pressure of emotion being held down. After a mild opening, in which the poet observes that the pleasure of summer was its easy victory over winter, and of winter our sure expectation of the summer to follow, we come upon a word charged in this way with unexpected meaning: he goes on to admit that there was something painful nevertheless in the year's movement through the intermediate seasons, that the contrasting pleasures met each other in a 'perpetual spring-with-autumn ache', and we are made to pause upon the word 'ache'; for a moment there is a ripple on the surface indicating an undercurrent of unstated feeling. Immediately the word is absorbed back into the image: it becomes the 'creak and groan' of the seasons' turning wheel. The poem has so far been in the past tense; now, for the concluding lines, there is a sudden switch to the present and in consequence an increase in our awareness of the underlying emotion:

> In which all move yet—I the same, yet praying
> That the twelve spokes of this round-felloe'd year
> Be a fixed compass, not a turning wheel.

'I the same, yet praying..' epitomizes the tension of this kind of poem. With all things moving in the inevitable cycle of the seasons and bound by the laws of time, the poet announces his subjection to the same rule, yet in the same breath prays to be exempted from it: in the very same moment, and with equal tenacity, both accepts what alone is actual and possible and resists it.

'Time' turns to a different aspect of the same theme. It is remarkable for a similar assurance and sensitive control of detail but its technical success is in this instance a more considerable achievement, as the poem embodies a much more complex response.

The vague sea thuds against the marble cliffs
And from their fragments age-long grinds
Pebbles like flowers.

Or the vague weather wanders in the fields,
While up spring flowers with coloured buds
Like marble pebbles.

The beauty of the flowers is Time, death-grieved:
The pebbles' beauty too is Time,
Life-weary.

It is all too easy to admire a flower
Or a smooth pebble flower-like freaked
By Time and vagueness.

Time is Time's ease and the sweet oil that coaxes
All obstinate locks and rusty hinges
To loving-kindness.

What monster's proof against that lovesome pair,
Old age and childhood, seals of Time,
His sorrowful vagueness?

Or will not render him the accustomed thanks,
Humouring age with filial flowers,
Childhood with pebbles?

The strategy is approximately that of 'The Felloe'd Year'. The
surface manner is almost unruffled; the movement is careful and
unhurried. It begins with an impersonal matter-of-factness, the
first three stanzas merely explaining the structure of its imagery;
after that the poet's feelings are introduced by mild insinuation.

The images in the first two stanzas present two perspectives on
time—time as an 'age-long' process making artifacts almost for
eternity and time as the creator of transience. Pebbles are emblems
of what is indestructible, flowers of what is transient; in the former
time shows its weariness of life, in the latter its grief that things
should die. It is appropriate that we should offer age the consolations of transient but blooming flowers and childhood the illusion of
permanence. A tension exists between the poet's simultaneous
awareness of the beauty for which time is responsible and of time's

basic indifference to it, time's 'vagueness'. It is the very mildness and ordinariness of this word that makes the repetition of it and its adjective cumulatively sinister. As well as time's indifference and unawareness of what it creates it conveys the accidental quality of time, its lack of a precise meaning or purpose—all, in fact, that Laura Riding meant by an unsystematized reality. The poet is torn between appreciation of time's products and recognition that in the light of time's final treachery such appreciation is sentimental. But the exposure of this element of sentimentality is the opposite of aggressive: the poet no longer pretends to be himself unaffected. The mood generated between these opposed responses is a gentle wryness, combining muted protest with resignation. 'It is all too easy. .' is a sigh of self-reproach. In the next stanza this turns to a distaste, expressed in the sibilants, for the cloying sweetness of 'time's blandishments'. 'Lovesome', an ugly synonym for lovable, focuses a sharper repugnance for the insidious deception being practised; it enacts a positive grimace of saddened self-mockery. This becomes sarcasm in the last stanza and the implied accusation that he has lent himself knowingly to this pretence: the consolations offered to childhood and old age are, after all, no more than humourings. But at each stage in this indictment there is the balancing contrary awareness. The pebble's perfect beauty is stressed in the deliberately poetical 'freaked'; 'loving-kindness' is an emotional word, rich in association, and conveys the poet's participation in the gesture it makes; and only a monster, it is implied, could refuse childhood and old age his love, however sentimental. The question-form of the last two stanzas contributes to this tension the further refinement of a suspended judgement, and leaves the conflicting elements in ironic equipoise; but in the irony—and this is even truer of the revised version in the *Collected Poems*—there is just the hint of a dangerous tone, a suggestion that the poet might indeed refuse 'the accustomed thanks'.

This is not the first occasion on which a question has concluded a poem of Graves, but 'Time', is, I think, the first example of the strategy used to reflect this kind of poise and resilience. If this is so, then it is the first in a long line of excellent poems quite individual to Graves and perhaps his most characteristic and notable achievement. *Poems 1926–1930* made a necessary break with much in his previous work and brought to fruition some of the more promising developments of his first period. Without the influence of Laura Riding Graves's poetry would perhaps have taken much longer to reach, or might not have reached, its present stature. But *Poems 1930–1933* can claim to be the first volume to give a settled idea of the nature and range of his mature poetry. The self-disciplinary endeavour of *Poems 1926–1930* has achieved its purpose of finally excluding irrelevancies and sentimental excrescences from his poems; in its successor Graves has been able to bring the new manner and attitude towards poetry to bear on the deepest sources of his inspiration—personal conflict and the love-theme.

5

'No More Ghosts'

UNDOUBTEDLY the two early volumes of Graves's second period included a number of undistinguished and unsuccessful poems: some that were in the nature of private jokes or merely lacked seriousness, others that showed failures of tone or in which the satire was indiscriminately aggressive. The poet himself in one of this last group, 'Front Door Soliloquy' (*Poems 1926–1930*), pinpointed the quality they chiefly held in common: 'This house is jealous of its nastiness'. But any impression that the manner of those few poems, whether trivial or nasty, is representative of Graves's writing at that time would be seriously wrong. It is an impression, however, that critics frequently have formed, not only of the poetry published during the early years of Laura Riding's influence but also of the poems that continued to benefit, as Graves confessed, from her constructive and detailed criticism until the conclusion of their partnership in 1938, a year which also saw the publication of his second *Collected Poems*. This too is false.

There are examples of the trivial, the smart and the nasty in the poetry of the later years, but they are a very small proportion of the total. A few pieces like 'Lunch-Hour Blues'—flippantly abusive, shallow in thought, vehicles for little more than a disorganized exasperation—are scattered thinly through the later sections of the *Collected Poems*. 'Lunch Hour Blues' is best described as a squib, thrown at the usual easy target, the respectable citizen. Here he is seen at the lunch-table, a man who in the ascetic service of his god money has ceased to employ his various senses—hearing, smelling, seeing and tasting nothing.

> He's thrown the senses from their seat,
> As Indian heroes do—
> An act more notable were not
> The mind unseated too.

Such facetiousness is more in the tradition of the Thomas Hood doggerels than of serious satire. Productions of this sort, we might conclude from a comparison with similar verses of D. H. Lawrence's, are also an occupational hazard of the professional exile.

More cunning in its denigration of the civic virtues is the paradoxical defence of 'self-praise' in the poem of that title.

> Praise from the mouths of others is
> (All citizens agree)
> The sweetest of experiences
> And confers modesty.

The dulcet tone is an insidiously effective weapon of satire. If forbearance from self-praise is the mark of their secret self-approval, then, the argument goes, outright self-praise will firmly distinguish the poet from the bourgeois 'dogs and swine' he so abominates. So far, so good; but the bestial imagery—and it is worked out with some laboriousness—is a danger-signal, indicating a complacency of the poet's own to match that of the citizens. Not honest self-praise but arrogance and a naïve vanity are behind the poem's conclusion, in which the poet rejects the company of his fellow-citizens because he claims to be 'Too squeamish for the sty'. This is not the first time that boastful egotism has made itself felt strongly in a poem of Graves's. Where it occurs, as in 'Rocky Acres' and 'To the Reader over My Shoulder', it seems, as here, to be compulsively associated with a crude attack upon the bourgeoisie.

A third weakness that occasionally betrays itself in the more accomplished poems, may be illustrated from 'The Eremites'. Seriously intended to throw a cynical—a kind of Freudian—light upon the unconscious motives informing the asceticism practised by 'our pious fathers', the intention is vitiated by a stronger desire merely to be scandalous. In an ecstasy of loathing the poet lists the 'unnatural lusts', the 'Attelan orgies of the soul', indulged by hermits (typifying the 'pious fathers') in their dreams and visions; assures us that 'these goatish men'

> Kept vigil till the angelic whores
> Should lift the latch of pleasure—

repeats his accusations, in fact, so often and with such vehemence that they become at last incredible.

Such misjudgements of satirical aim are rare at this time. His satires are usually exact, terse, penetrating. An average example, 'The Laureate', yields this—

> Once long ago here was a poet; who died.
> See how remorse twitching his mouth proclaims
> It was no natural death, but suicide—

with its calmly scrutinizing irony, its fine control of voice emphasis, and its nicely calculated surprises in the rhyme-words of the first and last line. His satires range from what Douglas Day calls *jeux d'esprit* to poems which arise out of the poet's central, most personal preoccupations.

'The Halls of Bedlam' belongs, no doubt, to the first category. It is an exuberant burlesque of society's 'normal' image of the poet— the 'sensational' image put forth, say, by the popular newspapers, which is a projection of the vague feelings about the strangeness of the creative artist, or merely the highly individualized person, that the word 'genius', a convenient receptacle for a variety of misconceptions, is commonly made to carry. An automatic respect and superstitious awe pass easily into delighted horror and the conviction that the poet's abnormality is a species of madness. The poem narrates with graphic detail and in the appropriately scandalized tones how, 'Forewarned of madness', an 'imminent genius' goes 'normally, normally' about this daily business, gossiping, arguing, checking the cash account, until on the third day the (poetic) 'fit masters him'. While he is admitted to the halls of Bedlam, where 'The artist is welcome', the chorus of family, friends and neighbours remain to make their gloating comments:

> A very special story
> For their very special friends—
> They burst in the telling:
>
> Of an evil thing, armed,
> Tap-tapping on the door,
> Tap-tapping on the floor,
> 'On the third day at dusk'.

Father in his shirt-sleeves
Flourishing a hatchet—
Run, children, run!

Neatly in the poem's close the tables are turned: the bland assumption that normality equals sanity is as blandly ignored, and the description 'mad' is found to be more aptly applicable to the man's behaviour before, rather than after, the fit mastered him—continuing, as he did, to gossip and argue and make 'The neat marginal entry'

Normally, normally
As if already mad.

One of the best of the satires (because closely related to the poet's most deeply felt convictions) is 'To Evoke Posterity'. It is on the theme that to write for the approval of posterity, instead of for yourself and in the service of your own truth, is (in a finely concentrated phrase) 'Ventriloquizing for the unborn', assuming a personality not your own. This, of course, according to Graves's and Laura Riding's poetic and moral principles, is the chief sin. The theme, as I have shown, is a frequent one in *Poems 1926–1930*. The poem finds in this betrayal of self the single, unifying explanation of all the falsities of public life. Pursuing not the truth of self but public applause, you will lose personal reality and *become* the empty thing owned by the public, and for that 'the punishment in known':

To be found fully ancestral,
To be cast in bronze for a city square...
A life proverbial
On clergy lips a-cackle;
Eponymous institutes,
Their luckless architecture.

From the context of this stated value these instances of becoming the property of posterity gather precise, condemnatory meaning. 'Ancestral' booms with the hollowness of a life lived not here but at a remove. 'To be cast in bronze', also unexpectedly bringing to the fore an ordinarily secondary implication of being so honoured, is to be dead; the phrasing even hints at entombment. It is the triteness and lifeless fixity of the wisdom offered by the clergy that is highlighted in 'proverbial'. 'Eponymous institutes' brings irresistibly to mind the soulless atmosphere and the physical ugliness of such buildings, of which it is the name and not the soul, its 'selfhood', that counts. The latter idea is one that Graves plays with again in a much later poem, 'My Name and I' (*Poems and Satires 1951*). 'Luckless' is brilliant as a description of such architecture: the luck of inspiration is what it lacks, and the word is used to distinguish generally the vital and meaningful from their opposites. The word is a buoyantly gay piece of understatement, typically expressive of Graves's 'sanguine temperament'. It suggests the element of mystery in personality, of the unpredictable and incalculable in life, to which Graves now attaches prime importance. He uses the word and the concept again in 'The Halfpenny', another poem of this period, and it has occasionally appeared since then in his prose writings.

'To evoke posterity' is a type of opening phrase and title common to several poems written during the later years of this period. The beginning of a poem with a kind of logical proposition—to do something equals something else—is a mannerism characteristic of a style and a way of thinking practised not only in the satires but more generally at this time and with more severity than at any other time in Graves's career. The poem is regarded as exclusively an evaluative medium; its imagery is pressed briskly into the service of moral analysis and judgement. The effect is not didactic but ironic. One reason is that the demonstration that succeeds the proposition is, as frequently in Donne's poems, a parody of logical procedure. But there is more to the irony than that. Though his tone is dryly intellectual, unlike Donne Graves does not employ an intellectual vocabulary or imagery. His analogies are likely to be simple but eccentric and unexpected. 'To walk on hills', begins one poem, again using the title-phrase, is a joint venture of 'legs', 'head', and 'heart' 'towards/Perhaps true equanimity'. Hill-walking, which, as the poem goes on to show, connotes looking for picturesque sights to be awed and thrilled by, is an emblem, in other words, for the sentimental-romantic search. 'Legs', by walking with no purpose but to exercise the body, and 'heart', by sentimentalizing landscape, combine to overthrow the strict and sobering rule of the mind.

A view of three shires and the sea!
Seldom so much at once appears
Of the coloured world, says heart.
Head is glum, says nothing.

Legs become weary, halting
To sprawl in a rock's shelter,
While the sun drowsily blinks
On head at last brought low—
This giddied passenger of legs
That has no word to utter.

There is a disparity between the dry tone and the imagery, which
results in an oddly distanced attitude, as though the poet intends to
show by it an indifference, or a superiority, to his subject-matter.
The attitude has been noted already in 'Hell', but here it is no longer
so savagely dismissive. The effect rather is humorous: the tone either
shows itself to be amused by or actively deflates the images. The
amusement runs through the whole passage; the deflating intention
is there in such phrases as 'the coloured world', suggesting the
simple colours of an illustration for children rather than the real
world, and 'the sun drowsily blinks', which again relegates the
whole romantic venture to the world of the nursery.

Another style characteristic of these years is also a development
from *Poems 1926–1930*. 'Parent to Children' is a representative
example. The opening lines set the tone:

When you grow up, are no more children,
Nor am I then your parent...

It is even brisker than the tone of 'To Walk on Hills'—brisk to the
point of curtness. The rhythms throughout the poem are clipped and
unsettled, the lines short and each three-lined stanza is a tightly
self-contained unit, separating with sharp precision each logical
stage in the argument from the next. It is as though the poem were
in note-form, jottings made of the essential points in a situation.
There is an austere restraint here but no attempt to appear indifferent:

The procreative act was blind:
It was not you I sired then—
For who sires friends, as you are mine now?

Yet I envisaged progeny,
And children I begot, to fear;
And these were you, though now are not you.

This is at once more intellectual and more passionate than 'To Walk on Hills' and the poems like it. The painful nature of the poet's awareness of his theme is implicit—curtly taken for granted, as it were—in the urgent movement of these lines, yet it is as an idea, a paradoxical idea, that he is painfully aware of it; the anguish belongs to the difficulty in comprehending the seemingly incomprehensible. The combination brings this class of poem much nearer to the Metaphysical style. There is a specific resemblance to Donne's poetry in the play with logical riddles—'were you' and 'are not you'—and the stress on logical correspondence. It is this rhythm of ideas rather than a verse regularity (though a basic iambic metre is also there) that the poem relies on for the controlling pattern necessary to poetry.

The aristocratic tone can be heard in many poems of this time, and was gradually becoming an indispensible ingredient of Graves's style. In 'The Cloak' the assumption of an aristocratic persona is the poem's whole strategy and here the tone is employed with most success, more flexibly and for less limited purposes than in 'Quayside' (*Poems 1926–1930*), one of the earlier examples of its use. The poet is actually represented as an exiled Georgian or Regency peer, the name and function of poet being the equivalent of the peer's title, and his attitudes to society identical with those of the exiled peer to his country. He arrives in France and seems content with his humble lodgings in Dieppe and the 'sharp' but 'wholesome' wine—

> The cares of an estate would incommode
> Such tasks as now his Lordship has in hand.
> His Lordship, says the valet, contemplates
> A profitable absence of some years.

He has no feelings of nostalgia for his homeland:

exile's but another name
For an old habit of non-residence
In all but the recesses of his cloak.

The satirical thrusts are the more effective for being more casually,
even carelessly, delivered than in the earlier poem. The politely dis-
dainful euphemisms, rotundities and understatements enact a more
subtly ironic, composed and poised attitude. The impersonation,
too, is a more faithful one, and the period quality of the allegory
achieves for the poet an almost genial detachment, as though he is
enjoying the act, an air of mock-solemnity implying ridicule of the
presumed cloddishness and lack of poise in the society that has
exiled him. The poem has the relaxed quality of humour—the
element of self-parody is essential to it—as distinct from the sharpness of wit. Rather than the power to make a clean dismissal, which
'Quayside' exemplified, the style here is concerned to demonstrate
the poet's ease and assurance in the role adopted and the values he
has chosen to live by. He is able to accept calmly now the isolation
inseparable from a life lived strictly according to personal conviction
that he first called 'exile' (but then with bitterness) in 'To M. in
India' (*The Marmosite's Miscellany*).

But perhaps the central achievement of these years is the formation of a balanced, all-purpose style, an amalgam of features taken
from each of the three special styles just analysed. A typical poem is
still concerned primarily with the 'evaluation of good and bad
elements in actuality',[1] but the process is not made to appear, as it
is in 'To Walk on Hills' and 'To Bring the Dead to Life', one of
definition. The skeleton of logic has been sufficiently though not
amply fleshed, and the tone is not self-denyingly dry but plain—
one might call it practical. Take, for example, 'Defeat of the Rebels'.
In the context of a colonial war the poet demonstrates the superiority
of self-disciplined over romantic behaviour. The rebels were foolish,
relying on romantic gestures to offset their unpreparedness and lack
of determination, and were therefore easily defeated by us. Since
they would not learn to be realistic and in the event proved cowardly

[1] *The Long Weekend*, p. 300.

they deserve no pity. But we too had fallen short of the necessary standards of efficiency and alertness: the gear they abandoned in flight was our own, stolen from us in the past, and would not have been 'But for our sloth and hesitancy'. The manner of the poem is that of a discussion, in which alternative moral positions are considered: the enemy, deceived by their own rhetoric,

> thought it enough
> To believe and to blow trumpets, to wear
> That menacing lie in their shakos.

> Enough: it falls to us to shoot them down...
> Such prisoners were unprofitable.

The style includes a measure of briskness and, in that last line, even of cold aristocratic disdain. It is impersonal in a way that recalls 'The Cloak'—it involves an assumed tone—but the distance between the poet and his persona has lessened considerably; it is, in fact, barely perceptible, and the tone can modulate swiftly into the direct expression of strongly committed moral feeling, as in that reference to the 'menacing lie', which brings it momentarily closer to 'Parent to Children'.

The years of his association with Laura Riding were for Graves a period of poetic self-realization. There were fewer instances of what in his Foreword to *Collected Poems 1938* (p. xiv) he calls 'digressions' from his true interests as a poet. Gradually he came to see himself as committed chiefly to two roles—as moralist on the one hand and as love poet on the other—and almost all his poems written between 1933 and 1938 were the result of his activity in one or the other of these roles or in both at once. 'Defeat of the Rebels' belongs to the first group. The values it refers to, the practical virtues of hard work and decisive action, are the moderate, everyday, strictly human values of 'Midway' but are not invoked in the bitterly self-castigating spirit of that poem. This region of practical morality is inhabited with more naturalness and assurance now.

Frequently these qualities are embodied in a manner and imagery that are not merely natural but homely, as, for example, in 'The

China Plate'. The plate (of the title) was discovered in a street-market, its value as an antique hitherto unnoticed, and was purchased cheaply. It was brought home and, prized rather as a showpiece than as a useful piece of crockery, was put on display on a prominent shelf and produced proudly to be inspected by admiring friends. The tale has been told satirically and the poet's implied disapproval is now made explicit—with the same brisk impatience as is shown in 'Defeat of the Rebels':

> Enough, permit the treasure to forget
> The emotion of that providential purchase...
>
> Let it regain a lost habit of life,
> Foreseeing death in honourable breakage
> Somewhere between the kitchen and the shelf—
> To be sincerely mourned.

Not only does the poem make its moral statement with a homely directness but the values affirmed are essentially simple. The clear, undoubting nature of the poet's allegiance to these values is conveyed through the crisp finality, the almost epigrammatic quality of the short last lines of each stanza. The poem gives expression, more strongly than before, especially in that last stanza, to Graves's conviction that he must accept the common terms of life ('Foreseeing death..') and frame his daily existence according to certain basic rules of conduct such as honour and hard work.

Several poems written during this period connect this simplicity with the coming of a new sureness and depth of feeling. In 'The Ages of Oath' it is the first article of a poetic creed. Graves confesses that in the past

> The lost, the freakish, the unspelt
> Drew me: for simple sights I had no eye,

and asks:

> Did I forget how to greet plainly
> The especial sight, how to know deeply
> The pleasure shared by many hearts?

In 'No More Ghosts' simplicity is identified with the solution to old problems, in particular the emotional disturbances arising from his neurasthenia and (perhaps) being part of an uncongenial society. Apart from 'Leaving the Rest Unsaid', in which the poet takes leave of the reader, this is the last poem in *Collected Poems 1938* and counterbalances the one Graves has chosen to open the collection, 'The Haunted House' (originally 'Ghost Raddled'): now the 'patriarchal bed' that harboured ghosts has been 'cut to wholesome furniture for wholesome rooms' and

> We are restored to simple days, are free
> From cramps of dark necessity.

'Defeat of the Rebels' and 'The China Plate' are representative examples of Graves's moral realism during these years, which was a development, but a distinctive one, of the sceptical-realistic mood that had been playing an ever more important part in his verse since its appearance in about 1925. They show some of the moral positives the firm possession of which he had been working for for over a decade. These criteria for living are few and traditional but give strength to his verse without in any way simplifying the moral situations presented. There is for instance, no avoidance in 'The China Plate' of the corollary to 'Becoming a good citizen of the house', which is 'death in honourable breakage'; yet the poem manages to convey convincingly that in facing the inevitability of death one is not only behaving honourably but regaining a 'lost habit of life'. Such strength is an impressive achievement and a testimony of moral courage in the poet. It is new to his work and has since become characteristic of it. But it is not his finest achievement. These poems show only one aspect of Graves's poetic temperament, taking no account of his urgent impulse to romantic protest against the conditions of life. It is in those poems, as I have argued, that incorporate both elements—the realistic and the romantic—of his disposition that his very best work lies; in them is most apparent the 'mistrust of the comfortable point-of-rest' to which Graves ascribes (in his Foreword to *Collected Poems 1938*) his continuing 'health as a poet'. The best example from this period—in a line with poems like 'Time', 'O Love in Me', and 'Vanity'—is the well-known 'Certain Mercies'.

It presents an image of the spirit as a prisoner of the body. The spirit asks:

> Now must all satisfaction
> Appear mere mitigation
> Of an accepted curse?

Can we, the spirit, not escape the curse; must we merely accept it and be grateful for the small mercies allowed us: that the water though rusty quenches our thirst, that we are hungry enough to find the rotten food edible, and that 'with patience and deference' we at least manage to avoid punishment;

> That each new indignity
> Defeats only the body,
> Pampering the spirit
> With obscure, proud merit?

The tension is between the desires of the spirit and the limitation on their realization imposed by the body—between romantic longing and reality. At first it seems that the balance of forces is not being kept. 'We' is identified with the spirit and the tone of the questioning expresses arrogant protest against an oppressive reality; the questions, that is to say, are merely rhetorical and expect each time the answer 'no'. But the last stanza corrects this impression, making it clear, for instance, that the poem is dramatic: that the 'we' (spirit) a character, whose arrogance is measured by the tone of its questions and judged by the words 'pampering' and 'obscure'. If its merit is 'obscure', even though also 'proud', then such merit is at least suspect, while 'pampering' leaves no room for doubt, unequivocally exposing the self-indulgence of the spirit's pride. Nevertheless the protest, though faulty in its arrogance, has been made, and the poem does not accept the 'accepted curse' any more than it supports the spirit in its pretensions. The question is truly left open, has the last word, and the poem ends where it began—in uncertainty. Uncertainty itself is what is accepted.

This kind of poise bears witness to Graves's increasingly precise awareness of his double nature, an awareness that is the result of a maturing of self-knowledge, chiefly of himself in love, throughout the period of his partnership with Laura Riding. Whereas during the first period it was a by-product of his poetic energies, apparent in occasional poems like 'Return', under the influence of Laura Riding its cultivation became a conscious purpose, was more ruthlessly pursued and was practised as a moral discipline. Poems such as 'Thief' in *Poems 1926–1930*, which were exercises in self-contemptuous antiromanticism, led later to 'Never Such Love', a more probing exposure of the illusions that possess lovers, and to 'Ulysses' (*Poems 1933*) and in the later 'thirties 'A Jealous Man', both penetrating psychological studies of man's moral inadequacies in his relationship with woman.

'Never Such Love' is an acidly ironic comment on the over-sanguine expectations of lovers who, not recognizing 'The heart's fated inconstancy', see in the man-woman relationship only the immediate promise of happiness, and who to satisfy uncontrollable greed enter into it in a blind haste. Their love is no more than

> the near-honourable malady
> With which in greed and haste they
> Each other do infect and curse...

The violence of their initial confidence, when they swore 'Never such love..ever before was', is followed inevitably by a correspondingly violent disillusionment, when at their love's ending they are overwhelmed with 'sorrow and shame'. Graves has here exposed the lovers' ignorance of the full reality of love and the 'greed and haste' that governs their actions. His own position of detachment is based on the awareness that both the happiness and the suffering are necessary aspects of the love situation, each a stage in an ever-recurring cycle of events: as it was love that caused the lovers to flourish so now they are 'by love withered'—'True lovers even in this', the poem concludes. In this attitude 'Never Such Love' is nearer than say, 'Vanity'—where the theme is similar—to the clear-eyed acceptance of love in all its aspects that characterizes Graves's poetry of the 'forties.

'A Jealous Man' is a comic-horrific study (after the manner of 'The Legs') of the nature of jealousy.

To be homeless is a pride
To the jealous man prowling
Hungry down the night lanes,

who has 'a mind dream-enlarged' and imagines

Tall corpses, braced together,
Fallen in clammy furrows,
Male and female.

It is intimated in these stanzas that jealousy arises out of an imperfect love—a love which is hungrily demanding, proudly ungiving
and resentful; which, in other words, is dominated by lust, the
principal emotion to inform the jealous man's fantasies. Contrasted
with the man's state of conflict is the woman's self-possession and
purity of motive:

Now out of careless sleep,
She wakes and greets him coldly,
The woman at home,

She with a private wonder
At shoes bemired and bloody—
His war was not hers.

The contrast—'His war was not hers'—deepens the moral implications of this particular psychological insight, providing a moral
standard by which to measure the poet's (obviously this is personal
experience) degree of failure in the love relationship. The insights
concerning this theme here and in 'Never Such Love', and in
slighter poems like 'Galatea and Pygmalion' or not completely
successful ones like 'The Eremites' and 'The Stranger', laid the
foundations for much of the assurance that informs the poetry of
Graves's next period.

These insights form an integral part of another more ambitious
group of poems. I am thinking primarily of three poems—'Green
Loving', 'The Challenge' and 'End of Play'. Each is an attempt to
define the difference between two kinds of love—to be more exact,
between divergent attitudes towards, and estimations of, the love
experience. In Graves's later view the first kind is the 'near-honour-
able malady' analysed in 'Never Such Love', and it is placed by

comparison with a love acknowledging new values. These are values that have already been enforced in a large number of poems written since 1926 and were associated with the personality of Laura Riding in 'Against Kind'. In the love-poems, however—'The Age of Certainty' and 'On Portents', for example—though clearly and confidently affirmed, they were presented in the barest outline. In the later group of poems Graves *explores* his thought—in a more complex series of images shared in part by all three poems.

The theme they hold in common is stated most succinctly in another poem, 'Fiend, Dragon, Mermaid', which celebrates the poet's release from the Fiend of pride, the dragon of neurasthenic despair, and the mermaid of his early love, the affected innocence of whose 'childish-lovely face' seemed to promise him shelter and consolation: 'though my blood is salty still/It swings to other tides than the old sea'. 'Green Loving'[1] contrasts the greenness—the immaturity and sensuality—of the poet's love with the 'clear sky, the clear eye' of woman's love, more objective and unself-deceiving than man's. 'True sky was never seen until today' and clear recognition of woman's qualities had been obscured by 'the gross fears of clay' and the fierce burning, the frantic nature, of the poet's desire for her. He concludes therefore with this injunction:

> Lover, ungreen yourself, let her far glance
> Find yours at her own distance.
> Too close your eyes before,
> And held no more
> Than dreaming images of your own substance.

He had loved selfishly, discovering in the loved woman only reflections of himself; his only resource therefore is to quell his possessiveness and to that end relinquish control of the relationship to her and let her choose what distance shall be between them.

This is an interesting poem but the symbolism is too contrived and schematic and Graves was justified in finally deciding to omit it in this form from his later *Collected Poems*. But the dropping of 'The Challenge' from those collections is more to be regretted. It is

---

[1] A revised version of the first stanza appears in *Man Does, Woman Is* (1964) as 'Variables of Green'.

unusually long for Graves, running to 67 lines, and could possibly have benefited from greater concentration. This may have been the reason for its abandonment, but it seems to me to be a successful poem: the array of images is marshalled without seeming laboured and the thought is worked out more thoroughly and runs more smoothly than in 'Green Loving'.

Here the theme of the two kinds of love is shaped into an allegorical narrative, borrowing some of its properties from medieval romance and employing a suitably archaic style.

> In ancient days a glory swelled my thighs,
> And sat like fear between my shoulder-blades,
> And made the young hair bristle on my poll.
>
> Sun was my crown, green grassflesh my estate...

The old love was ruled by lust, and it is made more apparent that 'fear' (presumably the same as 'the gross fears of clay') was the consequence of lust—fear of being denied satisfaction and an unadmitted fear, perhaps, of the body's death. The poet lived purely in the land of the senses—'green grassflesh' is a vivid and poignant variation on the more abstract colour imagery of 'Green Loving'—and the sun's pride was his symbol. He rashly vested all his hopes in the pleasures of a physical existence, forgetful of time's treacheries, age and death:

> Time was my chronicler, my deeds age-new,
> And death no peril, nor decay of powers.
> Glory sat firmly in my body's thrones.

Finally the sun's domination was challenged by another power—the moon 'That drained the wholesome colour from my realm'—and from that time his glory was over and his flesh was numb. The sun represents the male principle and the rule of the flesh; the moon represents the superior female principle, and, partly, the rule of the mind—the poet was 'dumbfounded by her reasoned look'. She dictates love's phases and man must suffer without protest the barren periods she imposes on any relationship with her. Though 'thievishly he longs/To diadem his head with stolen light', she is not to be possessed:

> The Moon's the crown of no high-walled domain
> Conquerable by angry stretch of pride;
> Her icy lands welcome no soldiery.

For the power of love that she wields is ultimately 'inhuman'; its authority is absolute and must be submitted to before the 'sick heart' can be 'renewed'. And as soon as the poet does submit the kingdom of 'grassflesh' is restored to him: 'In wind and sun and stream my joys I take', but the senses now enjoy their powers only by permission, serving a wider conception of love as symbolized by the moon—'Bounded by white horizons beyond touch'.

The important event in this poem is Graves's revival of the moon symbolism to render his experience of love. Absent from his poetry since his first period, it here imparts some of the emotional intensity of 'Full Moon', which in occasional images 'The Challenge' resembles, at the same time as it embodies the more complex perceptions into the nature of love of his second period. Good as the poem is, however, it does not come up to the standard of 'A Love Story' (written in the year following the publication of *Collected Poems 1938*), which is the definitive treatment of this theme and exploration of these images. The fact that, evidently, 'The Challenge' was an extended preparatory study for 'A Love Story' may have been the determining consideration in Graves's decision to omit it from his most recent collections.

The third poem that contrasts the two kinds of love, 'End of Play', is certainly the finest and most revealing on this theme to come out of his second period. It opens on the attack. Though few people have the courage to admit it, the old order in which our simple, innocent, sheltered loves and our sentimental religion flourished no longer exists—'We have reached the end of pastime, for always,/ Ourselves and everyone', the poet declares in staccato, harshly insistent rhythms. Where once life seemed

> to dawdle golden
> In some June landscape among giant flowers,
> The grass to shine as cruelly green as ever,
> Faith to descend in a chariot from the sun,

now 'a mirror and an echo/Mediate henceforth with vision and sound'. These at first baffling images, in which Graves attempts to define the distinguishing quality of the new love, gain a precise meaning as the poem proceeds. With the echo standing for reflective thought and the mirror for imagination, the meaning seems to be that thought and imagination serve to distance the subject from the impact of his experience, that experiences are strained through the sieve of the discriminating mind; the mind, no longer ingenuous, reflects on what it experiences. Other signs of our maturity are that 'we have at last ceased idling' and 'we tell no lies now'. One cause of our torment before was that, in the words of 'Green Loving', our eyes were too close to the object of our love so that we saw only projections of our own desires and fears. In 'End of Play' the point is made, with a sharper intention of repudiation, that such sensuous entanglement distorted reality and threatened to destroy us: our senses became 'lion or tiger' that 'Could leap from every copse, strike and devour us'. Now we are free from the shames of fear and lust that were laid in store for the 'innocents' of love. Rejection of the 'hypocritic pomp' of romantic love is balanced in the last stanza by the affirmation of a new romanticism:

> Yet love survives, the word carved on a sill
> Under antique dread of the headsman's axe;
> It is the echoing mind, as in the mirror
> We stare on our dazed trunks at the block kneeling.

The new love is the idea of love; it is what survives in the mind after the death of the old self—pride, credulity, the body's lusts and self-deceptions.

Graves has taken from the other two poems the essential perceptions concerning his youthful, unregenerate love and probed into them more relentlessly. This love was not merely 'green'—immature and exclusively physical—but 'cruelly green', and the nature of this cruelty is explored in the stanzas that follow: it takes the form of hypocritically concealing beneath a fair surface torments of disillusionment. Deceived by its blandishments, we saw things not as they were but as larger than life and indolently put our faith in miracles. To take another example of this more probing treatment, in the second passage quoted the terror that the poet feels for the tyranny of the senses is rendered, more strikingly than by the imagery of 'Green Loving', as the lurking menace of 'lion or tiger'. Again, in describing the love that presides over the new dispensation Graves gives a completer and more penetrating account of what it represents morally. It not only fosters a more objective, unsentimental view of life but also the limited virtues of hard work and honesty celebrated in the 'moral poems'—'we have at last ceased idling' and 'we tell no lies now'. 'End of Play' also goes beyond the other two poems in the degree to which it manages to express the poet's personal implication, the wrench of personality caused by the death of the old self and the rebirth of the new. The pain necessarily involved in extricating himself from past illusions is to be felt in the furious, nervous rhythms throughout the poem. Their tautness reflects too the effort of self-discipline required to ensure his liberation from the bonds of the old love. The new 'faith'—for that is what it is—is no longer expected to 'descend in a chariot from the sun' but is achieved by what Graves in his Foreword to *Collected Poems 1938* names 'practical persistence' (p. xiii).

The relation between the two aspects of his poetic sensibility, the realistic and the romantic, is much closer than ever before. The rhythm and tone he uses (in, for instance, the opening lines and the first passage quoted above) to prepare the way for the new romanticism avowed in the last stanza, paradoxically equal in asperity the most sceptical of the poems in *Poems 1926–1930*. It is apparent from this that his scepticism in the past has not, viewed in retrospect, proved aimlessly destructive but has cleared the ground for the building up of a more impregnable romanticism. 'We tell no lies now' is here completed by 'yet love survives'. The energy of moral commonsense that goes into the contemptuous dismissal of the old faith in miracles is evidently the energy generated by the faith in a different love which the last stanza affirms. In 'Certain Mercies' there was a tension between romantic longing and moral realism; in 'End of Play' there is a move towards fusion, for the brutal, 'self-humbling' dismissal of the daydream life that seemed to 'dawdle golden/In some June landscape' with the words 'we have at last ceased *idling*' has the same tone as the self-martyring austerity of the ideal asserted in the concluding stanza. In this move, as in the idea of death and rebirth and the very image of decapitation, the poem points forward to the White Goddess poems.

'End of Play' and 'The Challenge' are grouped along with 'On Portents', 'New Legends' (previously 'The Age of Certainty'), 'To Whom Else?' and a few other poems to make up the fifth and last section in *Collected Poems 1938*. Graves brought them together and let them sound the final note in this collection because he considered that in comparison with his other work they each evidenced 'a more immediate sense of poetic liberation'. In the Foreword he states that much of his poetry had been devoted to 'a close and energetic study of the disgusting, the contemptible and the evil' and confesses that this is 'not very far in the direction of poetic serenity'. It is one step, however; 'other steps', he adds in cautious anticipation, 'remain, and a few have already been taken'. He is referring, presumably, to this last group of poems, and particularly to the love poems that I have instanced, in which there are intimations of a new certainty. The steps they take are, in fact, as we have seen, towards the ethical and finally religious position embodied in the mythology of the White Goddess. Two more poems show, in their very different ways, progress in the same direction.

'The Great-Grandmother' is the fullest and most realistic celebration of a woman's qualities during this period. Where they were, in 'Down, Wanton, Down!' and 'A Jealous Man', a foil to man's lustfulness and the jealous fears created by his lust, here they exist in their own right. The great-grandmother is portrayed as morally stronger and deeper than the men of her family but by no means likeable or approachable. Though she lied to her son and told half-truths to her grandson, 'Yet she was honest with herself': what she represents is a sour spirit of truth bred of disillusion. She has lived a public life of necessary deception in order to keep intact a personal integrity, and has reserved for her great-grandchildren the private feelings she concealed from those nearer to her—

> Confessions of old distaste
> For music, sighs and roses—

Their false-innocence assaulting her,
Breaching her hard heart...

This woman's sour honesty, unsentimentality, clear-sighted distrust
of men's 'false-innocence', singleness of purpose and tacit but un-
relenting opposition to a male-dominated world make this poem a
more complete embodiment of Graves's own disillusionment with
masculine values than any other:

> She has outlasted all man-uses
> As was her first resolve:
> Happy and idle like a port
> After the sea's recession,
> She does not misconceive the nature
> Of shipmen or of ships.

It is the first poem to recognize specifically the 'hard heart' of
woman, her ruthlessness as a judge, her capacity for dissimulation
when other interests conflict with truth to herself—characteristics of
the Muse-woman familiar to readers of the later poetry; but Graves
admonishes us to 'believe her' rather than men, her kind of hardness
being more trustworthy than their hypocritical persuasiveness.

There could not be a greater contrast between this and 'Like
Snow', and yet both poems are easily recognizable harbingers of the
White Goddess poetry. In the White Goddess poetry woman is
presented in her two capacities—as an uncompromising, impersonal
custodian of Truth, a role which may entail considerable hardship
for man, and as the solution to man's self-torment and a repository
of all his hopes. In 'The Great-Grandmother' she appears in the
former role—'She does not misconceive the nature/Of shipmen or of
ships'; in 'Like Snow', though still potentially formidable, she is
represented primarily as a comforter:

> Like snow, warmer than fingers feared,
> And to soil friendly...

She is a sort of grace or benediction cancelling out past suffering,
nursing the poet through the terrors of winter and 'dark night'. The
contrast between the two poems extends to the style. The accents of
the first are plain and conversational, those of the second poem with

its dense alliteration and 'musical' quality are lyrical. The difference is, once again, the difference between Graves's realistic and his romantic impulses. Here they are kept separate; in the poems of the next period, as in 'End of Play', usually they interpenetrate and thereby strengthen each other.

Other steps remained to be taken before Graves's 'poetic liberation' was complete. By removing himself in 1929 to Majorca and making it his permanent home Graves dissociated himself from the remnants of a once flourishing civilization, a gesture of repudiation to the spirit of which he has ever since remained true. In his poetry he turned firmly away from the general themes of society and public belief, to which he had given his attention briefly and on the whole unsuccessfully in the years 1923 to 1925, and confined himself to a rendering of what he has called in the Foreword to *Poems and Satires 1951* 'the intenser moments of his spiritual autobiography' (p. viii). And in this sense his poems since then have never been other than strictly personal—as were, in fact, the majority of those written before he left England. But though estranged from his times he has not ceased to take an interest in them. It is evident that in the 'twenties as well as in the 'thirties he was strongly affected, as were other writers, by an awareness that the confident, seemingly secure pre-1914 era had been succeeded by an age which was, as he puts it in the Foreword to *Collected Poems 1938*, 'intellectually and morally in perfect confusion' (p. xxiv). In his introduction to *The Common Asphodel: Collected Essays on Poetry* (1949) he points out that his earliest theories of poetry were 'coloured by the contemporary view of humanity as convalescent after a serious nervous breakdown and resolved on a complete reorganization of its habits and ideas' (p. vii). In a neurasthenic state himself he identified himself closely 'with convalescent and reconstructive humanity'. Once cured of his neurasthenia, however, he ceased to identify himself with that world—in which ideas were regarded merely as hypotheses and ethical systems were without authority. He was even more alienated from the ethos of the 'thirties when, as he declares in *The Long Week-end*, it was fashionable 'to be reasonable about the confusion into which the new theories of physics, astronomy, sex, and economics had plunged thinking people' (p. 304). From a position fastidiously outside the process he recorded his reactions to these phenomena through the medium of historical fiction and in a few, related poems. He was attracted to Imperial Rome, the scene of the Claudius novels (1934), and in *Count Belisarius* (1938) to the Byzantine Empire of the sixth century as settings for his stories because of the parallel he saw between their decadence and the collapse of traditions in his own times. The protagonists, Claudius and Belisarius, are isolated men of principle moving in corrupt societies and represent the lost decencies valued by their author. To them he has attributed the same moral stance taken up in response to their circumstances as his own in response to the situation of the 'thirties. Claudius, besides, possesses qualities of perseverance, clumsy honesty and practical cunning, which, though comically extravagant, are actually Graves's own.

In two poems, 'The Fallen Tower of Siloam' and 'The Cuirassiers of the Frontier', he is similarly concerned to define his attitude towards society, plunged in confusion and by this time moving rapidly and blindly towards another world war. The tower of Siloam is the one mentioned in Luke xiii. 4, whose fall killed both innocent and guilty alike. In the poem it symbolizes the structure of European civilization tottering and about to collapse: its 'west wall' (Western Europe?) fissured and 'the underpinning/At the south-eastern angle' (the twin props of Christianity and Hellenism) rotten. The tower stood so grimly and caused such anxiety that when it did fall, killing those who had not foreseen this disaster, the poets were only relieved, being free now to ignore it. They were not public servants and it was no duty of theirs to shore up a building which was bound to founder. On the contrary it was morally imperative that they should dissociate themselves from its rottenness and the world's hollow, ludicrous pretence that all was well:

> Though kings
> Were crowned and gold coin minted still and horses
> Still munched at nose-bags in the public streets,
> All such sad emblems were to be condoned:
> An old wives' tale, not ours.

In 'The Cuirassiers of the Frontier' Graves tries out an alternative attitude. The poem is presumably an actual by-product of the researches into Byzantine military history undertaken for *Count Belisarius*. The cuirassiers are the 'Goths, Vandals, Huns, Isaurian mountaineers' who defend the frontiers of the Roman Empire. Their position with regard to Rome—apart from and yet belonging to it—parallels what Graves feels to be his own relationship to modern civilization. They are Roman citizens and Christians by adoption not birth and stand in the same relation to the Empire as children to a foster parent. Their vigorous qualities, however, are those of which an effete society is most in need: they are hardy, courageous, loyal, truthful, and live by a strict code of morality. In fact they, at the outposts, rather than the citizens of the metropolis—

> Her white-gowned pederastic senators,
> The cut-throat factions of her Hippodrome,
> The eunuchs of her draped saloons—

are in their vitality and loyalty the true heirs to this civilization, and know it:

> We, not the City, are the Empire's soul:
> A rotten tree lives only in its rind.

Connected with these experiments in clarifying his relationship to contemporary public life are a number of poems in which Graves reconsiders, more carefully and deeply, his attitude to the social traditions and beliefs that he had implicitly renounced in his autobiography and the poems of the late 'twenties. 'Recalling War', which undeservedly has been omitted from *Collected Poems 1965*, written at least twenty years after Graves had taken part in it, is his finest war poem. But, more than that, it is an attempt to set against the prewar accepted view of life the consciousness of evil that his experiences of fighting had released in him. This consciousness haunted the nightmares of his early poetry without achieving clear expression and only became his central concern, though in a different context of experience, in his second period; but 'Recalling War' is the first poem to render successfully the fullness of his original response. Its urgent tone and painful imagery, prompted evidently

by his horrified prevision of a world war like the first, are ballasted
with an intellectual perception and moral assurance that could only
be the consequence of hindsight and are, in fact, products of that
disciplined self-examination first undertaken in *Poems 1926–1930*.

> Fear made fine bed-fellows. Sick with delight
> At life's discovered transitoriness,
> Our youth became all-flesh and waived the mind.
> Never was such antiqueness of romance,
> Such tasteless honey oozing from the heart.

The bitter sarcasm of these lines finds its justification in the dis-
tressingly lucid exposure of the contradictory attitudes, the divided
state brought about by war, that it effects—and in the diagnosis of
youth's desperate, self-delusive romanticism as a renunciation of the
mind's control, a refusal to find meaning in anything but the
moment's satisfaction. Graves's standpoint in this passage is clear
and forceful, but at the centre of the poem there is an ambivalence
that registers a more intricate apprehension of the situation.

> War was return of earth to ugly earth,
> War was foundering of sublimities,
> Extinction of each happy art and faith
> By which the world had still kept head in air,
> Protesting logic or protesting love,
> Until the unendurable moment struck—
> The inward scream, the duty to run mad.

This records a conflict of feelings—revulsion from the underlying
ugliness of the naked earth when stripped of its 'sublimities' set
against the inability to deny its truth as a picture of reality, which
the mere protestations of logic and love are powerless to change; the
poet nostalgically regrets the 'Extinction of each happy art and faith'
and yet feels that they were the world's subterfuges to avoid recognizing this truth, and that it proudly and gracefully 'kept head in
air' so that it might not see what was at its feet. The happy arts and
faiths are the traditional social and moral supports of the civilization
that failed to survive the 1914–18 war. The element of nostalgia for
its unshattered certainties in this complex of feelings is a new

development since the sweepingly valedictory *Goodbye To All That*. The poem embodies the two irreconcilable attitudes to his society that appeared separately in 'The Fallen Tower of Siloam' and 'The Cuirassiers of the Frontier'.

The same may be said of 'A Country Mansion', an even more impressive poem. The conflict of attitudes is given an expanded and more firmly distanced treatment, however, and through a careful weighing of the pros and cons of the case—rebellion against, or acknowledgment of, his cultural heritage—the poet achieves a finer, more balanced definition of the degrees of sympathy and antipathy that he feels. Our culture is represented as an ancient country house, which in the beginning was owned by a single family and passed from father to son in an unbroken line but now, a haunted anachronism, of ever diminishing relevance in the contemporary world, has survived its true heirs and is occupied by a succession of life-tenants only. In its prime 'the fruit-trees grew/Slender and similar in long rows'—an evocative illustration of its youthful vitality and elegance, and of the perfection of type ('*similar* in long rows') made possible by a flourishing civilization. The verse appreciates these qualities, yet in choosing to stress the similarity of the trees Graves prepares us for the individual's rebellion against type that will inevitably occur as soon as that civilization begins to pall. The same delicate balance of appreciation and potential criticism is maintained in another image: it is claimed that in 'the venerable dining-room'

> port in Limerick glasses
> Glows twice as red reflected
> In the memory-mirror of the waxed table,

where 'twice as red' implies at once the enrichment of objects and customs by tradition—'the memory mirror'—and an improbable inflation of their significance. A more openly disrespectful tone begins now to make itself heard. The house's continuing power to attract allegiance from the young is compared with the feats of Old Parr, who at the age of 105 'did open penance, in a sheet,/For fornication with posterity'. There is something senile, obscene and boastful about such tenacity of life. At last one son, like Graves,

172

rebelled and broke free. Though he had spent a happy childhood in the house and might be buried there,

> Yet foster-cradle or foster-grave
> He will not count as home.

His relationship to his inheritance is the same as the cuirassiers' to Rome—but with this difference: he does not propose actively to defend its traditions. These belong properly to the past and he is poised between respect for the past and a self-respect that prevents him benefiting from its gifts:

> No place less reverend could provoke
> So proud an absence from it.

Poise and fineness of definition do not make the sum of this poem's distinction. There is the seemingly effortless synthesis in the verse of pointed wit, verging at times on the epigrammatic, and conversational flow; related to this there is the large inclusiveness of the symbol. The poem allegorizes its author's rebellion not only from his family but also more generally from the upper middle-class milieu of his early years, English society, and modern civilization— the mansion is made to symbolize the community in each of these manifestations. The range of reference is wider than even this indicates. At one point a veiled allusion to the War brings an illustrative precision to the accusation that youth has wasted itself in the service of a declining civilization: the inhabitants of the house, to give it new life, 'Pour their fresh blood through its historic veins'; the wording strengthens the accusation by stressing that the sacrifice may involve bloodshed. At another point, with psychological plausibility, Graves identifies the nightmares of neurasthenia with the house's hauntings —both alike signs of the past's tyranny over the present, a tyranny of no longer valid obligations; referring to a bedroom that at first had caused little disturbance to its occupants, he adds:

> But gradual generations of discomfort
> Have bred an anger there to stifle sleep.

An examination of this poem provides a fitting conclusion to a survey of the poetry Graves wrote during the years 1926 to 1938. A period as it was for him in many ways of coming to terms with the past, 'A Country Mansion' is of all the poems the most balanced and temperate in its judgement of it. He was now looking forward with something like clairvoyance to years of a more positive achievement. A few steps, he declares in the Foreword to his 1938 collection, had been taken in that direction. 'No more' and 'no longer' and similar phrases, occurring like fragments of a larger theme in several of these poems, are the negative expressions of his resolutions for the future; but in 'No More Ghosts', where the negation of the title-phrase is announced with the most buoyant confidence in the body of the poem, it is rounded with a complementary assertion:

> No new ghost can appear. Their poor cause
> Was that time freezes, and time thaws;
> But here only such loves can last
> As do not ride upon the weathers of the past.

6

'Poetic Liberation'

AT THE outbreak of the Spanish Civil War in 1936, following official advice, Graves and Laura Riding left Majorca. There followed three years of wandering in Europe and lastly in the United States. Not long after the publication of his *Collected Poems* in 1938—Laura Riding's *Collected Poems* appeared in the same year—they parted company. She remained in America, abandoned poetry and 'discovered her American self'; he, in 1939, sailed for England. He married again and, having been rejected for active service because of his age, retired to a Devonshire village for the duration of the war. As soon as it was possible, in 1946, he returned with his family to his house in Majorca and has lived there ever since.

Although he wrote comparatively few poems between 1938 and 1945, much of his time being devoted to the production of a miscellany of prose books, those that he did write were of a high standard. But they were remarkable for other reasons too. The promise of a new development that Graves had seen in some of his more recent works, which had led him in his Foreword to *Collected Poems 1938* to anticipate for his poetry a different kind of assurance, something more nearly described as 'poetic serenity', had been richly fulfilled. The first signs came with the appearance of four new poems in a small selection of his poetry, issued in 1940, confidently entitled *No More Ghosts*. Two of them, 'A Love Story' and 'To Sleep', are the most impressive in the collection of eighteen poems that Graves contributed two years later to *Work in Hand*, a composite volume which also included work by Alan Hodge and Norman Cameron. Although, as we have seen, a few of the last poems in *Collected Poems 1938* were already showing a change of direction, this handful of poems is as striking in its evidence of a poetic renewal as was *Poems 1926–1930* measured against its predecessor, *Poems 1914–1926*. The

175

appearance of *Work in Hand*, like *Poems 1926–1930*, amounted to the announcement of a new period in Graves's writing.

A year later, trying to make sense of certain obscure medieval Welsh texts, he embarked on a series of discoveries that were to become the strongest thread in the intricate argument of his most original prose work, *The White Goddess: A Historical Grammar of Poetic Myth* (1948). Through successive drafts this book developed into an extraordinarily ingenious—partly scholarly, partly imaginative—reconstruction of the beliefs and cults of Bronze Age matriarchal religion. His contention is that the various goddesses of prehistoric matriarchal societies were all versions of a single Goddess: the rites that characterized their worship were the same, representations of them in mythic iconography emphasized the same symbolic features, and the same powers were attributed to them by later writers. A large part of Graves's purpose was to restore the mythical stories, which he assumed had been deliberately distorted by the conquering patriarchal priesthoods, to their original form and to work out a plausible 'reading' of them; much of the excitement of the unfolding argument springs from the fact that this is at the same time a gradual recovery of prehistoric myth as an elliptical but meaningful medium of communication. The most profound effect of these researches for Graves was the rediscovery of myth as a *poetic* language. He was working on the first draft of the book between 1943 and 1944, and this was immediately reflected in the subject-matter, language and imagery of the poems he was then writing. The myths, by the symbolism they provided and the more evocative use of language they invited, facilitated at once a greater concentration of meaning and the embodiment of a richer emotional content than his poetry had been able to encompass before. But the important fact to note is that the radical change of mood and tone signified by the poems in *Work in Hand* (1942) had already been completed a year before the White Goddess and her mythology had been thought of. In these poems the new position he takes up in relation to his experience is one which he had attained without the help of the mythology but which the mythology, once discovered, enabled him to consolidate.

A primary concern of this survey of Graves's poetic progress has been to emphasize the continuity between the interests, moral attitudes and styles of the different periods as well as the changes that took place. There have been two main breaks in his career, in 1926 and in 1938, and yet in neither case did he completely sever his connections with the past. This is more true, perhaps, of the second break, when there was less to discard than there had been in 1926. *Work in Hand*, in fact, derives much of its strength from the merging of three streams of development. Two of them belonged respectively to his first and second periods; for this group of poems, besides building upon the achievement of the Laura Riding years, can be seen to have revived characteristics of his early verse that had disappeared from view in 1926 not to emerge again until the later 'thirties. The presence of emotion in the best poems of the first period—whether painful as in 'Full Moon' and 'Cool Web' or lyrical as in 'Pygmalion to Galatea'—was the chief characteristic revived. These poems embodied the poet's recognition of an intelligible pattern in his experience, particularly of the man-woman relationship, without at all diminishing in emotional intensity the expression of that experience. In the self-disciplinary years that followed, in pruning his poems of sentimentality Graves managed to deny his positive emotions any place at all in the majority of them; so that when towards the end of the second period he discovered in these emotions once more material for his poetry he was able to reap the harvest of this earlier recognition.

The chief contribution of the intervening years was intellectual and moral. In the two previous chapters I have outlined the nature of Graves's achievement during this period and the degree to which he was indebted for it to Laura Riding. I drew largely upon quotations from *Anarchism Is Not Enough* (1928) to give an idea of her thought as it was in the early stages of their partnership. In the later stages he certainly became less heavily dependent on her ideas and branched out on several paths of his own; but her absence from the surface of his poetry was only a sign that her influence was being assimilated at a deeper level. In 1938 she published *The World and Ourselves* which like *Anarchism Is Not Enough* outlines an ethic of the emotions and behaviour. The moral position it reveals was basically the same as it had been ten years earlier, but in the later book she drew attention to the positive rather than the negative facets of her convictions. And it was this new emphasis and the greater 'serenity' with which she held these convictions that were reflected in Graves's latest poems in the *Collected Poems*—and, more strikingly, in *Work in Hand*.

I quote, then, from *The World and Ourselves* for the light it throws on the tone of the new poems and the attitudes with which Graves confronts his experience in them. In Laura Riding's terminology people, modes of thinking, feeling and behaving can be divided into 'inside' and 'outside'; 'ourselves'—chiefly though not exclusively some writers and some women whether they write or not—are the inside and 'the world' is the outside. This is not the old opposition of the individual and society, which is 'a physical opposition between all the members composing a society'; 'inside' defines a non-social personal reality, and the division between an inside and an outside reality makes a 'quality distinction—between the life of the mind and the life of physical necessity' (pp. 226-7). Body and mind are words used to describe different realities, different ways of being. 'An inside person is one who subordinates bodily to mental experience', and 'mental values are real by the living, instantaneously reconciling order they introduce into the varied elements of our experience and the rescue of self they thus accomplish from the uncertainties of time' (pp. 218-19). The distinction between the body and mind, therefore, is a moral one: between the 'inside values...which result from self-relation to the permanent generalities of existence' (p. 209) and the outside values of those people who only 'exist from moment to moment, without continuity, permanence, responsibility, personal identity', who 'exist only in incidents; have consciousness only in terms of what they experience rather than in terms of self' (p. 376). The distinction is expressed by another opposition—that between the truth and the facts: 'the more our desired certainties have to do with truth rather than facts, with knowledge of ourselves rather than of what may temporarily happen to us, the less it will matter what actually does happen and the less spectacular will our happenings be' (p. 43). The terminology is not exactly the same as that of *Anarchism Is Not Enough* but the ethic it defines has changed very little. The main difference is that the personal reality, the reality of life lived by 'mental values', is evoked not as a bleak though truthful bareness but as an enrichening experience bringing order and peace into our lives. It is the spirit of this description of it that Graves captures in 'No More Ghosts' when he refers to 'the ordered ease' of his existence.

Laura Riding's picture of reality has for its corollary a definition of the inside person's moral responsibilities. *The World and Ourselves*, I should explain, was an attempt to formulate a way of relieving the moral disorders of the world in 1938, a specifically inside way, and only incidentally a definition of insideness. In this situation, then, the problem was 'how to be ourselves all the time, how not to break the moral continuity of our lives' (p. 104). Secondly: 'goodness itself, and the knowledge that it confers of the difference between the good and the bad results of civilization, are to be attained not in the reform but in the definition of self. We cannot temper the violence of outward changes until we have inside ourselves all that is unchangingly ourselves and nothing that is not' (p. 433). And lastly: 'those of us who are selves…daily redeem ourselves from the world with an increasing accuracy of self-knowledge'. The tone and moral bearing of nearly all the *Work in Hand* poems are an exact reflection of a life lived according to these values. In the period of his literary partnership with Laura Riding Graves's poetry defined his intellectual belief in, and argued for, these values but only occasionally reflected in tone or in the poet's attitude to himself the confident, contented living of them. Between 1926 and 1933 he used this standard of 'goodness' as a rod with which to castigate the world and himself, and even later, as in 'End of Play', the verse enacted the bitterness of the struggle to possess this goodness; the poems of *Work in Hand*, on the contrary, have a 'poise of being' that testifies to the achieved possession.

The third development that can be felt as a source of strength in these poems began in the first period and continued throughout the second. It was the gradual and obviously painful maturing of self-knowledge. This has already been amply illustrated in previous chapters and only a brief recapitulation is necessary here. The most interesting evidence, from the point of view of this and the next chapter, of the progress in self-knowledge during Graves's first period is in the sporadic use of a set of related images to express the poet's psychological insights which, besides reappearing in *Work in Hand*, anticipated the mythological symbolism fully worked out in *The White Goddess*. As I have explained in my previous discussion of Graves's earlier poems, the occurrence of this imagery indicated the poet's recognition of a pattern in his experience; in this recognition we have the first signs of his growing self-knowledge. I am thinking, for example, of the moon imagery, used to express different aspects of the love relationship, in 'Reproach', 'Full Moon' and the concluding stanzas of Part I of *The Marmosite's Miscellany*; again, of the conception of the divided self, dramatized in 'Return' and other poems as rival selves, himself and a cursed or despairing alter-ego, precursors of the rival heroes in the Myth who alternately destroy each other in their struggle to enjoy the undivided favour of the Goddess. Other poems in the first period depicted, though not in an imagery that has lasted, emotional situations that were proto-types of those embodied in the mythological poetry. Most important was the idea of the self's death and rebirth, which was treated successfully in 'The Stake'. The pursuit of self-knowledge in the second period was a self-disciplinary measure, an exercise in self-criticism. It produced such penetrating psychological studies of man's moral inadequacies in his relationship with woman as 'Ulysses', 'Never Such Love', 'A Jealous Man' and, in part, 'End of Play'. These insights contributed much of the assurance that informs the *Work in Hand* poems, and are, for example, concentrated in a single poem, 'To Sleep', to give a previously unequalled rendering of his self-tormenting love.

The complement to Graves's developing awareness of man's moral inadequacies in the man-woman relationship, was, as we have also seen, the growing conviction that woman is morally superior to man and that men, especially poets, can find wisdom only in submission to the female principle. It is the subject of a long letter that Graves contributed to *The World and Ourselves*. It was an attitude that, having its seed in such poems as 'The Ridge-Top', 'The Red Ribbon Dream' and 'Pygmalion to Galatea'—projections of an ideal woman—found tougher expression in 'Down, Wanton, Down!', 'A Jealous Man' and, most notably, in 'The Great-Grandmother'. This estimate of woman, is the all-important fact in *Work in Hand*, where as a *felt* truth, it plays a large part in the reorganization of the poet's emotions.

My comments on a selection of these poems should make plain in what way they are a personal affirmation of Laura Riding's beliefs—explicit or, more commonly, implicit—and at the same time combine the opposite virtues characteristic of his best writing in his two earlier periods. When compared with my comments in the next chapter on the later volumes, those to appear after the inception of *The White Goddess*, it should become equally plain that the values they affirm, the attitudes they express, and the technical strategies they frequently adopt are the essential ones of his later poetry and yet exist independently of the subsequent mythology. By recognizing this we put ourselves in a better position to understand the symbolic function of the White Goddess and the myths concerning her that Graves has assembled.

'The Worms of History' outlines his moral and religious position. It is the first poem since 'The Figure-Head' (*Welchman's Hose*) and 'Knowledge of God' (*Mock Beggar Hall*) to attempt a definition of Graves's religious beliefs, or—to be more precise—of the sense in which his agnosticism can have the epithet 'religious' applied to it. It argues that the traditional God has died. Adam, believing that goodness (the word used is 'excellence') is inseparable from 'divinity', mourned the death of goodness; but because he could not escape his need to believe in and worship a supernatural being he had to find 'lesser powers' to worship, and so made deities of certain 'royal monsters' (man-gods like Alexander, Pompey and Napoleon, the instances given in *The White Goddess*[1]). To this process the poem opposes the belief that God is but man's name for 'excellence'; that

[1] 3rd ed., 1952, p. 478. All references are to this, the latest, edition.

the concept of the supernatural is itself responsible for the reign of the 'royal monsters' and the consequent evil and for man's failure to live by standards of true excellence. For Graves there is a distinction to be made between natural religion (represented by the rites of the Goddess) and supernatural religion; though God died, 'excellence' did not die with him:

> It was those lesser powers who played at God,
> Bloated with Adam's deferential sighs
> Which were his mourning for divinity:
> They reigned as royal monsters on the earth.
>
> Adam grew lean, and wore perpetual black;
> He made no reaching after excellence.
> Eve gave him sorry comfort for his grief
> With birth of sons, and mourning still he died.

The values implied are those defined in *The World and Ourselves*, though felt individually and embodied in a quite personal myth. The title of the poem explicitly connects it with the terminology of that book. For 'history' and 'time' belong to the outer reality of mere happenings unrelated to the 'permanent generalities of existence'. Another quotation will give a more precise idea of the connection. The author asks: 'what is there beyond the mere sorting of [the relatively good from the relatively bad in] history? The knowledge of what are the really good things, and the ordering of life by such knowing, rather than by setting off the available best against the worst' (p. 76). When the supernatural idea died, the poem is saying, men assumed that only relative, temporal values were left to them, and so ceased to know and seek 'the really good things'. The 'worms of history' were the evil released by the worship of the wrong things, the 'royal monsters'. 'The really good things', on the other hand, are absolute good, for which 'excellence' is the poem's precise and restrained, classical description. The poem celebrates, then, the end of time lived in history, that is in the outer reality, and the beginning of time lived according to excellence, the values of the inner reality.

It is, moreover, the death of a specifically male God and male values—which is why the 'sorry comfort' provided by Eve's giving birth exclusively to sons is mentioned: the only possible comfort for Adam's grief would have been the sense of inner personal realities, of inner goodness, that the presence of daughters would have communicated. Though it is not made explicit, the strongest impression received from this poem of the nature of excellence is that it is to be found in the here and now. Adam 'made no reaching after excellence' because he associated its possession with a happy time in the past and a prelapsarian state of innocence, and now assumes that it is for ever beyond reach; whereas, as the poem concludes, 'excellence lives' —in the present and eternally. There is, again, a relevant sentence in *The World and Ourselves*: 'whatever we truly have—is alive with us, of us—is therein good'. This living in the present of ultimate values is woman's natural virtue (in another passage Laura Riding writes: 'women are concerned with what *is*—immediately and ultimately', p. 93), and it is one of the reasons why she presides in Graves's moral world.

Elsewhere in this volume excellence is identified with the state of mind of the true lover. 'The Oath' and 'Despite and Still' are, as it were, formal announcements of the poet's confidence in the love-relationship. Although this confidence is not new, the simple directness and almost light-heartedness with which it is stated are. There has not been till now such a plain, unequivocal acceptance of the dual nature of love: these poems combine an assured sense of love as an ultimately undamageable truth with an undeceived awareness that suffering is an essential part of it. In the best of his earlier love poems, 'Vanity' and 'Sick Love', love is not an undeniable condition of existence but a state of happiness, which, the poet bitterly points out, does not last. In 'The Oath', on the contrary, the lovers

> Take timely courage
> From the sky's clearness
> To confirm an oath.
>
> Her loves are his loves
> His trust is her trust;

it is only hinted, but the recognition is firm, that the sky is not always clear. Clear sky and thunderous sky: this is in its simplest form the pattern that Graves has discovered in his experience of love. Love, for Graves, is the prime inside reality discussed in *The World and Ourselves*, and a phrase from that book already quoted describes it: 'the rescue of self...from the uncertainties of time'. From now on, by seeing each aspect of the love situation as a stage in an inevitable cycle and in each poem that deals with a single stage keeping the whole cycle in view, he manages to express his loyalty to an unchanging principle, an idea of the values affirmed by love in *all* its aspects which enables him to accept each particular concrete experience of it. What is acknowledged in 'Despite and Still' is 'the thing's necessity'; in acknowledgement of this the poet resolves 'to love despite and still'.

My comments on these three poems are meant to bring into focus the attitudes that, stated openly here, are implied in the confident demeanour of all the poems in *Work in Hand*. In some cases the demeanour is chiefly a matter of tone—in, for example, 'The Beast' (revised and retitled 'The Glutton' in *Collected Poems 1959* and omitted from *Collected Poems 1965*). The theme of this poem (which I quote in full) is lust. By setting it against 'Leda', a poem of the 'thirties treating the same subject, I want to bring out the poise of the later poem as compared with the overflowing disgust of the earlier.

> Beyond the Atlas roams a love-beast;
> The aborigines harry it with darts;
> Its flesh is esteemed, though of a fishy tang
> Tainting the eater's mouth and lips.
> Ourselves once, wandering in mid-wilderness
> And by despair drawn to this diet,
> Before the meal was over sat apart
> Loathing each other's carrion company.

In the earlier poem the poet only felt 'horror' at lust, and the terms in which he addressed his heart, personified as Leda—'beneath your god/You strained and gulped your beastliest'—expressed mere revulsion from the act and from himself. In effect he was disowning a part of himself. The moral verdict on lust is no different in 'The Beast' but the tone is. The poem is in the third person, and the beast is described with a neutral politeness and gravity which is never

quite ironic. The evil it represents does not need to be actively dis-
owned; it is regarded instead as no longer part of the poet's true self.
The tone is of a person who has achieved 'firm, inner self-possession',
an expressive phrase employed by Laura Riding to define the state of
mind of the successfully inside person. In Graves's poetry it denotes,
besides the controlled tone, a willingness to let the poem speak for
itself, and this is one of the most notable characteristics of all his
later work. In 'The Beast', for instance, there is no pressing forward
of the poet into the poem; the poem is all in the emblem and the
careful placing of certain words so that the implied comparison—
between gluttony and lust—emerges gradually and the words rever-
berate with the maximum of unstated meaning. Such words are
'fishy', 'tainting', 'mid-wilderness', 'despair', and 'carrion'. 'Fishy'
has sexual connotations, and 'tainting' a moral as well as a literal
sense; 'mid-wilderness' suggests 'lost in confusion of values' and
that the poet's present standpoint is outside the wilderness; 'despair'
is made to imply that they were 'drawn to this diet' for lack of anything better; and 'carrion' brings with it all the associations of predatory greed, an idea that epitomizes Graves's analysis of the nature of
lust.

An indication of the stability reflected in the bearing of these
poems is the ease with which emotion is now handled. 'The Shot'
is typical in joining self-criticism with a plain acceptance of positive
emotion; which, as I have argued, is a combining of characteristics
from the two previous periods. The poem opens in the later manner
with a studiously detached observation—'The curious heart plays
with its fears'. The point of this is explained by the ensuing emblematic illustration: it is as if one should wilfully smash a hole in a
ship's side and expect it miraculously not to sink; denying that what
one fears can happen is to be under the illusion that one's happiness
is impregnable. But where in the late 'twenties and the 'thirties the
impersonality of such an observation would have turned to icy
distaste and the implied criticism to self-contempt, here the tone is,
at first, merely uncommitted. The translation to an emotionally
engaged tone is therefore swift and sure. In the four lines that
follow the poet admits his involvement in the case presented:

O weary luxury of hypothesis—
For human nature, honest human nature
(Which the fear-pampered heart denies)
Knows its own miracle: not to go mad.

A 'fear-pampered heart' is one that by its preoccupation with its own conflicts excludes a wider conception of human nature. Exposure of its narrowness, however, is subordinated to the weightier purpose of affirming the value of, and the poet's gratitude for, the knowledge that 'honest human nature' has to offer. In the language of *The World and Ourselves* this is knowledge of what is 'unchangingly ourselves', a reality inaccessible to the discontented state of mind which pursues hypothetical miracles. A comparison of this poem with two poems from *Poems 1926–1930*, 'Ship Master' and 'Midway', reveals vividly the changes in Graves's point of view. Both presented pictures of human nature, but the tone of the former was bitterly jeering and the picture was very black, and in the latter, though the intention was apparently affirmative, human nature was defined negatively as a position between opposite extremes—'Midway is man's convenience'. 'The Shot', on the other hand, while displaying greater moral assurance allows the affirmation to be an emotional as well as a mental one. Midway is now more than a 'convenience'; it is the achievement of courage and essential sanity.

In 'To Sleep' self-criticism is itself conveyed through an emotionally engaged tone and imagery, which prepares the way for the deeper and more complete affirmation of the poem's conclusion. It opens with a contrast between true love and the partial love that, having its source in jealous doubt, gives rise to the lustful fantasies of frustration. At night, tormented by these thoughts, sleep eluded the poet:

> Loving in part, I did not see you whole,
> Grew flesh-enraged that I could not conjure
> A whole you to attend my fever-fit...

At first, when he imagined her speaking, her voice echoed his own. Now he has discovered that to love her with complete trust he must recall 'All scattered elements of will that swooped' in 'jealous

dreams' or like the 'dawn birds' 'in curiosity' dashed their brains
out against the window-panes;

> Now that I love you, as not before,
> Now you can be and say, as not before:
> The mind clears and the heart true-mirrors you
> Where at my side an early watch you keep
> And all self-bruising heads loll into sleep.

There is a deep seriousness in the treatment of personal emotion in
this poem that has long been absent from Graves's work, and a
plainness in expressing it (plot, style, tone) that is one of the chief
virtues of the later poetry. The poet identifies himself with the
emotion without embarrassment and without self-indulgence. It is
to be felt, though briefly and unostentatiously, in the obsessively
echoing phrases 'you whole' and 'whole you' of the first stanza and
in the repetitions in the last stanza of 'now that' and 'now' and 'as not
before', which succeed in conveying a sense of relief and even triumph
in the restrained tones of a formal syntax. At the same time the poem
embodies a moral and psychological insight into the nature of his
self-tormenting love more complete than that in any previous poem
of his. Lust is defined as the result of failure to give oneself wholly
in love. It is both the lover's desperate pursuit of compensation for
this failure and an attempt to take love by force so as to reassure
himself that he has not failed ('I did not see you whole', 'flesh-
enraged', 'fever-fit', 'scattered elements of will'). The 'jealous
dreams' are expressions of this predatory will, and the curious 'dawn
birds' of distressful uncertainty that unsuccessfully seeks relief in
imagined possession of the woman. Because his love is willed he sees
her not as herself but as in part reflecting himself.

This moment of doubt presents the key situation of Graves's love
poetry. In Chapter 5 I remarked on it in 'This is Noon', a poem
which reveals the surest recognition in the first period of the basic
pattern in his experience. That and the moral discoveries resulting
from the introspections of the second period contribute to the more
detailed insights of 'To Sleep'. This situation was until recently still
at the centre of his poetic impulse. The first poem in *Man Does*,

Woman Is (1964) speaks of the 'close caul of doubt' in which the poet must fix his mind during the time that precedes the conception of a poem.

'To Sleep' concludes with the picture of a contrastingly unpossessive love. The poet's belief in the possibility of such a love is evidently the source of the 'firm inner self-possession' that all these poems display. The quality of feeling which informs the invocation of this standard is, with the exception of 'The Challenge', something new in Graves's poetry. The last two lines reveal an attitude of contented submission to the loved woman who keeps watch at his side; she alone can bring the peace he needs by rescuing him from himself. But the terms in which submission is expressed are even more interesting. The poet belittles himself, comparing his relationship to the woman with that of an anxious child to its mother; but there is no bitterness in this self-abasement, in fact there is relief and an almost placid contentment. Seeing himself as childlike is obviously a way of accepting his inability to live up to this standard of whole love all the time. It is a point of view, an impersonalizing strategy, that Graves left behind with his 'nursery' period, but it has been revived to answer a more serious purpose. Comparison with Herbert's 'The Collar', which uses the same strategy, should make it clear why I see in this submissiveness a religious frame of mind. There has been an important change of emphasis since, for example, 'End of Play': whereas that poem concentrated purely on the mind's need and ability to see that love triumphs over the weakness of flesh by its own efforts of 'practical persistence', here there is awareness also of the further necessity of resigning oneself to a power outside the poet's and lover's control. This attitude is the central fact of four other poems. In 'Dawn Bombardment' submission is to a woman or goddess who appears in a dream, in 'A Withering Herb' and 'A Love Story' it is to the 'sovereign moon', and in 'Mid-Winter Waking' to the Muse: an impersonal truth, a condition of the poet's existence, in 'A Love Story' and 'A Withering Herb', in the others, more benevolently, a guardian over him. All are embodiments of what I referred to earlier as the female principle. It is in this way of confronting his experience now, in this conception of his relationship to it, that we locate what may properly be called a religious stance—not in the fact that a Goddess is named and celebrated in some of his poetry. Graves has made it clear that the White Goddess in her many mythological forms is a symbol. He is an agnostic and has frequently stated his disbelief in supernatural religion. 'True religion', he wrote in the late 'fifties, 'is of natural origin and linked practically with the seasons, though it implies occasional states of abnormal ecstasy which can be celebrated only in the language of myth'.[1]

In 'The Beast' Graves controls emotion by the employment of a finely judged tone, in 'The Shot' and 'To Sleep' by juxtaposing with it the lucid and steady perceptions of self-knowledge. A different means—and in the light of future developments a more significant one—is adopted in 'A Love Story'. The same perceptions are at work but here, where the charge of emotion is evidently much stronger, control is exercised and an impersonality maintained chiefly through the tight organization of a complex imagery. The first stanza presents a scene in which a full moon rising against a red winter sky, a snow-covered landscape and 'owls raving' convey a spine-chilling impression of dying love. In boyhood, horror of these 'solemnities' at first dissuaded the poet from falling in love; he accepted the fate of unfulfilment that they implied. But later, falling in love, he

> made a lodgement
> Of love on those frozen ramparts.
> Her image was my ensign: snows melted,
> Hedges sprouted, the moon tenderly shone,
> The owls trilled with tongues of nightingale.

The result was that winter returned with vindictive fury and 'the pallid sky heaved with a moon-quake'. The scene, personified in the last stanza as 'Queen Famine', symbolizes an aspect of the whole truth about the man-woman relationship: the whole truth being that it is a constantly changing cycle of situations. By mistaking a temporary phase of sanguine romanticism for the full reality of the relationship the lover has earned this death, the vengeance of Queen Famine. The lines quoted are a fine example of strong feeling held

---

[1] 'Answer to a Religious Questionnaire', *5 Pens in Hand*, New York, 1958, p. 117.

in check by the impersonality of the means of expression. The pain-fulness of the emotions is completely contained in the precisely evocative imagery—the bare suggestion of difficulty in 'lodgement', for instance—and the poet's sardonic judgement on this romantic phase is inherent in the unnaturalness of sprouting hedges and singing owls. The point is not merely that, like 'The Beast', the poem is allowed to speak for itself, but that different means of expression are employed—a set of meticulously related images whose combined power of suggestion is one of symbol. In the early poetry the moon symbolism occurred sporadically—on each occasion to express a different emotion. For nearly the first time—the exception, 'The Challenge', is not so fully realized as a poem—Graves has made of it, in 'A Love Story', the powerful vehicle for a whole range of various experience. Though the moon appears only in her baleful aspect, that aspect can be seen to form part of a whole, coherent reality. The 'solemnities' described in the first stanza, the moon rising against the angry red of a wintry sunset, belong to one phase of the moon and one time of the year; the poem's conclusion, in which the poet resigns himself to the moon's control of the 'phases' of his experience, hints at other 'phases' and the need to wait patiently for them. The critical spirit of his second period is respon-sible for the more penetrating insights expressed by the symbolism now—in, for example, the passage I have quoted, where this parti-cular kind of falling in love, defined in terms of chivalry and romance, is carefully distinguished from what is represented by the moon. Self-knowledge arrived at in the second period has made of this early imagery, then, a symbolism capable of expressing most of what Graves since 1938 has wanted to say. The inexhaustible detail of the White Goddess mythology has enabled him to pry into all the corners of his theme with increasing particularity, but the essence of it is in this poem. We can already feel here what the benefits of a fully-grasped mythological symbolism are: briefly, it gives the poet the chance to express powerful emotion and to organize a wide range of experience while at the same time remaining impersonal.

Such impersonality implies acceptance. In 'A Love Story' it is acceptance of the poet-lover's fate, and the attitude is once again better described as submission. The poem's last stanza is the most forceful expression of this attitude in the whole volume. The poet concludes that his confident expectations of love had been misplaced. Accordingly he

> ...recomposed the former scene,
> Let the snow lie, watched the moon rise, suffered the owls,
> Paid homage to them of unevent.

Graves now pays his homage exclusively to the female principle in experience—whether presented as incarnate in an actual woman, or as Goddess, or as the poet's Muse. It is particularly interesting that in this respect the poetic Muse and woman, whose qualities are now his only moral standard, have the same roles. To write poetry is for Graves inseparable from the effort of relating himself to the values discovered in his experience; which only restates a definition quoted by Laura Riding from Gerald Bullett in *The World and Ourselves*: 'the values implicit in poetry are the values by which we live at our best' (p. 244). The fusion brought about by the White Goddess mythology, a fusion of woman, Goddess and poetry, was therefore only the final and most complete expression of an identification that had already taken place in Graves's mind by about 1940—between the loved woman who by nature possesses the personal reality, the poem in which the values of this reality are implied, and the Moon-Goddess who symbolizes that reality.

The exercise of control through a powerful, subtle and extensive symbolism is one of two representative strategies adopted by Graves to absorb the greater impact of emotion in his later poetry. There have been many examples of the other strategy—a certain kind of indirectness in approaching a poem's central theme—since the publication of *The White Goddess*, but this also can be illustrated from *Work in Hand*. 'Language of the Seasons' is a particularly fine example. In the country, the poet says, our lives are ruled necessarily by the 'four seasons'; the fact is brought home most painfully when there are 'unseasonable frosts', 'usurping suns and haggard flowers'. In the city we were not aware of the seasons, only of 'weather', and—here Graves introduces the real subject—

Framed love in later terminologies
Than here, where we report how weight of snow,
Or weight of fruit, tears branches from the tree.

At one level this is an observation on the contrasting terminologies of traditionalist and modernist poetry. A deeper level, disclosed only in the last two lines, can be glimpsed in the precise epithets 'usurping' and 'haggard'. The not yet stated analogy between the seasons and love endows them with a double meaning: 'usurping' carries a suggestion of the lover's presumption in expecting summer happiness before it is due (as it was presumptuous 'to serenade Queen Famine' in 'A Love Story'); 'haggard', again a word more usually associated with persons, intimates that the lover's presumption has been punished (as it was by Queen Famine). Each is an image implying pain, and it is the constant threat of pain in love that, beneath the apparently casual observation, is the message of the last two lines: love *necessarily* causes pain. Perhaps it is this characteristic technique of oblique reference to disturbing emotions that a phrase in 'The Shot' is meant to define. After asserting that the heart, grateful for the unchanging personal reality known by 'honest human nature', will not let self-tormenting fears obscure it, the poem goes on to describe how this may be prevented from happening: the honest man will merely 'hint the fact'. *Hinting the fact* is clearly inseparable from the way Graves has learned to accept his own difficult nature; it is a procedure partly dictated by caution but chiefly by a determination not to be shaken by the pains of disappointment and betrayal from his loyalty to the positive values that he has also discovered in his experience. Not all his future poems will be content with this indirect approach, and many of them will bear the impression of at least as much suffering and bitterness as the poetry of his first and second periods contained; but they never will quite lose sight of these values or give way to disillusionment and cynicism. This too is evidence of Graves's essentially religious point of view now.

7

The White Goddess

THE REMAINDER of the poems written during the war years were added to the poems of *Work in Hand* to make up his next volume, *Poems 1938–1945* (1945), in which the first White Goddess poems make their appearance. A few more, written in the next two years, were included in *Collected Poems 1914–1947* (1948), which came out in the same year as *The White Goddess*. Graves has drawn on her mythology ever since, though to serve a variety of purposes. She dominates *Poems and Satires 1951* (1951) and her influence is still strong in *Poems 1953* (1953), but in the latter new interests are beginning to prevail; allusions to the actual mythology are few and then only to the basic situations of the Theme, realized with the utmost spareness of detail. This started a process that has continued until the present day.

I am not concerned here with *The White Goddess* as a theory about matriarchal religion but as a work that made available to Graves a means of communicating a unified view of his experience. It is with the importance of the White Goddess Theme to the poet that Graves himself is concerned, and its peculiar relevance to his particular 'spiritual autobiography' must be of prime interest to the reader of his poetry. It is helpful, however, to know something of the theory.

Graves has on several occasions described the White Goddess and outlined what, using a striking phrase from a letter of Alun Lewis, he calls 'the single poetic theme of Life and Death'; the clearest account is that given in one of the *Oxford Addresses on Poetry* entitled 'The Personal Muse' (pp. 57–81). Originally, he writes, the White Goddess was the goddess of the vegetation rites practised by the earliest Mediterranean societies and was worshipped in several guises and known by different names. A common name for her was the 'Triple Goddess'—because she represents the female principle in its three archetypal roles: as the mother of man, as his bride, and as the hag who buries him. In these capacities she respectively creates, fulfils and destroys him. As the Moon-Goddess she has her three phases of waxing moon, full moon and waning moon; and as the Goddess of the Year she presides over the three seasons of spring, summer and winter. In these prehistoric matriarchal communities she was worshipped by the whole group. Some time in the second millenium B.C., however, her shrines were taken over by invading patriarchal tribes, who introduced instead the cults of warlike male deities, Bull-gods and Thunder-gods; the process of suppression was accelerated during the Christian era, and Goddess-worship has, according to Graves, survived only as a personal faith confined to those individuals who have become dissatisfied with the prevailing values of modern patriarchal society. As the Muse she is venerated by poets; at first the Muse-trance was a collective one induced at set lunar festivals but it is now only experienced by the few truly dedicated poets, at irregular moments of intense poetic concentration. The poet may feel her power when he falls in love; but it is 'poetic love' only when he acknowledges its origin in the Triple Goddess and pledges himself to serve her. But poetic love also demands 'the recognition of the Muse-goddess as incarnate in some particular woman, who must be loved and trusted whatever happens. Though a sudden sense of the Goddess's creative power may overcome a poet when he first falls in love, and be enhanced by his rediscovery of her ancient titles and emblems, only a personal Muse can open the arcana of poetry to him.'

The Theme, as Graves summarizes it,

recounts the birth, life, death and resurrection of the Demigod of the Waxing Year; the central chapters concern his losing fight against the Demigod of the Waning Year, his rival for love of the all-powerful and inscrutable Threefold Goddess, their mother, bride and layer-out. The poet identifies himself with the Demigod of the Waxing Year; the rival is his twin, his second self, his weird. All true poetry...celebrates some incident or other of this ancient story; and the three main characters are so much a part of our racial legacy that they also assert themselves in dreams and paranoiac visions.

The Goddess is 'the Mother of All Living, the ancient power of love and terror—the female spider or the queen-bee whose courtship means murder'. The Theme goes back to a seasonal war between the Spirit of Growth and the Demon of Drought. In Palestine, for instance, the Goddess, 'Anatha, incarnate in a priestess-queen, annually ordered the crucifixion of her sacred consort as a means of placating the Demon of Drought; then took the executioner into her bed until the autumn rains should come—after which she destroyed him, chose another sacred king: in theory, the crucified man risen from the dead'. In this story the poet is the sacred consort who is murdered and brought back to life by her. Elsewhere Graves distinguishes obsessive poetic love from on the one hand human love and the Petrarchan idealization of women as distant saints on the other; and the poet-lover's murder and resurrection are here described by him as 'a love-ordeal which puts his sense of certitude to the supreme test', for the love offered by a Muse-woman is 'an absolute if unpredictable love.'

The story's interest for Graves is that he finds reflected in it an image of the pattern of events which he has seen in his own inner experience. It embodies his understanding and religious acceptance of the conditions of life as he has felt them; and he sees the Goddess as the Magna Mater, the 'Mother of All Living', who presides over them. Primarily, however, she is the Goddess of Love, and the rites which the Myth interprets enact for Graves the stages of a love-affair—the initial falling-in-love, fulfilment, betrayal and the possible or hoped-for restoration to the woman's favour. In her ability to create and destroy in love she is 'the ancient power of love and terror—the female spider or queen-bee whose courtship means murder'. It is clear from the terms used here that she personifies, as did Attercop, 'the All-Wise Spider', the violent oscillation from love to terror in Graves's own experience, particularly evident in his earlier volumes. This characterization of the Goddess also throws new light on the allegory of 'The Pier-Glass' in its first version, and suggests a different interpretation: in which the murderess represents woman in her destructive role, punishing her lover for some undisclosed shortcoming. The precipitous uncertainty of Graves's feelings expressed in the early poetry was to be accounted for as much by his neurasthenia as by his experience of love; significantly, therefore, he now claims that the three main characters in the Myth, the Goddess and the two rivals for her love, 'assert themselves in dreams and *paranoiac* visions'. Perhaps the rivals, the poet's ego and alter-ego, of 'Return' first appeared to him in a paranoiac vision.

Love involves the poet in repeated experiences of death and resurrection. Since poetry springs always from love and the values it creates, this is to say that being a poet—living for the poems he may write—involves him in the same process of death and resurrection. The Theme represents this process as a spiritual progress—from suffering (punishment imposed on man for his pride, jealousy, dominativeness, possessiveness in love) through submission to enlightenment—and in so doing gives expression to a sense of certain values. The mythology asserts always the female as against the male principle in human affairs. The Muse-poet protests against 'the patriarchal system: in so far as it values the intellect at the expense of instinct; and force at the expense of persuasion; and written laws at the expense of custom'. He 'sees history as a dangerous deviation from the true course of human life—an attempt to deny women their age-old moral ascendancy. A poet's absolute love, his readiness to trust in woman's wisdom, whatever may ensue, represents a nostalgia for human truth'.[1] In a lecture on 'The White Goddess' printed in *Steps* (1958) Graves writes that she symbolizes 'the supreme power, glory, wisdom and love of woman' (p. 102); in addition woman possesses a spontaneity and 'intuitive certitude' which is her chief gift to man. The Goddess is a deification, then, of these qualities. Towards men she has a benevolent and a corrective part to play; but the Myth largely concerns her activities in the latter part—as judge and disciplinarian of men. Her graciousness is chiefly a promise and a hope rather than an experienced fact. In the *Oxford Addresses*, for example, Graves interprets the story of Anatha and her competing lovers, Aleyan and Mot, as an image of the 'new, peculiar not yet fully explored, poet-Muse relationship. Anatha may well discipline Aleyan for showing signs of marital possessiveness: may betray him with his cruel, destructive twin as a means of asserting her personal freedom. But if Aleyan survives the ordeal,

[1] *Oxford Addresses*, p. 63.

after dying cheerfully for her sake, she will surely—he tells himself—raise him up again and destroy his rival' (p. 81).

Graves's relationship to the mythology and his ideas concerning the Muse and the Muse-poet raise several questions, most of which can only be answered through analyses of specific poems. But some can be dealt with at once. When he asserts, as he does in his talk on 'Sweeney among the Blackbirds' (printed in *Steps*) and elsewhere that 'poetry...cannot be separated from the state of being in love' (p. 110), what exactly does he mean? He evidently does not mean that all true poetry is love poetry, for in his Clark lectures (*The Crowning Privilege*, 1955) he singles out for praise Clare, most of whose poems, as Graves notes, were about Nature. The reasons he gives for commending Clare's best poems are these: 'he meant what he said, considered it well before he wrote it down and wrote *with love*' (p. 50, my italics). The meaning of 'with love' is illuminated by a remark made in his first lecture where he states his disagreement with those who believe 'a poet may be heartless or insincere or grasping in his personal relations and yet write true poems' (p. 21). To write 'with love', we infer, is to write truthfully and with all one's positive emotions engaged; a poet who is heartless, insincere or possessive in his life will be the same in his art—will write only loveless and therefore bad poems. Graves is of Ben Jonson's opinion that the good poet must first be a good man. Poetry must be written out of the poet's most intensely felt experience and in response to the deepest spiritual truths known to him—and for Graves these are to be found in the love-relationship. The guarantee of a poem's sincerity and spiritual 'goodness' is the poet's personal Muse. 'Whenever a poem reads memorably', he writes in the Foreword to *Collected Poems 1965*, 'this is almost always because a living Muse has directed its need and, however individual the poet's choice of words and rhythms, impressed her secret images on them'. In some way the poem must feel her influence, and this can only happen if the poet loves her wholeheartedly and submissively. In a broadcast talk entitled 'The Poet and his Public' (also included in *The Crowning Privilege*) he says that the poet who writes for the Muse is one who 'treats poetry with a single-minded devotion which may be called religious' (p. 187). Given Graves's equation of poetry and goodness, this also means that the response to experience that Muse-poems embody is a religious one.

A second question is suggested by this word 'religious': what does Graves understand by it? He is not a believer in a supernatural deity or a life after death, and he disclaims any intention of setting up the White Goddess for universal worship. His attitude to religion is that of some anthropologists who, he reminds us in his lecture on the White Goddess (*Steps*), give *de facto* recognition to all sorts of deities—male and female. 'No god at all can be proved to exist, but only beliefs in gods, and the effects of such beliefs on worshippers' (p. 95). It is the effects, for Graves, that deserve the name of religion. The invocation of the Voodoo deities of Haiti, for example, 'causes ecstatic behaviour in their worshippers and produces *if not miraculous, at least inexplicable, phenomena*' (p. 101, my italics); conversely, the inexplicable phenomena of poetic inspiration, the source of creative power, have led Graves to attribute it to 'the Lunar Muse, the oldest and most convenient European term for the source in question' (p. 96). The Goddess may be a metaphor or may not; he cannot tell, because he has no other explanation to offer for the experiences to which he gives her name than that she causes them. But much about any deity is unknown and unknowable and, as in the case of their worshippers, it is the quality of Graves's acceptance of the inexplicable, the seemingly miraculous, in his experience that can be called religious. Religion is a condition of mind. He depicts it as offering a 'subjective vision' of perfect being in his discussion of 'The Poet's Paradise' in the *Oxford Addresses*: 'the love-feast, for all who attend it in a state of grace and with complete mutual trust— by no means a simple condition—strengthens human friendship and at the same time bestows spiritual enlightenment: which are the twin purposes of most religions. Whether the soul visits a non-subjective Paradise or Hell on quitting its body, let theologians dispute' (pp. 128–9).

Since 1944, when Graves discovered the 'ancient titles and emblems' of the White Goddess, he has depended on her mythology primarily to provide analogies with, and a point of view in relation to, his personal experience; but in the early stages he also wrote a number of what he called 'magical poems'. These are either versions of ancient Celtic or Greek texts, or poems directly celebrating the Goddess and her mysteries. The latter rely for their meaning more heavily than his other poems on their author's investigations into pre-historic religion: to understand them fully the reader needs a de-tailed knowledge of the stories and emblems referred to and of the interpretations Graves puts on them. Probably because of this he has decided to omit a number of them from *Collected Poems 1965*. One that he has retained, however, 'To Juan at the Winter Solstice' (*Poems 1938–1945*), though obscure in some of its incidental allu-sions, is clear in its general import, and its images have an emotional power and suggestiveness which lose only a little in precise signifi-cance from an incomplete knowledge of their sources—much can be inferred from the poem itself. It provides one of the fullest accounts in the poetry of the Theme.

The poet chooses the time of the winter solstice—when the sun heroes of ancient legends traditionally were born—to recount the Theme to his young son, Juan. There is only one story worth telling, he begins: it is, of course, the story of the Love-Goddess and the unalterable sequence of events which her devotees—those who dare assume the role of her sacred consort—must suffer for her love. For a poet the conception of reality represented by the Goddess and her ritual is the only one, and so awe-inspiring is it, he goes on, that it can be communicated only in the archaic symbolic language of trees, beasts, birds and stars, whose traditional meanings are enriched by a patina of mythical-religious associations. Is it of these, he asks, that his son will wish to tell? Then he will tell of the stages in the appointed fate of the sacred victim, surrogate for the sun-hero, whose life begins and ends in woman. The poet asks again:

> Or is it of the Virgin's silver beauty,
> All fish below the thighs?
> She in her left hand bears a leafy quince;
> When with her right she crooks a finger, smiling,
> How may the King hold back?
> Royally then he barters life for love.

This records the moment when the Goddess through her priestess-queen, at the New Year festival, chooses her lover. But I quote this stanza to illustrate the succinct precision and emotional resonance with which the language of myth conveys its meaning. It describes the goddess Aphrodite, whom, since her cult was associated with the sea, Graves for his own purposes here identifies with a sea-goddess, probably Rahab; but it is not necessary to know this to feel the impact of the first two lines. They evoke powerfully her double nature: of an unearthly, magical beauty ('silver' suggests the moon), chaste and possibly unattainable, she is yet also promiscuous and treacherous like the mermaid. The same ambivalence is expressed in her gestures. In one hand she holds 'a leafy quince'—if its symbolic meaning of immortal love, love at the expense of life, is not known to the reader, 'leafy' sufficiently enhances the suggestion of succulence and desirableness, and implies further an area of shade and peace surrounding the gift; at the same time, however, with her other hand she beckons him—inviting and yet smilingly inscrutable. What she has to offer, this says, is both sweet and terrible.

The King accepts her invitation because his love is too great for caution. His eagerness to serve her whatever the cost—to give his life for her love—is the believer's willingness to surrender himself to a non-human power. The poem is at no point merely a description, but works all the time to reveal this view of the incidents described. A characteristic example of the way words are charged with emotional force by the mythological context occurs in 'royally', and it serves to illustrate also the way this view is enforced. It takes on all the associations of royalty that belong to the Goddess Theme and that the concept originally carried: service, trust, self-sacrifice, recklessness, courage and above all, the 'virtue' (in the Elizabethan sense) inherent in a sacred king marked out by a cruel but special fate from his common subjects—all these are added to the normal senses of magnanimity and style. The word, almost by itself, celebrates a code of behaviour and implies the religious foundations on which it is based. The stanza as a whole affects us more as revealing an immutable spiritual reality than as stating, albeit in a novel way, a few home truths concerning love; and this impression is largely attributable to one peculiarity of the picture it presents. The generalizing agency of myth is not alone enough to convert a love story into the affirmation of religious faith. Here Graves achieves that effect by portraying the Goddess in the symbolic pose in which she is frequently depicted in early religious iconography, for example on Cretan seals, and at the same time making the stereotyped gestures—the left hand proffering the quince, the finger of the right hand winsomely crooked, and the smile—live with a felt meaning. He achieves the effect in the next stanza by giving back to the mythical events narrated a sense—and the emotions—of the solemn ritual they were originally devised to reflect and explain:

> Or of the undying snake from chaos hatched,
> Whose coils contain the ocean,
> Into whose chops with naked sword he springs,
> Then in black water, tangled by the reeds,
> Battles three days and nights,
> To be spewed up beside her scalloped shore?

In these lines the hero undergoes a ritual death and rebirth. The 'undying snake from chaos hatched' was Ophion, the serpent demiurge created by Eurynome, the Goddess of All Things. He was the destructive principle to her creative principle, and at the midsummer festival his part was taken by the rival, the executioner and successor of the sacred king, representative of the Demigod of the Waning Year. Thus in the Isis story Osiris was killed and replaced by Set. But this is not the end of the story: the last chapter recounts his resurrection as the Goddess's son Horus at the winter solstice. The essentials of this process are vividly there in the verse and do not rely on annotation to make their impact on the reader. It adds something to the meaning, however, to know that the snake also represents wisdom—knowledge through self-destruction, suffering—and this ritual, besides earning the hero his right to be reborn to the Goddess's love, is at the same time his final initiation into her mysteries and bestows enlightenment.

To summarize: we can see, in the first place, how with the aid of myth Graves has managed to concentrate a multiplicity of meanings and considerable emotional power into his images, and in what profusion it has supplied him with these images, which are however linked and ordered by the 'single theme'. Secondly, it has enabled him to make of the vicissitudes of the man-woman relationship something like a Mystery play, which gives ritual shape to the varied incidents of a love story; all the painfulness of love is here but impersonalized by its association with the full conception of love's meaning embodied in the Myth—of which suffering is only a necessary part.

'To Juan at the Winter Solstice' presents the Goddess in her central function—as a symbol of the power and mysteries of love. But this is not the only role she has in Graves's poetry. Conceiving history 'as a dangerous deviation from the true course of human life—an attempt to deny women their age-old moral ascendancy', he occasionally represents the Goddess as a force in history, symbolizing the suppressed female principle, taking her revenge upon the male-dominated world for wilfully flouting her authority. In 'The Destroyers' (*Collected Poems 1914–1947*), a satire on man, unfortunately omitted from *Collected Poems 1965*, she is depicted in a cruel mood—taking secret satisfaction in ridiculing the degraded state to which man has brought humanity: 'Gusts of laughter the Moon stir'. This means that the savagely scornful tone of the poem derives special propriety, effectiveness and impersonality from the poet's self-identification with her super-human and omniscient point of view. But the advantages of seeing the Goddess in this light—as a kind of Platonic idea of femaleness revealed in history—are more than technical: it affects the moral status of the poem. Graves's researches into the origins of religion have provided him with a longer perspective on human development. His satiric denunciations are backed by a broad moral interpretation, applying generally and in detail, of that development. Thus the attack directed, in this poem, against the 'restless and arbitrary male will' (Graves's description of the poem's theme in *The White Goddess* (pp. 477–8), where it first appeared), is the more telling for being supported by a long view of history, one that finds its crucial episode in the second millenium B.C., when matriarchy was supplanted by the institution

of patriarchy, and can draw on it for evidence of the evil consequences of man's domination since.

The poem takes the form of an address to Perseus, the type of
the 'destroyer', whom Graves describes in his comments on the poem
in *The White Goddess* as 'the Gorgon-slaying warrior-prince from
Asia, remote ancestor of the destroyers Alexander, Pompey and
Napoleon' and 'the man who first tilted European civilization off
balance, by enthroning the restless and arbitrary male will under the
name of Zeus and destroying the female sense of orderliness,
Themis'. The passage I have in mind occurs in the third stanza:

> You who, capped with lunar gold
> Like an old and savage dunce,
> Let the central hearth go cold,
> Grinned and left us here your sword
> Warden of sick fields that once
> Sprouted of their own accord.

Technically this is a *tour de force*—the pattern of internal and end
rhymes creating an effect of angrily insistent, jeering scorn. The
thought is nevertheless complex. The lines recall the time generally
when bands of armed herdsmen worshipping male gods invaded
Greece and overran the Goddess's chief shrines, introducing a civilization that was ruled by a male military aristocracy and sustained
itself by conquest, and allowing the arts of agriculture practised by
the peaceful matriarchal peoples to be forgotten. In particular there
seems to be a reference to the Achaeans' capture of the Earth-
goddess's shrine, followed by the substitution of Apollo's cult, at
Delphi, popularly believed to be the centre of the earth, and the
consequent dying of the oracular flame. Their offence was their
wilful-ignorant neglect of the essential arts of life. In the setting of
matriarchal religion this constituted the omission (hinted at in the
last two lines) of the necessary fertility rites sanctified by the
Goddess. But the strength and complexity of this passage is more in
the two-dimensional nature of the imagery than in the concentrated
allusiveness in the one dimension of historical narrative. The same
words that adumbrate, with the utmost economy, a factual historical

context also evoke general absolute moral realities; for the 'central hearth' and the 'fields' are, symbolically, the inner life ('central' in that sense, too) of instinct, spiritual truth and reverence, as opposed to intellect in the service of greed and the 'arbitrary male will'. And still the Laura Riding ethic is at the centre of Graves's attitudes. Her actual words perhaps are echoed here, for in the *The World and Ourselves* she states what is in fact the theme of the poem: 'a confused outer brutality envelops the inner hearth of life where we cultivate all that we know to be precious and true' (p. 17).

The Goddess appears in yet another characteristic guise—as the Muse, the source of the poet's inspiration—in 'Advice on May Day' (*Poems and Satires 1951*). It is a light poem, which has not been reprinted, but the assumption on which its advice to the poet rests is a serious one: that the aesthetic discipline to which the Muse insists her poet should conform is at the same time a moral discipline exemplary for the man. 'Never sing the same song twice', the first stanza begins, 'Lest she disbelieve it'. This is to say that every poem springs from a unique impulse which the poet must obey without question. If he seeks to circumvent the rigours of the creative process by imitating his previous achievements—by repeating himself—then it will be a betrayal of his inspiration and morally dishonest, and in *that* sense will earn the Muses's disbelief. The last stanza advises: 'Make no sermon on your song'. The implication here is that the poem is a gift to the poet and should be treated as such: his task is to reveal plainly and briefly what his inspiration brings, and no more. Where a 'smile' out of place or 'half a word' too much might ruin a poem by the glimpses they offered of a conceited or comfortable attitude in its author, to preach a sermon from it would be gross evidence of prolixity and complacency. A recent formulation of this view occurs in the Foreword to *Collected Poems 1965*: Graves disclaims 'the least authorial pride' in his work, and gives as his reason for doing so— that he cannot 'regard himself as the originator of lines which move readers no less than he was himself moved to write them'. The middle stanza I quote more fully:

> Never sing a song clean through,
> You might disenchant her;

Venture on a verse or two
(Indisposed to sing it through),
Let that seem as much as you
Care, or dare, to grant her...

Singing a song 'clean through' would be trying to get at the heart of the experiences that caused it. 'Seem' implies that this is what Graves would like to do but that he doubts whether it is practicable. The alternative attitudes towards the Muse that he recommends the poet to take up—modesty and fear—hint at the reasons for his doubt: modesty because poetic expression is intrinsically limited—certain feelings and certain truths are beyond the reach of language; fear that grappling head-on with some of his experiences would kill his poetic powers. The moral of the first stanza is 'be honest', of the last 'be humble'; of the middle stanza it is perhaps 'be not ambitious'. It is evident that the Goddess idea not only enables Graves—as it does in 'To Juan at the Winter Solstice' and 'The Destroyers'—to express in his poetry a unified moral, and at times religious, view of his experience, but it embodies an estimation of poetry as in itself a kind of moral exercise—one in which the struggle with words and form is also spiritually beneficial to him. To be a poet means to practise certain disciplines, certain virtues such as honesty, humility and temperance—in the act of writing, or by means of it, as in one's life.

The character of the Goddess has one other aspect, more rarely seen in the poetry but perhaps, for Graves personally, the most important. Commonly her story is an allegory of the necessary conditions of life and her function is represented as disciplinary, but occasionally behind this image appears another, more shadowy one in which she is the tantalizing possibility of a perfect state. As such she is the object of an aspiration that Graves has expressed sporadically at every stage of his development: when, for instance, he asked his love to be 'the distant light,/Promise of glory, not yet known/In full perfection' ('Sullen Moods'), or when he evoked Lucifer, 'the star of morning', in the Epilogue to *The Feather Bed*; and in the 'thirties the same impulse informed his prayer 'That the twelve spokes of this round-felloe'd year/Be a fixed compass, not a turning

wheel' ('The Felloe'd Year'). The earliest and one of the best celebrations of the Goddess in this aspect is the dedicatory poem to *The
White Goddess*, later revised and included under that title in *Poems
and Satires 1951*. Here she is presented in all her other roles—as the
pagan Mother of All Living, the Muse, and the Goddess of Love—
but she is also one who impelled her devotees to scorn the moderate
aspiration of the classical ideal and to look for her

> In distant regions likeliest to hold her
> Whom we desired above all things to know,
> Sister of the mirage and echo.

It is interesting to note the connection here with the imagery of 'End
of Play'. There the 'mirror' of imagination and the 'echo' of the
mind were the mediators between the poet's experience and his *idea*
of love—the idea which was later to be embodied in the White
Goddess Theme. The statement of this new love, after the bitter
repudiation of the old, was firm but dour. Strangely, in the later
poem scepticism about the reality of what the new love has to offer
is more extreme: not only must we know her as an 'echo'—that is,
at a remove, but she may be ('may' because she is only the 'sister'
of the mirage) an illusion of our imaginations. And yet it does not
read like scepticism: despite the possibility that she is illusory the
poet's tone is perversely confident, even jubilant. There is even a
bold emphasis laid on the paradox of wanting *knowledge* of what may
be a mirage. Whether she is so or not, the idea of her is, in the poet's
view, sufficient justification for the quest and the single-minded
pursuit of it. The 'distant light' may have come no nearer but it
shines more intensely now—so as to dazzle the poet; the 'promise of
glory' may be no more likely of fulfilment, but the poet's imagination
of that glory and his obsession with it are infinitely greater; so that
we, the poets, he says, 'forget cruelty and past betrayal'.

In the traditional picture of the Goddess

> Whose broad high brow was white as any leper's,
> Whose eyes were blue, with rowan-berry lips,
> With hair curled honey-coloured to white hips

the Myth has given Graves a more vivid image of this glory and at the same time of the paradoxical nature of his yearning (note the disturbing effect of 'white as any leper's') than he had possessed before; and this explains why the romanticism of this poem is more full-bodied than that of any previous poem of his.

The Goddess is, severally, the poet's conscience, the supreme wisdom of woman which has, disastrously, gone unheeded throughout history, and a goal of perfection; above all, she is the spiritual reality in the love experience—and this is the justification of her authority in her other roles. In order to communicate that reality Graves has made it unfold itself in the dramatic sequence of the Nature ritual sacred to the Mother-goddess of prehistoric matriarchal societies. The crucial episodes in that ritual were the actual or symbolic death of the sacred king at the midsummer festival, just before the days begin to shorten, and his supposed rebirth as the Goddess's son at the Winter solstice, the turning point of the year when the days begin again to lengthen. Graves has made of this pattern of death and rebirth the central mystery of love. In doing so he has equated his experience with the spiritual experience symbolized in the majority of known religions, not only in the fertility cults.

As we have seen, this pattern was already emerging during his first period. 'The Stake', the poem that opens *The Pier-Glass*, was the clearest example, but we can discern fragments of the pattern in several other poems. Its source can be traced to Graves's almost literal experience of death and rebirth in France during the First World War recorded in 'Escape' (*Fairies and Fusiliers*)—an incident that became emblematic for the poet. (He refers to it in a poem of the 'fifties revealingly entitled 'The Second-Fated':

> Fortune enrolled me among the second-fated
> Who have read their own obituaries in *The Times*...)

The postwar volumes represented the torments of neurasthenic nightmares in imagery that goes back to that poem—as a nightly descent into Hell followed by a rebirth into morning sunlight. Death in love may be the subject of 'The Pier-Glass', as it certainly is of the Prologue to *The Feather Bed*, in which the poet describes his visit to the Witches' Cauldron and his sight of the 'dead snake'. 'Morning Phoenix' (*The Pier-Glass*), a poem which Graves has revised and under the new title of 'A Phoenix Flame' reprinted in *Man Does, Woman Is*, images the poet's death and, partly identifying it with his nightmares, expresses his longing to be 'A *morning* phoenix with proud roar/Kindled new within' (my italics). 'Return' and 'A False Report' (now retitled 'Angry Samson') are both celebrations of the poet's rebirth. The pattern repeated itself on a larger scale when Graves's first marriage came to an end and he was revived from this death by his love for Laura Riding. Telescoping this with his later experiences, he narrates in 'The Second-Fated' how, after 'a brief demise', he 'visited first the Pit...And next the silver-bright Hyperborean Queendom', and how he learned to despise the

> factitious universe
> Ruled by the death which we had flouted;
> Acknowledging only that from the Dove's egg hatched
> Before aught was, but wind—unpredictable
> As our second birth would be, or our second love...

'The Second-Fated' while buoyant in mood confesses to uncertainty: this 'second love' or 'second birth' is 'unpredictable'. In 'To Juan at the Winter Solstice' the death and resurrection of the sacred king is mentioned as a stage in his ritual journey through the year; in the myths, however, there is frequently a doubt as to whether or not the 'star-son' born to the Goddess at midwinter is in fact the sun-hero reborn—whether, for example, Horus is the new self of Osiris. In 'Darien' (*Poems and Satires 1951*), another magical poem, Graves takes advantage of this obscurity to explore the ambiguity, in his account of poetic love, of the claims he makes for it. He narrates how once 'at full moon' (meaning the time of the poet's ritual murder) he came upon the Muse 'without warning'. He spoke to her but she would not meet his eyes, and knowing this to be a sign that the time had come when he must die at her hand he was possessed with 'a great grief'. When he asked her to look at him,

> She answered: 'If I lift my eyes to yours
> And our eyes marry, man, what then?

Will they engender my son Darien?
Swifter than wind, with straight and nut-brown hair
Tall, slender-shanked, grey-eyed, untameable;
Never was born, nor ever will be born
A child to equal my son Darien,
Guardian of the hid treasures of your world'.

The poet eagerly accepted his fate:

'Mistress', I cried, 'the times are evil
And you have charged me with their remedy
...Only look up, so Darien may be born';

and went on to praise him in the language of myth as the incarnation of spiritual truth and wisdom, as the immortal soul, and 'the new green of my hope'. Darien, the Muse's son, is both the poet's reborn self—purified by death in the service of a transcendent love—and, as a standard of perfection celebrated by the poet in his oracular function, a 'remedy for the times'. He offers himself for sacrifice *in order that* he may be created anew, restored to the Goddess's love; but when she asks whether their instantaneous love will engender her son Darien the question indicates a radical uncertainty at the centre of this experience. It is partly a threat—'you know what suffering such love entails'—but partly that she doubts the outcome and has not yet decided whether to give her love. There is an ambiguity, too, in the words she chooses to convey the matchless qualities of her son—'Never was born, nor never will be born/A child to equal my son Darien'—which could mean that he will never be more than a product of the imagination. It is to secure her love that the poet willingly embraces the suffering involved, but he too is uncertain how real Darien is: despite the extravagance of his praise he can say, in conclusion, no more than that he is 'the new green of my hope'.

Graves has named this hope Darien from Keats's 'On first Looking into Chapman's Homer'. Keats describes a similar state of feeling—anticipation of renewal through the poetic imagination. He writes of the 'realms of gold' and the 'western islands' (the paradisal Apple Islands of Graves's mythology) enjoyed by the poets and likens his feeling on entering for the first time the poetic kingdom ruled by Homer to those of

> stout Cortez when with eagle eyes
> He star'd at the Pacific—and all his men
> Look'd at each other with a wild surmise—
> Silent, upon a peak in Darien.

The kind of romantic mood expressed by these lines is in complete harmony with the almost religious joy of Graves's poem—based equally on a 'wild surmise'.

Of the poems written since 1942 those that I have been considering so far are all concerned directly with the White Goddess—with, in other words, the large general meanings of the Theme. They can be regarded as imaginative explorations into the possibilities of the language of myth, in which the poet's personal experiences symbolized in the story of the Goddess and her changing relations with her lovers have been totally absorbed into the mythological context. A poem like 'Darien' is dramatic and emotionally charged, but still it does not represent Graves at his most intensely involved—it does not have quite the immediacy of, say, 'A Love Story'. The finest of his later poems are renderings of the human relationship, in which the Myth is present only as an unobtrusive framework for the experience.

An example from the same volume as 'Darien', *Poems and Satires 1951*, is 'The Young Cordwainer'. For the idea of the poem's general situation Graves is indebted to a legend recorded in an obscure medieval French ballad called 'Le Petit Cordonnier'—which explains the title. Otherwise, apart from two images, the river and the periwinkle, which also appear in the ballad, and which according to his interpretation of it in *The White Goddess* (pp. 322–3) bear a folklore meaning derived originally from some ritual in honour of the Goddess—both symbolizing death, the episode in the poem is entirely Graves's own. Like 'Darien' it describes the death of the lover at the hand of the loved woman, but despite the legendary setting the experience described affects us as taking place between a man and a woman rather than between the poet and the Goddess;

it has a more intimate and ultimately more moving quality. It is a dialogue, after the style of ballads and in an adaptation of the ballad verse-form, between the woman and the lover's dark, other self—in Graves's language 'his twin, his second self, his weird', the rival and successor to the sacred king of the Myth.

> SHE: Love, why have you led me here
> To this lampless hall,
> A place of despair and fear
> Where blind things crawl?
>
> HE: Not I, but your complaint
> Heard by the riverside
> That primrose scent grew faint
> And desire died.
>
> SHE: Kisses had lost virtue
> As yourself must know...

Note that it is *he* who has led *her* to this 'place of despair'; and it is he who now gently but firmly persuades her to, and assists her in, the completion of the necessary murder. He leads her past the loathsome 'bandogs' and up the stairs; he reminds her that the primrose of true, tender love has for its fellow the baleful periwinkle of death; he overcomes her dread of the deed that must be performed, taking her up and up until finally they come 'To a locked secret door/And a white-walled room'; and there he shows her 'the state bed' where a man garlanded with blue periwinkles lies awaiting his approaching execution. With a sword beneath her pillow and wine to revive her, she is now ready to 'perfect all'. The man on the bed is the young cordwainer of the title: it is he who is to be killed. She will use the sword, but his death will have been brought about by the combined efforts of her and the dark 'twin'.

The three characters, the primrose, the periwinkle and the sword are the only properties that Graves has taken from the White Goddess story. The poem relies for its effect primarily on an imagery that in Graves's poetic history dates back to his first period. The house, 'the lampless hall' where 'blind things crawl', the terrors of the stairs, recall the 'haunted' atmosphere of his early nightmare poems and some of the love poems. They evoke the same mood of despair in love that was symbolized in the early poetry by the dragon. The 'state bed' is an actual reminiscence—it was on 'the huge bed of state' that the woman in 'The Pier-Glass' murdered her lover; in fact, 'The Young Cordwainer' is as it were a rewriting of that poem—clear and explicit where that is vague, showing as it does a fuller understanding of the situation, and sharper in its impact.

The idea of the lover's warring light and dark selves first emerged, of course, in 'Return', and the rival lovers of the Myth are a further objectivation of the conflict. But in 'The Young Cordwainer' greater attention is paid to the psychology of the experience—to what exactly each character represents and how they are related—than in either the early poem or the Goddess poems that have been cited, and greater subtlety is employed in revealing it. The dark self, the alter-ego, has been called into being by the despair caused by the death of the woman's love for her lover. Therefore together she and the alter-ego are instrumental in bringing about the (spiritual) death of the ego (which, we infer from the first stanza, has died for the lack of the light and hope bestowed by love). Although the allegory makes of the lover's divided self two distinct characters, with separate parts to play, yet the poem skilfully insinuates the identity of the young cordwainer and his twin: while it is HE, the despairing self, who is assumed to have felt it when 'Kisses had lost virtue', yet it is the young cordwainer who is doomed to suffer the final death-blow of despair. It adds to the human reality of the poem that the woman, though cast for a leading role in this drama of love, should be portrayed as a *reluctant* performer—as much as man the involuntary subject of a non-human power.

The poem is chiefly concerned to explore the experience of *death* in love, but the imagery just hints at a possible sequel. There is a strong suggestion in the stanzas that describe the fearful, breathless ascent to the 'secret door' of the 'white-walled room' that this is an image of the sexual act culminating in sexual death—and release. The cleanness of the 'white-walled room' (also called a 'confessional', suggesting a place where the *poetic* act takes place) is an ambiguous concept. Whether it implies exhaustion and penitence or renewal and purification is undisclosed. As is indicated in 'Darien', it is an essential part of the experience that it should be undisclosed.

The ability to be in uncertainty about a central fact is integral to Graves's faith; it contributes a tough invulnerability to, without qualifying, the romantic affirmation of such poems as 'The White Goddess' and in others, like 'The Young Cordwainer', gives dramatic reality to his expression of that faith. There is at least one poem, however—'Instructions to the Orphic Adept' (*Poems 1938–1945*)— from which doubt of the poet's resurrection from death and despair, and uncertainty as to what state of being will ensue, have been banished. It is in part a translation from Orphic texts, but it is un-likely that this fact alone accounts for the poem's unusual definite-ness. The explanation seems to be that what is defined, this state of perfect being that succeeds the experience of death, is not an assured possession; it is an achievement of a kind that might justify Graves's ambiguity or inexplicitness in other poems.

The instructions are those that accompany the adept's initiation into the final mysteries of the Orphic religion. They are an expan-sion of the single commandment with which the poem opens: 'remember/What you have suffered here in Samothrace'. The adept is then warned of the temptations that upon his death will beset him during his passage through Hades and told how to overcome them. He will come to two springs; the first is Forgetfulness and though his throat will be parched he must avoid it; instead he must proceed to the second and there ask if he might drink:

> To the right hand there lies a secret pool
> Alive with speckled trout and fish of gold;
> A hazel overshadows it. Ophion,
> Primaeval serpent straggling in the branches,
> Darts out his tongue. This holy pool is fed
> By dripping water; guardians stand before it.
> Run to this pool, the pool of Memory,
> Run to this pool.

The guardians will ask him if he does not 'fear Ophion's flickering tongue'. He must disclose that he is a 'Child of the three-fold Queen of Samothrace' and say:

My feet have borne me here
Out of the weary wheel, the circling years,
To that still, spokeless wheel:—Persephone.

Then he will be admitted to the company of other initiates, will rule Hell's 'twittering ghosts', pronounce oracles, and be served by the priestesses who will pour libations to his 'serpent shapes'.

The secret pool, alive with 'speckled trout' (the singing spotted fish which in Greek and Celtic legend, according to Graves, symbolize poetry), recalls the pool overhung with the nine hazels of poetic art from which Gwion, in 'The Romance of Taliesin' (*The Mabinogion*), received the gift of inspiration and oracular powers. 'Ophion/Primaeval serpent' is, as in 'To Juan at the Winter Solstice', a symbol of wisdom-out-of-suffering or, in an alternative definition, 'universal fertility out of death' (*The White Goddess*). The pool from which the adept must drink is however called Memory, not Poetry, and the theme of the poem is stated in the first precept of the Orphic doctrine—remember what you have suffered. For Graves, the spirit dies and is renewed in poetry; the serenity into which it is reborn is poetic wisdom; and poetic wisdom is the transcendence of past sufferings *by not forgetting them*—by seeing them as necessary to the spirit's purification. The process represents, as G. S. Fraser, connecting this poem with 'The Worms of History', perceptively remarks, the transformation of 'pain into the excellence of art'. In his new incarnation, as the speaker of oracles, the poet himself assumes the 'serpent shapes' of wisdom. That inspiration will last, however, cannot be counted on; the poet retains the gift only on the condition that he repeatedly gives proof that he deserves it. It bestows a serenity, therefore, that may at any moment be withdrawn; and it is the subjection to the capriciousness of this inspiring power that the guardians have in mind when they ask the adept if he is not afraid of 'Ophion's *flickering* tongue': poetic enlightenment is piercingly intense but intermittent. This is why the condition of perfect being (identified with poetry) is not, in Graves's conception, an assured possession.

In one respect 'Instructions to the Orphic Adept', remarkably, anticipates an idea of poetic love that Graves has been developing in his most recent poems. He names it, after the Goddess of the Orphic, Jewish and Sufi Wisdom-cults, the Black Goddess—blackness in these cults symbolizing wisdom. He writes of her in 'Intimations of the Black Goddess' (included in *Mammon and the Black Goddess*): she is sister to the White Goddess and leads those poets 'who have served their apprenticeship to the White Goddess', who have suffered death and recreation at her hand, to their final goal, 'a miraculous certitude in love' (pp. 162–4). This state is represented in 'Instructions to the Orphic Adept' as Persephone. In an imagery that in turn derives from a poem of the previous decade, 'The Felloe'd Year', Graves tells how after years of being bound to the cycle of the changing seasons, alternations of good and evil, the poet has been at last released—in the words of *The White Goddess*, 'excused further Tearings-to-Pieces, Destructions, Resurrections and Rebirths' (p. 139). And in the poem's opening lines he figures man's search for wisdom as a journey into the blackness of Hades: 'your mazed spirit descends/From daylight into darkness, Man...'—an image which he reworks in the recent poem entitled 'The Black Goddess' (*Man Does, Woman Is*).

'Instructions to the Orphic Adept' is, like 'To Juan at the Winter Solstice', classed as a 'magical poem' in *Collected Poems 1914–1947*. In these poems, as in others that directly celebrate the White Goddess or describe her intervention in human affairs, the Single Theme is treated as a revelation of religious truth or as affording in the form of a historical theory a broad foundation for a *Weltan-schauung* and an ethical system. But the majority of the poems that Graves has written during his third period deal with a specific human relationship, and either the Theme is used as a mould to give a general shape to the poet's perceptions concerning it—as is the case with 'The Young Cordwainer'—or it is a shadowy, barely discernible presence animating the poem's values.

These two kinds of poem were from the start being written con-currently with the Goddess poems; an example of the former kind that has been much admired, 'Theseus and Ariadne', appeared first in *Poems 1938–1945*. Ariadne, falling in love with Theseus, had rescued him from the minotaur; he had promised marriage but after

a brief stay on the island of Naxos had deserted her. The poem begins
several years after this episode. Theseus is now married to Phaedra
and, far away in place and time, has only dream-like memories of his
early love affair.

> High on his figured couch beyond the waves
> He dreams, in dream recalling her set walk
> Down paths of oyster-shell bordered with flowers
> And down the shadowy turf beneath the vine.
> He sighs: 'Deep sunk in my erroneous past
> She haunts the ruins and the ravaged lawns'.

He imagines her as a ghost inconsolably haunting the scene of her
betrayal. He does not know that she still lives and that the god
Dionysus, taking pity on her, had made her his wife.

> Yet still unharmed it stands, the regal house
> Crooked with age and overtopped by pines
> Where first he wearied of her constancy.
> And with a surer foot she goes than when
> Dread of his hate was thunder in the air,
> When the pines agonized with flaws of wind
> And flowers glared up at her with frantic eyes.
> Of him, now all is done, she never dreams
> But calls a living blessing down upon
> What he would have mere rubble and rank grass;
> Playing the queen to nobler company.

The arrangement—the appearance sharply succeeded by the reality
—expresses the poem's purpose: in juxtaposing Theseus's romanti-
cized and Ariadne's truthful memories of the past, his complacent
assumptions about the present and the actual present that confounds
his suppositions, Graves is drawing a comparison between the points
of view, and by implication the characters, of man and woman. By
the time-shift—between an imperfectly remembered past and an
unknown present—he contrives a finely organized effect of irony, a
moral irony that, for example, exposes Theseus's dishonesty. The
circumstances of the implied classical legend—give dramatic reality
to the poem's critical weighing of contrasting attitudes, achieve for
the protagonists an archetypal status, and provide a frame of refer-

ence, in scene, characters and events, glancing allusion to which enables the poet to concentrate his meaning and, as it were, to bury his ironies—to make them more dangerously latent in the verse.

The unfolding of Theseus's character is done with supreme skill. The first six lines do not yield their full content—data for the moral placing of Theseus—until the second passage, describing Ariadne, has done its work. Thus until we have read on to the end of the poem we are not in a position to gauge the *degree* of viciousness embodied in the erstwhile lover's words of apparent self-reproach. The assumption that she would die for love of him is in the event, as we see, bland egotism, a sort of stupidity; more culpable is the destructive satisfaction he feels at the thought of it—a satisfaction masked as pity by the sweet romantic melancholy of 'She haunts the ruins and the ravaged lawns', but coldly exposed in the poet's brusque rephrasing of this thought: 'What he would have mere rubble and rough grass'. The balancing of these two lines against each other is immensely suggestive; it opens up vistas on the narcissism of a certain kind of sentimental romanticism—that precludes reverence for, even implies antagonism towards, another person's identity. It is evident now that what at first, in the reference to his 'erroneous past', we took to be self-reproach for his betrayal of love is in fact pious self-congratulation on his present disengagement from such disreputable escapades: the error was not his faithlessness but to have been involved at all. We recognize in this a male characteristic —the apotheosis of will at the expense of feeling. The poem in almost every line expands with this kind of suggestiveness. Descriptive phrases are loaded with moral implications: 'high on his figured couch' conveys the lordly self-importance, the assumption of an almost godlike aloofness, in his musings; 'set walk'—that it should, in his mind, be 'set', unalterable—betrays the inflexibility of his own imagination and the inability to accept change. Or an image will suddenly, on rereading, gather from its context symbolic overtones —as in the line 'Dread of his hate was thunder in the air': where the mention of 'thunder' relates Theseus to the Thunder-god Zeus of patriarchal religions, as opposed to Ariadne, a type of the Moon-goddess, and Dionysus, alluded to in the last line, a type of sacred king—thus transforming Theseus into a personification of the whole male ethos.

The shallow, self-regarding character of man, represented by Theseus, is contrasted with the deeper sensibility of woman as embodied in Ariadne. He, vague and self-centred in his feelings, escapes to a glamorized past; she, simple and constant in her feelings and responding directly to her surroundings, lives solely in the present. Against the dream-like perfection of the scene conjured up in his reverie is set the dignity and immediate life of the other, actual scene: not living in the past, she is alert and confident. The same point was made in the concluding lines of 'The Worms of History': 'excellence lives' in the present, and the gloss that I added, quoting Laura Riding, that 'women are concerned with what *is*—immediately and ultimately', is also relevant here. For Ariadne's living in the present, too, is a living by ultimate values. In Theseus's words there is an almost lachrymose insistence on the power of time—'the ruins and the ravaged lawns'—whereas the suggestion is that Ariadne inhabits a mental world unaffected by time: the house has aged but she walks 'with a surer foot'. The 'moral ascendancy' of woman, an assumption on which several of the *Work in Hand* poems rest, is here given full and convincing reality. There is the gentle but firm hint of a Cordelia-like divinity in her being (she is married to a god and 'calls a living blessing down'), a divinity, however, that is not supernatural but living—a quality of life, which, it is implied, is beyond man's attainment.

We can feel the implied presence of the White Goddess mythology in the hint of a moral kinship between Theseus and Zeus and in the off-stage presence of Dionysus, but it is there most effectively in the poet's way of enforcing his estimation of woman's moral qualities—by bestowing upon her a faint aura of Goddess-like 'divinity', something worthy not merely of neutral recognition but of man's reverence. This estimation of woman 'Theseus and Ariadne' shares with earlier poems, and in particular the poems of *Work in Hand*; but not until Graves had worked out her supreme role in the Single Theme and discovered her counterparts in the mythology of the ancient world could he paint her portrait with such sensitivity and precision. In other respects also it resembles and perhaps betters the *Work in Hand* poems. It presents a more rounded and perceptive picture of man's moral nature than does 'To Sleep'—with greater economy and less overt emphasis. And as much as 'The Beast' the poem speaks for itself, endowed possibly with a finer quality of independence by the greater complexity of what it succeeds in saying.

In 'To be Named a Bear' (*Collected Poems 1914–1947*) the Theme is again used as a background—but to dramatize not a whole relationship but a single aspect of it. As with 'Theseus and Ariadne', there is room for comparison between it and the pre-Goddess poems of *Work in Hand*. In its technique of oblique reference to the poem's central, originating emotion, it recalls in particular 'Language of the Seasons'. The disclosure of this emotion—and therefore our understanding of all that goes before—is reserved, as it was in the earlier poem, for the concluding lines.

The poem opens with a neutral observation on the habits of bears: by marking certain trees in a forest they map out the boundaries of their hunting grounds, and they love sweet things like the bees' honeycomb and blueberries. The poet then asks if he has not aptly been named a bear, for he too is 'Unkempt and surly with a sweet tooth' (a recognizable piece of self-dramatization). The mythological significance of these remarks is made clear in the following lines: like the bear-dancers in the cult of the Arcadian Bear-goddess, Artemis Calliste ('Callisto') he tilts his head towards 'the starry hub'. (The universe was pictured as a mill-stone, turned by the two constellations the Great Bear and the Lesser Bear; at the hub was the Goddess, whirling around with the universe but without motion.) He aspires, that is to say, to the changeless state of the Goddess. His taste for wild, sweet things, too (which the danger, for example, of being stung by bees will not cure) is not just an idiosyncrasy of physical appetite but a yearning for the dangerous but sweet love of the Goddess. Like the dancers he worships Callisto, but he envies those animals that sleep through the hardships of the winter months—

> That yawn awake when the skies clear
> And lank with longing grow
> No more than one brief month a year.

The analogy is now complete; as a result, by these closing lines the emotion held back throughout the poem—the pain of unsatisfied longing felt unremittingly by the poet—is suddenly released. Even here the shock of this revelation is, momentarily, delayed, for it takes a moment to recognize the personal reference sheltering behind the mild 'no more' and the well-bred appearance of not speaking of himself.

The strategy is exactly that of 'Language of the Seasons'. The meanings of the earlier poem are more neatly and tightly concentrated; the later poem moves towards its surprise ending with an innocent, relaxed air. This gives 'Language of the Seasons' a sharper impact, but 'To be Named a Bear' has the advantage of a symbolism with a wider range of association. For example, 'honeycomb and blue-berries', as images linked with the Theme, are thereby harnessed, as I have intimated, to a complex of romantic ideas concerning wildness and sweetness: that what is wild is alone natural and true, that the sweetest, most desirable things are also wild and dangerous and are more precious for being so, and so on; these merge with another set of ideas concerning honesty and sincerity, that centre on the wildness, clumsiness and surliness of the bear (an association frequently to be encountered in Graves's work). A disadvantage of this kind of poem is the occasional inaccessibility of an image. Thus 'the starry hub' will not give up all its meanings to someone who is unfamiliar with the author's investigations into classical mythology.

'Theseus and Ariadne' is characteristic of one way of using the mythology adopted by Graves: it embodies the poet's thought in a third person narration of a legendary relationship. 'To be Named a Bear' illustrates another way: the poet here identifies himself with a character in the ancient story or ritual—in this case the bear-dancer. An early example of the first kind of poem is 'Ulysses' (*Poems 1930–1933*); in the same volume there is a group of prose-poems called 'As It Were Poems' which anticipates the second kind. The poet summarizes several legends and asks the same question about each one: 'where was I?' In the legend of Troy he was in the person of Ajax, cheated, goaded into rage, and labelled mad; in the legend of

Robin Hood he was Friar Tuck, 'the gross fool of the green-wood'; in the story of the Golden Ass he was the 'impassioned ass', subjected to cruelly ridiculous ordeals but rescued by Isis; in the legend of Isis he was the drowned Osiris: he casts himself for roles that are at once humiliating and heroic, as he does also in the later mythological poetry. Both betray the same impulse—to raise his sufferings, while resisting the temptation to inflate their importance, to archetypal status.

The Theme provides an objective correlative for Graves's experiences. In so far as it implies a scheme of values and exemplifies them in a body of mythology it also gives substantial backing to his affirmation of these (invariably romantic) values. The further strengthening of the romantic attitudes previously expressed in such poems as 'On Portents' and 'The Felloe'd Year' is one of the most important consequences of the White Goddess mythology. His poems now frequently express the desire for the extraordinary or the impossible, but he represents this, for example in 'The White Goddess', not as a faint-hearted avoidance of the real but as a spiritual quest of considerable difficulty. The paradoxical nature of his desires is admitted and the pain in store for one who pursues such a paradoxical ideal is frankly confronted—recognitions intrinsic to the Myth—in the very moment of asserting the supreme value of this quest. This removes from Graves's romanticism any suggestion that the idly fanciful or the easy wish-fulfilment has played a part in its make-up. Other poems are romantic in the sense that they present what is most valued by the poet as not to be found in life as a whole but only in life as it is lived at certain special, intense moments —moments which therefore detach themselves from the apparently unbreakable sequence of time.

Life seen in this aspect is celebrated in 'Through Nightmare' (*Poems 1938–1945*). The poet tells the loved woman never to question the primary reality of the paradise where sometimes in her dreams she finds herself. There, he says, she will meet those rare people—'The untameable, the live, the gentle'—who are alone worth knowing: who are not the slaves of time, do not allow worldly, temporal pressures to distort personal moral truth:

They carry
Time looped so river-wise about their house
There's no way in by history's road...

Time is outside them and they have a private existence apart from
it—but in a place by no means easy of access: paradise is subjective,
a state of being, achieved only by the pure of heart. One reaches this
condition of purity on but few occasions—she is 'seldom/In their
company seated'—and only after a spiritual journey of great hardship: the poet's beloved has had to 'travel/Through nightmare to
[their] lost and moated land'. We are made to feel, once again, that
Graves has brought to bear upon this celebration of the extraordinary, of a romantic ideal, a steady awareness of the pervasively
ordinary and the painfully actual: the 'lost and moated land', far
from being a never-never land divorced from reality, is the ultimate
goal of spiritual endeavour. The White Goddess mythology helps to
enforce this impression; for the Island of Avalon is being alluded to,
the 'Apple Island' with its moated castle where heroes after a life
spent honourably and dangerously took their rest, and where the
dying Arthur was transported by Morgan le Faye.

'The Portrait' (*Poems and Satires 1951*), an intensely romantic
celebration of the loved woman, illustrates even more impressively
the resilient quality of this romanticism. The poem is organized on a
simple principle: each stanza presents a contrast in some characteristic between the Muse-woman, the poet's inspiration, and
other, less gifted women. While she speaks unaffectedly in her own
voice to everyone

those other women
Exercise their borrowed, or false, voices
Even on sons and daughters.

Her feelings and actions are so governed by an inner reality that as a
totally private being she is invisible to 'those other women', whose
own carnality is so grossly evident. 'She is wild and innocent,
pledged to love/Through all disaster'; 'those other women', who
have no experience of such love, are scandalized, condemn her as a
witch and a harlot and snub her in the streets. This characterization
of a woman who lives from within herself is not detailed, and the

virtues she exemplifies are simply named—she is sincere, self-contained, 'wild' 'innocent' and constant; but the picture of her, the poem's values embodied in her, acquire definition and solidity from the comparison with the specific, nicely observed imperfections of ordinary women, and we are persuaded accordingly that these values, although romantically absolute, nevertheless constitute a feasible moral standard—one that is applicable to reality as we know it. By contrast with women who inhabit their artificial social selves even in their closest personal relationships, the loved woman's habit of speaking 'in her own voice' is a sign that she lives completely from within herself. Her invisibility bespeaks a spiritual, as opposed to their total absorption in a physical, existence. Even 'wild' is not an empty gesture of praise but betokens in this context a refusal, as 'innocent' implies her inability, to conform to the externalities of their moral world—one in which true love goes unrecognized.

Though the White Goddess is not directly mentioned and no use is made of her mythology, the Theme is nevertheless felt to be present. The assimilation of woman's powers to witchcraft (in Graves's view, an abusive term applied by Christians to the 'old religion') indicates that she is possessed by the Goddess. This fact throws more light on her character and makes a sharper division between her and ordinary women. She is the Muse-woman and as such is separated from the body of womankind not merely by the poet's preference but by belonging as it were to another and superior race, having a different faith and code of behaviour. This assessment of her standing communicates itself in the poem's conclusion. The poet is studying her portrait, and reads in the expression of her eyes a probing question:

> And you, love? As unlike those other men
> As I those other women?

The right to judge her love is one that belongs peculiarly to the Personal Muse, whose part it is to be the poet's conscience. At the same time, by making his ability to live up to romantic values the supreme test of a man's quality, the question completes the poem's presentment of romantic faith as something tough and invulnerable.

The tendency for the Theme to recede into the background of Graves's poems becomes more noticeable in the later volumes of this period. *Poems and Satires 1951* and *Poems 1953* are each about equally divided between poems featuring the Goddess or the legends associated with her and poems in which they are only latently present or which are completely independent of them. However, even in those that are independent the all-absorbing subject is still the man-woman relationship, and undoubtedly Graves's treatment of it has been indirectly influenced by the crystallization of his perceptions on the 'one poetic theme' that occurred in the previous decade. It is safe to assume that the most enduring effect of this crystallization was to throw into sharper relief and concentrate his attention upon a few, major perceptions concerning his experience. As a result he began writing poems which make no reference to the Theme but present some moment in or aspect of the love relationship with a restriction to bare essentials, a fierce impatience of unnecessary detail, rarely equalled in his previous poetry. They include some of his finest poems. Two of them, 'Counting the Beats' and 'The Survivor', appear in *Poems and Satires 1951*.

The theme of 'Counting the Beats' is the threat of death made ever present and accentuated by the intensified awareness of life that results from being in love.

> You, love, and I,
> (He whispers) you and I,
> And if no more than only you and I
> What care you or I?
>
> Counting the beats,
> Counting the slow heart beats,
> The bleeding to death of time in slow heart beats,
> Wakeful they lie.
>
> Cloudless day,
> Night, and a cloudless day;
> Yet the huge storm will burst upon their heads one day
> From a bitter sky.
>
> Where shall we be,
> (She whispers) where shall we be,

When death strikes home, O where then shall we be)5
Who were you and I?

Not there but here,
(He whispers) only here,
As we are, here, together, now and here,
Always you and I. 20

Counting the beats,
Counting the slow heart beats,
The bleeding to death of time in slow heart beats,
Wakeful they lie. 24

As frequently in Graves's best poems the strength of this is its
maintenance of a tension between conflicting awareness; here it is
the simultaneous awareness of the different realities of love and
death. A balance is kept between the claims of body and spirit as it
was in 'Certain Mercies'. The poet's affirmation of a present,
realized 'excellence', the 'now and here' (immediately and ultimately) of love—a value and therefore outside physical process—is
set against his pressing consciousness, which cannot be reconciled
with it, of the fact of physical dissolution. The poem is an acutely
painful presentment of the painful paradox that we live in two
worlds at once, a material world and a world of values.

The means employed to register this tension are of an extreme
simplicity; the obligation to plainness in diction and spareness of
detail that Graves now imposes upon himself is obeyed here more
literally, this side of silence, than in almost any other of his poems.
The essence of the poem is in the rhythms and the stanza form,
which enact, generally speaking, a nervous, jerky expansion followed
by a sudden contraction of feeling. The first stanza, for instance,
gives us in its first three lines, with a mounting urgency as the lines
lengthen, the poet's desperate efforts at self-persuasion and then in
the short last line a return to a lower-pitched, rather hopeless
bravado. Similarly, the second stanza is a crescendo of pain, as stage
by stage the terrible implications of the image are exposed, which
suddenly drops to the disturbed stillness of 'Wakeful they lie'. For
the rest Graves relies on the snowball repetition of key phrases to
reinforce the effect of mounting panic in each stanza.

Yet, though the means are simple, the thought-feeling of the poem is not. Consider, for example, the play on tenses in the fourth stanza —'where then shall we be/Who were you and I?' All the unbearableness of the poem's conflict is concentrated, with the effect of a metaphysical puzzle, in the stressed 'were' coming after the repeated 'where shall we be?' of the first three lines. The poem is a subtle dramatization of the conflict. One has to balance against one's consciousness of an attempt by the poet—in, for instance, the first stanza—merely to lull his own and the woman's fears the recognition of a sort of truth in the assurances of stanza five: he is right to insist that *their* reality is both in the here and now and for always, and that its *meaning* cannot be invalidated by time; he is only wrong to believe that at this moment such a thought can bring comfort. Simply by repeating the key second stanza as the poem's conclusion —thus denying the lover the last word and having the poem turn back upon itself—Graves underlines the effect of emotional deadlock and indicates the impossibility of release from it.

'The Survivor' also makes its effect without the help of the White Goddess mythology. But, like 'Counting the Beats', it is outstanding for the previously unequalled power with which it treats an experience central to the Theme: the lover's psychological death and rebirth into a new love. For Graves the literal death anticipated in 'Counting the Beats' and this metaphysical death are, as subjects for contemplation, virtually indistinguishable: they both represent the destructive principle active in life, and they pose the same unanswerable questions. In 'Counting the Beats' the question is one that preoccupied Alun Lewis: 'what survives of all the beloved?';[1] the question in 'The Survivor' is more—'assuming that in love resurrection follows death, do I accept or do I resent the necessary horrors of dying?' The poem presents a straightforward comparison between the soldier who on the battlefield undergoes, as Graves had done, an experience like death but survives to fight again and the lover who suffers the death of one love affair only to begin another with the same fervour and a renewed trust in love's everlastingness. The

[1] From a letter quoted by Graves in his Foreword to *Ha! Ha! Among the Trumpets* (1945).

soldier, having nearly died and then recovered, stands on the parade-ground, 'sword upright in fist', with courage unabated. But, the poet asks, is this joy?

> Will your nostrils gladly savour
> The fragrance, always new, of a first hedge-rose?
> Will your ears be charmed by the thrush's melody
> Sung as though he had himself devised it?

In the last stanza the poet asks the same question concerning love: is it joy for the man, after his and his beloved's double suicide and his subsequent resurrection, once more, vowing oaths of fidelity, to give himself in love to 'a young and innocent bride'?

There is the same synthesis of simplicity in form and imagery and a complex sophistication in attitude as in 'Counting the Beats'. Again the poem maintains a fine tension between conflicting emotions: gratitude for the new love and a near-cynicism arising out of the poet's awareness of the circumstances which had given birth to it—a combination, say, of the simple faith of 'The Oath' and the scepticism of 'Never Such Love'. The effect is less that of powerful, conflicting emotions being held in check than of a perfect blending of opposite points of view. One is reminded that Graves's aim now is to achieve a perfect ambivalence of expression. In a lecture entitled 'The Dedicated Poet' (*Oxford Addresses*) he writes: 'The supreme gift bestowed on the poet by the Muse is that of poetic humour: a grasp of the identity of opposites, the wearing of Welshman's hose. Sometimes, in fact, when a poem has been assiduously refined and refined under the white blaze of inspiration, its final draft becomes so perfect in its ambivalence as to make the poet humorously doubt whether the insertion of a simple 'not' will perhaps improve it' (p. 23). It is characteristic of his later style, and even more so of his most recent poetry, that for the rendering of this ambivalence so much should depend on the use of the question form; the whole poem is shaped round, poised upon, a single un-answered question, 'Is this joy?'.

More subtle in attitude towards the twin experiences of love and death than the mythological poems 'Darien' and 'The Young

Cordwainer', which treat the same theme, its thought is also more compressed; in fact it is in this concentration of meanings into a few, perfectly ambivalent words that the poem's complexity lies. Take the picture of the soldier in the first stanza. 'Sword upright in fist' gives us the quality of fierce confidence in his ability to fight again; it also suggests, though, a toy-soldier, a caricature of soldierly attitudes, and there is a touch of mockery at the elements of artificiality in the stance adopted; but at the same time, when brought into contact with the other term of the comparison, the phrase becomes a cynical image for the lover's renewed vigour, implying not love but an obscene readiness for lust. The questions of the second stanza, similarly, balance opposite conceptions of the new love. 'Will your nostrils gladly savour/The fragrance, always new, of a first hedge-rose?' means 'will you be able to appreciate the innocent love of a woman again?' but conceals a further doubt: the 'always' in the 'always new' hints at a disturbing paradox, that the newness of the first hedge-rose, the freshness of beauty newly experienced, is yet something old and an experience that has occurred before and will occur again; the doubt is whether the 'new' love is really new and not an illusion of love. The same doubt applies to the spontaneity of the 'thrush's melody'. It seems to be the unique result of an unpremeditated impulse; its freshness would make one believe this, and yet we know that the bird has *not* 'devised it' himself and that the song is repeated as it were by rote; again the poet embodies a double view of love—it is fresh, innocent, spontaneous and at the same time learned and artificial. But the poet, according to Graves, is gifted with the ability to comprehend the *identity* of opposites not merely their oppositeness, and the unifying vision that binds these contradictions together is of love as a force outside the lover's control, each love-affair being a new and total assertion of a known and inescapable power. The ability to make almost every word reflect this finely controlled ambivalence was not a new attainment for Graves, but from the time of *Poems and Satires 1951* it was to become a more frequent one.

In surveying the poetry written between 1943 and 1951 I have been concerned to show that despite Graves's concentration of his poetic energies upon the working out of a single theme the resulting poems are surprisingly varied, both in the approach to their material and in the degree to which they depend on the mythology. This is a fact that critics and reviewers rarely keep in mind when commenting on the later poetry. Generalizations frequently ignore too the changing moods and the different positions taken up by him in relation to his experience during the White Goddess period. The moods range from submission, romantic celebration and awed veneration to the irony of 'Theseus and Ariadne' and the scepticism of 'The Survivor'; each volume has shown new developments. While this is true of the second half of *Poems 1938-1945*, the additional poems in *Collected Poems 1914-1947* and *Poems and Satires 1951*, it is even more marked in *Poems 1953*.

The poems in this volume are further distinguished from those of the preceding volumes by their unity of mood. It gives *Poems 1953* as a whole a strongly individual character. Graves informs us in the Foreword that he had written more poems in the two years since the publication of *Poems and Satires 1951* than in the previous ten, and certainly those included here, considered as a group, leave the impression that a new incentive had given impetus to his writing at this time. The common mood is robust, 'manly', often belligerently so; the texture and rhythms of the verse invariably reflect a dogged determination. In 'The Sea Horse' the poet presents himself as the 'indomitable hippocamp' who has 'ridden out worse tempests' than the present one; he has drawn on his knowledge of past sufferings in love for strength to endure the renewal of them. In 'The Encounter', which describes a meeting between the poet and his dark self, he confronts his habitual lucklessness with 'lips in rage compressed'. As always, love and poetry are identified, and so in 'To Calliope' Graves addresses the Muse in the same proud terms as he uses elsewhere in this volume to the loved woman, the cause of his suffering; he asks:

> Am I not loyal to you? I say no less
>   Than is to say;
> If more, only from angry-heartedness,
>   Not for display.

'Angry-heartedness' describes the mood of these poems very well.

It is this that fortifies his refusal to yield to despair, and which in the valedictory poem, 'Leaving the Rest Unsaid' (a revision of a 'thirties' poem) he turns impudently against the reader. Assuring him that death has not yet overtaken his poetic powers, he proudly declines to write *Finis* on the last page:

> But no, I will not lay me down
> To let your tearful music mar
> The decent mystery of my progress.

The theme of nearly all these poems, or the situation implied in them, is a painful reversal in the poet's love affair, and the defiant attitude in his unyielding response to this situation. More specifically, the new attitude conveys the poet's revaluation of male pride as a factor in the man-woman relationship. While still accepting the lover's cruel fate—to be destroyed by the woman he loves—he does so with a fearlessness that is proud rather than, as in the past, submissive. Thus in 'I'm Through with You for Ever', punished by the anger of his beloved, he nevertheless declares his 'impenitence' for his offence. It is characteristic too of this volume that in 'The Mark' the moral advantage should be with the man, his resoluteness in love being contrasted with the woman's unsureness; and in 'With Her Lips Only', unusually, it is the man not woman who is the judge, and her falseness to her feelings is 'challenged' both by an 'urgent lover' and an equally 'urgent husband'.

'Challenge' is a key word in *Poems 1953*. For example, when, in 'Hercules at Nemea', the Muse seized the hero's fool's-finger (which signifies 'slow-witted', 'he who thinks too late') in her teeth and held it fast, the poet, identifying himself with Hercules, reports:

> And I stared back, dauntless and fiery-eyed,
> Challenging you to maim me for my pride.

This bravado is the new mood at its most extreme. The tone sounds at first like a regression to the boastfulness of the early 'Rocky Acres' and 'To the Reader over My Shoulder'. But here it is used dramatically as part of the characterization of Hercules, who is portrayed in the poem as slow-witted and foolishly rash. In fact he emerges as something of the comic figure that Graves made of him in *The Golden Fleece*. 'See me a fulvous hero of nine fingers', he brags, adding 'My beard bristles in exultation', an observation which like the word 'fulvous' makes the vainglorious gesture of these lines faintly ridiculous. But, as in the novel, the hero's simplicity and clumsiness and the larger-than-life extravagance of his emotions are no less morally attractive for being comic. The poet, by showing his awareness of the element of absurdity in his romantically extreme attitudes, renders them insusceptible to the realist's mockery which is anticipated and shared: the poet is amused by his own unreasonable pretensions but this in no way qualifies the intensity of his commitment to the feelings of 'pride' and 'exultation'; on the contrary, it adds a careless impudence to his assertion of them. This complexity of attitude, as much as the defiant manner, is a new development since, for example, 'To be Named a Bear', a poem that uses the device of impersonation for a simpler effect.

There is a corresponding move towards greater toughness in the style of these poems. 'Esau and Judith' is typical. As in 'Theseus and Ariadne' the nature of the man-woman relationship is defined by means of a legendary analogy, though its source in Genesis reflects a shift in Graves's scholarly interests from classical and Celtic to Hebrew mythology; these found their eventual expression in the theories of *Adam's Rib* (1955) and *Hebrew Myths* (1964). The poem relates how Esau, cheated by Jacob of his birthright and his father's blessing, a voluntary outlaw from his tribe and an enemy of the Israelite God, took to wife Judith, a priestess of the Goddess. He could not escape, however, the taint of his heredity; he had been formed in the patriarchal tradition and could not change, nor understand any other; a curse, therefore, lay upon their relationship. The poem differs from, say, 'Theseus and Ariadne' in the straightforward, matter-of-fact quality of its narrative. It states, strongly and plainly, rather than celebrates, the glory of woman.

The lines which pass judgement on patriarchy, similarly, have the strength of plainness and economy. In explanation of Esau's plight the poet asks:

Had Isaac and Rebekah not commanded:
'Take thee a daughter from my father's house!'—
Isaac who played the pander with Rebekah,
Even as Abraham had done with Sarah?

This is barely more than a recital of the facts—that Abraham to save his life allowed Pharaoh to sleep with Sarah and that Isaac for the same reason was prepared to allow the king of the Philistines to sleep with Rebekah; however, the hard, grim consonants give authority to the lines, and their very spareness of comment, which makes impersonal the scornful verdict they imply, renders them the more effectively dismissive.

Both these poems, though their source is the White Goddess mythology, are completely self-explanatory; they tell their own story, a claim that Graves makes in the brief Foreword to this volume for all his poems now. He eschews mythological detail of the kind that we have in 'To be Named a Bear' and the intricately worked imagery which is at its best in 'Theseus and Ariadne'. Instead he relies on plain statement and the bare outlining of a situation to make his points. This is even more noticeable in those love poems which are largely independent of the myths. Thus 'The Straw' opens with a list of the features in a symbolic landscape as evocative as that of 'Theseus and Ariadne' although compressed into less than two lines:

Peace, the wild valley streaked with torrents,
A hoopoe perched on his warm rock.

This, as we learn later, is the peace of requited love. The contradictory elements which make up this peace are already implied in the images. Warm and steady like the rock, vital and natural and variegated like the wild valley, it yet contains the turbulence of the torrents. The hoopoe, a royal bird and therefore representative of the poet as sacred king, is like the poet in its apparent contentment; but it is also a prophetic bird (this much is made clear when, in the third stanza, the poet like a character of the ballads speaks to it), a bird possibly of ill omen, and as such it contributes to the faint intimations of unease in this scene.

232

In poems like 'The Straw' one can trace the beginnings of the terseness that is the outstanding stylistic feature of Graves's most recent poetry. But there is also here the same quality of sturdy strength as we noted in 'Hercules at Nemea' and 'Esau and Judith' and which, though it does appear again (notably in *Man Does, Woman Is*), belongs peculiarily to *Poems 1953*. With the scene set, the poet comes directly to his theme: he has a presentiment of disaster. He wonders why nervously his fingers should tremble, causing the straw to twitch and jump. His love is returned by her; what has he to fear? And with a reasonable, pragmatic air character-istic of this volume he turns to address the hoopoe: 'These ques-tions, bird, are not rhetorical'—his nervousness is there plainly for anyone to see. Maintaining the same tone of severely impersonal argument he makes this stern pronouncement:

> Requited love; but better unrequited
> If this chance instrument gives warning
> Of cataclysmic anguish far away.

The hard 'k's and 't's and the aggressively firm rhythm, expressive of a strongly curbed anger, project an image of the poet as more than anything self-respecting and proudly unbending. When he asks the question that concludes the poem—'Have I undone her by my vehemence?'—it is not, as in the earlier poems, in a spirit of self-abasement: the responsibility for the 'anguish' foreseen may be nobody's but his own—too urgent, too possessive in love—but the poet refuses to blame himself for it. He accepts his 'vehemence' as an integral part of the love experience, which it is inappropriate either to blame or praise, as much as he accepts unflinchingly its inevitably painful consequences.

'The Foreboding' acknowledges more directly the emotions that occasioned the poem. The painful feelings are nearer to the surface, both in the picture presented and in the poet's tone, than in 'The Straw'. It describes how once in a moment of clairvoyance the poet saw his other self, seated at his desk, evidently in despair and motionless like a corpse, except that 'the pen moved slowly upon paper/And tears fell'. It is a prevision of the time when his love will desert him. Then he will feel 'no protest, no desire', but now he feels both.

> And I turned angrily from the open window
> Aghast at you.
> Why never a warning, either by speech or look,
> That the love you cruelly gave me could not last?

Fear is transformed, typically, into 'angry-heartedness': a 'manly' astonishment at the injustice of this predestined suffering. The more directly engaged quality of the opening is balanced, and controlled, by the franker indignation expressed in the close. Notwithstanding these differences, however, 'The Foreboding' and 'The Straw', though terser, are the same kind of poem; they have the same kind of strength. Take a word like 'anguish' in the stanza quoted from 'The Straw': it is a charged word, yet without losing any of its power it is at the same time in its context no more than a plainly descriptive, the entirely right, word for its purpose. The effect is partly due to the, as always, unhectic working out of the images (tremor... earthquake...cataclysm), the tidy dovetailing of one into another, but even more to the robust tone. Similarly, in 'The Foreboding' 'tears', a nakedly emotional word, has no more than its due resonance: it takes its place as just one item in a total picture of numb misery. Again, however, in trying to account for the poem's peculiar effect one's attention focuses on the tone, the tone, for instance, of the lines that follow, which are quoted above. These might be described as communicating strong emotion with a reasoning inflection. It is a formula that also fits 'The Straw'. It could be applied equally well to many of the poems written since 1953, which are remarkable for this same achievement: the transmutation of extreme emotion into impassioned thought.

The growth of a mood of masculine protest accounts for the new position taken by Graves in some of the Goddess poems. They are not openly rebellious—the Goddess is still the unquestioned ruler of the poet's fate—but the poet's attitude to her is ambivalent. In 'Dethronement', for example, undeservedly omitted from *Collected Poems 1965*, he identifies himself with her in her cruellest guise, as he did in 'The Destroyers', but this time he does not conceal a con-

234

flicting animosity, which finds simultaneous expression in the poem.

The title refers to the Goddess's dethronement of the poet-lover cast in the role of sacred king. He is urged to submit to his fate. She does not want his praise, which would be 'ill-conceived':

> Your true anguish
> Is all that she requires. You, turned to stone,
> May not speak nor groan, will stare dumbly,
> Grinning dismay.

He must flee the hounds which pursue him as they once pursued Actaeon:

> Run, though you hope for nothing: to stay your foot
> Would be ingratitude, a sour denial
> That the life she bestowed was sweet.

But he will not escape them; they will tear him to pieces 'assuredly/ With half a hundred love-bites' before he is considered worthy of resurrection. Graves has here dissociated himself from the lover to whom the poem is addressed. In the first quotation he apparently takes the part of 'the laughing, naked queen', deriding with a polite understatement the lover's innocence in hoping to influence her decisions: such hopes would be merely 'ill-conceived'. In the last sentence of the stanza he goes further towards sharing her point of view: the picture of the lover frozen with a buffoonish grin on his face is a cruelly humiliating one. Yet in both sentences, especially in the violence of the latter, can be heard an undertone of bitterness which betrays the poet's secret participation in the victim's suffering. The ambivalence is sharpest, however, in the former sentence. Firstly, there is a disparity between the connotations of 'anguish' and its epithet 'true'. The Goddess justifiably requires truth of feeling, ultimate sincerity, from her servants, but in choosing 'anguish' to describe the necessary pain entailed, Graves intends to stress its extremity, its unbearableness, which presumably nothing could justify; the two words work on different emotional levels. This leads to a clash between the two functions of the sarcasm in the next line, 'Is *all* that she requires'. The first is to mock the lover's folly in giving her what she does not require—praise instead of suffering;

the second is to enact the Goddess's sadistic enjoyment of her cruelty and thus convey the poet's resentment of it. Exaggerated mimicry of her presumed tone—that is to say, the poet's overplaying of his part as her advocate—is the technique used again in 'to stay your foot/Would be ingratitude'. There is a cooing sadism in the mildness of the remark that prevents us from taking at face value the submissiveness it purports to express. And in the cruel sarcasm of 'half a hundred *love*-bites' (my italics) mockery of the poet-lover and bitter protest on his behalf are about equally mixed.

The achievement of 'Dethronement' is to stretch the Theme so as to admit a new complexity of attitude, and to create thereby the possibility of a more supple—at once detached and intense—relationship between the poet and his material. On occasions the fusion of opposite reactions is so complete that they are barely perceptible and difficult to identify in the total effect. This explains the impact of another poem in this volume, 'Rhea'. The poem celebrates woman as typified by the Earth-Goddess. It depicts her dreamlessly asleep, divinely impervious to the terrors of the storm that rages around her. While oak and ash, the royal trees that symbolize her lovers, are torn up by the roots and the 'divine Augustus' and the 'divine Gaius' tremble with fear, she lies apart untouched and uncaring. For the elements are her children and she regards their destructiveness, with maternal indulgence, as no more than high-spirited play. The poet admires her splendid self-possession but is uneasily aware at the same time that a callous quality is part of it.

> On her shut lids the lightning flickers,
> Thunder explodes above her bed...

She lies, however,

> Not dead but entranced, dreamlessly
> With slow breathing, her lips curved
> In a half-smile archaic...

These lines combine a tender picture of a sleeping woman with the picture of an untouchable goddess in whose carelessness there is something (perhaps blamelessly) cruel: the proximity of the exploding thunder to her not only sets off, by contrast, the graceful loveliness of her pose but hints at a mysterious kinship between her and it, as though in fact the thunder and lightning are emanations from her. The two conceptions run parallel until they momentarily fuse in that last phrase, 'her lips curved/In a half-smile archaic'; she has the (as envisaged by Graves) enigmatic—both child-like and cruelly indifferent—half-smile of a *kore* carved in the archaic mode. The poet's fear and love are at this moment one and the same.

Poems 1953 is rich in good things, and it contains several poems not here examined which would equally repay close study. Auden in an essay entitled 'Poet of Honour' (*Shenandoah*, Winter, 1962) has singled out 'The Sea Horse' for especial praise, and Ronald Gaskell in his *Critical Quarterly* essay has some illuminating comments on another, 'With Her Lips Only'. But the volume has its failures, and though throughout the third period these formed an insignificant proportion of Graves's total output there are enough to warrant a cursory glance at them. Unlike many of his early poems and some of his second period, his poems now never fall short in clarity: they are well constructed and the images always work out. The Graves of the 'fifties and 'sixties is too conscious a poet to let anything appear in print which is not at least competent. The weakness of the occasional imperfect poem is, then, usually moral rather than technical. Graves is more prone to such weakness in his satirical productions than in his love poetry. 'The Blue-Fly', for example, an attack on the male lover, expresses little more than an uncontrolled physical revulsion from him. He is depicted as the blue-fly that for five days and nights had undisturbed enjoyment of a peach. Humming all the time, romantically, 'O my love, my fair one!' it went about its disgusting business. The poet is merely abusive: 'The ignorant, loutish, giddy blue-fly', he points out, when magnified 'looks farcically human'. The motive is wholly vindictive, repayment for some undisclosed injury. What kind of injury, however, is not difficult to infer:

> Nature, doubtless, has some compelling cause
> To glut the carriers of her epidemics—
> Nor did the peach complain.

The poet, it seems, has been displaced in the woman's affections

(the peach did not 'complain') by some inferior rival; the lines hiss
with venomous resentment of her inexplicable behaviour and with a
furious jealousy very nearly given full rein. Comparison with, say,
'A Jealous Man' will provide a convenient measure of this poem's
failure to dramatize and impersonalize the poet's emotions.

Undoubtedly 'The Blue-Fly' is intended as a serious poem, and
it keeps its place still in the collections. As a rule, however, since
1938 Graves's satires have been light-hearted productions. Whereas
in the 'thirties the satirical vein ran through much of his best poetry,
now, as he announces in the Foreword to *Poems 1938–1945*, he
makes a careful distinction between his 'inspired' poetry and his
merely destructive pieces: 'I write poems for poets, and satires or
grotesques for wits'. Each volume contains instances of both kinds,
but in *Collected Poems 1965* the satires have been reduced to a
handful. None of them, retained or abandoned, has the seriousness
of 'To Evoke Posterity'; most are amusing if occasionally laboured
jokes; some are unamusing exercises in vituperation; a few, amongst
them the best, have the elegance of 'The Cloak'. 'Queen Mother to
New Queen' (*Poems and Satires 1951*), for instance, is urbanely but
incisively ironic about man's self-esteem and an unloving attitude
to sex: the Queen Mother advises her daughter, if the King should
desire sensual distraction, to

> Make no delay or circumvention
> But do as you should do, though strict
> To guide back his bemused attention
> Towards privy purse or royal edict.

'From the Embassy' (*Poems 1953*), making use of the same aristocratic persona, is a sly comment on the growing recognition of his
poetic stature in official quarters. As a poet, he says, he has always
had the ambassadorial privilege of being in but not of the non-
poetic world; but now the latter, becoming interested in what he has
to offer, is beginning, so to speak, to relax currency restrictions;

> I meet less hindrance now with the exchange...
> And shy enquiries for literature
> Come in by every post, and the side door.

The last phrase rips off the polite mask assumed by the Establishment, to reveal beneath its grateful interest and 'shy' deference the modishness and opportunism that really govern its actions.

In the poetry that appeared during the remaining years of this period, until the publication of *Collected Poems 1959*, there was a sudden drop in intensity. Some are very slight indeed. Sixteen poems were issued with the Clark lectures and other essays on poetry in *The Crowning Privilege* (1955) and another nineteen new poems appeared alongside a miscellany of stories, talks and essays in *Steps* (1958); of these only just over half were reprinted in *Collected Poems 1959*, and three have been omitted from the latest collection. The best of them, 'The Lost Jewel', still has the old urgency, but the light-heartedness of the satires is now the dominant mood in all but a very few of the others. In a preface to a reading of the poems published in *Steps* Graves confessed that the poems he was then writing had too much cunning and lacked exuberance (p. 236). It seemed for a while that he had perhaps reached the peak of his achievement with *Poems 1953*, even that he was beginning to 'mellow'. He had never written poems so undisguisedly and con-tentedly autobiographical as 'The Face in the Mirror' (his own face) and 'The Second-Fated' (himself). These are both fluent, attractive poems, saved from complacency by their self-amusement, but com-pared with previous performances they have a touch of showmanship and their self-acceptance strikes one as comfortable. 'Mistrust of the comfortable point-of-rest', as Graves suggested in the Foreword to *Collected Poems 1938* (p. xxiv), has always been an indispensable ingredient in his best work and the temporary loss of this attitude accounts for the lower standard of his poems during these years. In one of the few poems of any intensity written at this time, 'Gratitude for a Nightmare', he discusses the dangers of security and respecta-bility to the poet. The nightmare that bestrides the poet in dream, though feared, is regarded by him as identical with the source of his inspiration which, if it ceased to terrorize him, would dry up. To

> earn respect as a leading citizen
> Granted long credit at all shops and inns—
>
> How dangerous! I had feared the shag demon
> Would not conform with my conformity...

But the demon does come and 'all's well'. The problem concerns Graves again in a talk reprinted in *Steps*, 'Sweeney Among the Blackbirds'. There he decides that the roles of poet and citizen are reconcilable if he keeps a sense of humour; with humour 'a poet can go mad gracefully, swallow his disappointments in love gracefully, reject the Establishment gracefully' (p. 127). Not surprisingly therefore, grace—personal 'charm' perhaps defines the quality more accurately—and humour are the notable characteristics of the majority of these poems. Charm can run to prosiness, as in the tedious 'The Naked and the Nude', and is responsible for the button-holing manner of poems like 'Around the Mountain', which begins:

> Some of you may know, others perhaps can guess
> How it is to walk all night through summer rain...

The humour, at its best, makes for a mildly self-mocking treatment of themes that had once engaged the poet at a deeper level. 'A Slice of Wedding Cake' exemplifies the playful, relaxed air of this kind of poem:

> Why have such scores of lovely, gifted girls
> Married impossible men?
> Simple self-sacrifice may be ruled out,
> And missionary endeavour, nine times out of ten.

The final section of *Collected Poems 1959* comes as something of an anticlimax to over forty years of writing. The impression they make does not answer to the fairly consistent self-portrait that Graves has built up in the body of his work—of the poet as an elective exile and a rebel, uncompromisingly individual, a tough romantic obsessed with 'the single theme of life and death' symbolized in the White Goddess mythology. They leave us with the pleasant if conventional picture of a poet who has honourably solved his poetic problems and is now prepared to rest on his laurels. How wrong we were to assume this has been proved since. As in 1926 and 1938, in 1959 Graves was poetically reborn. He has perhaps been more prolific in the first half of the present decade—certainly he has written more poems in this period that will last—than in any previous comparable stretch of years.

8

The Black Goddess of Wisdom

IN THE first five years of the 'sixties Graves has already published four volumes of poetry—*More Poems 1961* (1961), *New Poems 1962* (1962), *Man Does, Woman Is* (1964), and in a limited edition *Love Respelt* (1965)—and another collection. His astonishing productivity in these years is one sign that he has entered a new period in his writing. It is not the only sign: from the vantage-point of his most recent work it can be seen that these poems are a progression of moods and attitudes leading to a new experience and a new conception of love; to this conception he has given the name of the Black Goddess. While the most complete embodiment of this experience is in *Love Respelt*, there are hints of it in the preceding volumes; the poem actually entitled 'The Black Goddess' appears in *Man Does, Woman Is*, and several other poems in that volume use imagery peculiarly descriptive of her; the beginning of these images are to be traced in *More Poems 1961* and *New Poems 1962*.

In all the poems of the 'sixties theme and manner express, more than anything else, the poet's ability to survive and then to transcend suffering. *Poems 1953* heralded this development; but angry robustness gives place in *More Poems 1961* to a different kind of robustness. The poet-lover neither resists his fate nor submits despairingly to it; both would be more demonstrative postures than these poems generally allow. Both, too, would indicate a flaw in the quality of the poet's acceptance of his experience: underlying the attitude of this volume is the tight-lipped acknowledgment, more unquestioning than ever before, that the lover's fate is irrevocable and that protest would be irrelevant—acknowledgment of, in the words of an earlier poem, 'the thing's necessity' ('Despite and Still'). All the poems start from the curt assumption that love necessarily involves suffering; the only uncertainty is whether the lover can bear it. The poet asks in 'Patience':

Must it be my task
To assume the mask
Of not desiring what I may not ask?

The answer being implicitly affirmative, what is really in question is the poet's ability to maintain such an attitude of stoical self-denial. His cry is not to be released from his 'task' but for the patience to carry it out: 'O, to be patient/As you would have me patient...' The question is the same in 'Symptoms of Love': can the lover '*endure* such grief...?' (my italics). This word is, as it were, the *leitmotif* in *More Poems 1961*. To his usual romantic list of epithets for love Graves can now, in 'Under the Olives', add one more: 'Innocent, gentle, bold, *enduring*, proud' (my italics).

The style of these poems is a more extreme development of the spare terse style of *Poems 1953*. In keeping with the stated theme of several of them, refraining from protest they express a tighter self-restraint than do the poems of the earlier volume. Emotion is not excluded but held in check, so that it is felt as a constant pressure behind the verse; the characteristic tone implies a severely curbed pain. The poems are frequently brief; either they run to no more than seven, eight or ten lines a piece, or if longer the lines themselves are short, composed sometimes of five and six syllables each. Their syntactical simplicity and the baldness of their statements, or the fact that occasionally a poem consists of but a single sentence, add to the effect of brevity. 'The Cure', a poem of seven lines, is typically short, swift in movement and direct. It opens brusquely, 'No lover ever found a cure for love'; except, it continues, by the inflicting of such a painful wound, killing hope, that it was worse than love itself. Here abruptly the poet breaks off, adding only the summary dismissive verdict, 'More tolerable the infection than its cure'. We are left with an impression of the poet's fierce taciturnity, of an incipient rebelliousness cut short.

In 'Symptoms of Love' the economy of the means employed to make the poem's effect is as conspicuous as in 'Counting the Beats'.

Love is a universal migraine,
A bright stain on the vision
Blotting out reason.

> Symptoms of true love
> Are leanness, jealousy...

In lines so clipped much of the poem's intention is contained in the
curt rhythms, expressing a self-punishing naked truthfulness—in,
for example, the brutal stress on 'blotting'. Every word has the
maximum impact: the telescoping of the two images in 'bright
stain', for example, gives to the phrase a compressed, complex
power: 'bright', implying instantaneous illumination and immediate
pain (the brightness of a migraine flash), conflicts—the contrast is
heightened by the contrasting vowel sounds—and combines with
the suggestion of something slow, dark and indelible (as a migraine
is not) in 'stain', to epitomize the paradox of love.

Most striking of all, Graves has in these poems carried to its
limit the discipline of leaving unsaid what it is not absolutely necessary to say. 'Under the Olives' is in this respect representative.

> We never should have loved had love not struck
> Swifter than reason, and despite reason:
> Under the olives, our hands interlocked,
> We both fell silent:
> Each listened for the other's answering
> Sigh of unreasonableness—
> Innocent, gentle, bold, enduring, proud.

What we have is the plainest of statements, but one which at every
point connotes an ambience of unstated feeling. The last line gives
us the most definite clue—though it is still only a hint—to its
character. It is a mixture of pain and satisfaction; while love induces
gentleness in its subjects, it also requires from them the tougher
qualities of boldness and endurance. The epithet 'enduring', in
particular, raises nearer to the surface of the poem a sense of the
difficulty of the lovers' relationship: points to the element of pain
in 'struck', for example, and of conflict in 'despite'. It explains the
resoluteness enacted in the verse-movement, which is made thereby
to carry the further implications of cruelties survived and obstruc-
tions overcome. There is an intimation of something unsimple and
laborious in love in the mere doubling of negatives in the first line.

Even the pause after 'We both fell silent' is eloquent—enacting the ensuing silence and the fullness of the moment that cannot be expressed; in the pause, as again in the line-division between 'answering' and 'sigh', we feel happiness, awe, uncertainty and an awareness of difficulty.

Stoicism is not the only attitude communicated in these poems but it is the central one, out of which the attitudes of the next two volumes seem to have developed and which prepared the ground for the affirmation of *Love Respelt*. Graves's practice in the majority of these poems of keeping very close to an actual human relationship, using the mythology only sparingly and simply, is also indicative of the direction in which he is now moving. This new approach to his theme and the tone of resolute stoicism are evidently related phenomena, each expressions of the poet's now more naked exposure to his experience. In 'Intimations of the Black Goddess', a lecture given in 1963, Graves wrote: 'Only during the past three years have I ventured to dramatize, truthfully and factually, the vicissitudes of a poet's dealings with the White Goddess, the Muse, the perpetual Other Woman'.[1] The stress is on 'dramatize' and 'factually': it is not in the subject-matter of his latest poems that he found evidence of a new daring—the 'vicissitudes' of love was his theme throughout the White Goddess period—but in the bare, unmetaphorical treatment of it. This preoccupation with the literal human experience of love goes with, and perhaps derives from, the poet's concentration on love as a joint venture: woman is man's partner, though still the dominant one, rather than his conscience or the impartial administrator of justice. In 'The Sharp Ridge', for example, the poet at a crisis in their relationship pleads with her to

> Have pity on us both: choose well
> On this sharp ridge dividing death from hell.

The theme is now more often the 'difficult achievement' of love ('The Starred Coverlet'), an achievement towards which *both* struggle and which involves them *both* in suffering, than the cruelty and mystery of womanhood. In doing what she must do, periodically

[1] *Mammon and the Black Goddess*, p. 151.

withdrawing her love, she is not exempt from the pain she inflicts. The lover who, in 'The Intrusion', recoils with horror from the picture of 'her white motionless face and folded hands/Framed in such thunderclouds of sorrow', at the same time is made to realize that this is an image of her suffering. He is urged to 'give her no word of consolation' because her grief is 'Divine mourning for what cannot be', but nevertheless her evident need of 'consolation' accents her purely human plight; she is in the same position as the man—of having to suffer the fate of which she is only the involuntary instrument. It is a fate they share in common, and the separate roles they play are each as difficult as the other's. In 'The Falcon Woman' Graves, for the first time, considers the woman's role from her point of view. To be a man who honourably keeps his promises and builds too much upon the loved woman's promises, made in 'carelessness of spirit', to which she cannot be held, is, he admits, hard; but is it less hard for *such* a woman 'in carelessness of spirit/To love such a man?'

In his third period Graves was concerned with, separately or as a whole, the phases of love and the pattern of events in the man-woman relationship; each position taken was in answer to this pre-occupation. Implied or stated in many of the poems now is a more fundamental question: not 'what experiences must the lover undergo?' but 'what *is* love, what makes it as a *single* experience different from any other?' The exclusive concentration on the essence of this reality accounts, in part, for the spareness and brevity of most of these poems.

The opening poem of *More Poems 1961*, 'Lyceia', sets the tone, indicates the sort of interest that Graves now has in his theme. Lyceia is the wolf-goddess, and 'All the wolves of the forest/Howl for Lyceia'; they compete for her love but she keeps them at a distance. The poet therefore asks: 'What do the wolves *learn*?'(my italics). Love is regarded as offering a *schooling* in a radically different outlook than is available to the ordinary person. This view of love had to wait until *Love Respelt* for its complete expression. As yet, according to Lyceia, they learn nothing but 'Envy and hope,/Hope and chagrin'. But that there is more to be learned is the import of other poems in this volume: in 'The Starred Coverlet' lovers are enjoined on different occasions to learn patience, to endure, and

> to lie mute, without embrace or kiss,
> Without a rustle or a smothered sigh,
> Basking each in the other's glory.

The 'glory' is that of a distinct reality, the nature of which is the theme of several poems. They agree precisely on their definition: it strikes 'Swifter than reason and despite reason' ('Under the Olives'). Graves presents this life of unreason as a positive and rare achievement: he explains in 'The Laugh' that he had been at first baffled by it because 'the identity of opposites/Had so confused my all too sober wits'. The *marriage* of opposites—of two people 'unyielding in/Their honest, first reluctance to agree' ('Joan and Darby')—has gained for them entry to this special world, which defies and is inaccessible to reason and logic: if they were 'birds of similar plumage caged/In the peace of every day', he asks in 'Seldom Yet Now',

> Would we still conjure wildfire up
> From common earth, as now?

Not obeying known laws love is unpredictable, incalculable—to be 'Neither foretold, cajoled, nor counted on' ('Turn of the Moon')—and is the more precious for being so. The most intensely romantic expression of this reality, 'Two Children', comes the nearest to portraying the new kind of love celebrated in *Love Respelt*. In his youth, the poet records, it was 'a fugitive beacon' chased by him in his dreams; it 'set a nap on the plum, a haze on the rose'; it is 'Child of the wave, child of the morning dew': the stress here is on the elusiveness, the apparent insubstantiality, and the almost *miraculous* nature of love.

New Poems 1962 is the crucial volume for the understanding of the development of Graves's new faith. Primarily it is the 'factual' record of a period of despair and disillusionment with the neverending cycle of death and rebirth—some of these poems are more bleak than anything else Graves has written. But in two or three memorable poems it introduces us to a new mood of ecstasy and 'certitude' that signifies his release from the cycle and the discovery of the Black Goddess, and grew in the course of the next three years to be the dominant mood of his poetry.

'A bitter year it was', the poet says in 'The Wreath', and asks: 'What woman ever/Cared for me so, yet so ill-used me...?' 'Trance at a Distance' announces with stark matter-of-factness that 'She has raised a wall of nothingness in between' them. The gesture of weary helplessness, despairing resignation, which 'Hedges Freaked With Snow' makes, epitomizes the prevailing mood of this volume: the poet decides that there shall be 'No argument, no anger, no remorse ...no grief for our dead love', only 'the smile of sorrow'. In 'Possessed' he advises the lover, though he is certain that his love is returned, to 'Build nothing on it'. The themes of unreason and endurance recur—'Unreasonable love becomes you/And mute endurance'—but the emphasis is on 'mute'; it is a more passive endurance than that urged and reflected in *More Poems 1961*. The poet responds to his suffering no longer even with the tones and rhythms of a strongly curbed pain but with the dead tone and flat rhythms of one who, while still having the strength to suffer, is withered by his knowledge of what must happen time and time again. 'Horizon' presents such a moment of withered self-knowledge:

> Do as you will tonight,
> Said she, and so he did...
> Knowing-not-knowing that such deeds must end
> In a curse that lovers long past weeping for
> Had heaped upon him...

There is bitter awareness of the inevitability of betrayal in the bald 'and so he did', and a soured tiredness in the falling movement, like a sigh, of 'lovers long past weeping for', both of which express the final defeat of hope. Even his assertion of a revived faith, in 'Uncalendared Love', has the same bleak inflections. Those, he says, whose love is ruled by time are subject to the continuous seasonal death and rebirth. But he lays claim for himself and his beloved to a love unchanged by time:

> But you with me together, together, together,
> Survive ordeals never before endured...

Ours is uncalendared love, whole life,
As long or brief as befalls. Alone, together,
Recalling little, prophesying less...

The triumph of 'ours is uncalendared love' is immediately qualified
by what follows, which creates the impression rather that the lovers
had no choice in the matter; it is more their doom than their achievement, an ordeal rather than a privilege. 'Recalling little, prophesying
less' is a grimly negative statement of that living-in-the-present
celebrated with such simple confidence at the beginning of the White
Goddess period in 'Theseus and Ariadne' and 'Worms of History'.
Here it is a state of being without the comfort of roots in the past or
any sort of promise for the future: the lovers inhabit a vacuum of
loneliness. The verse has a kind of resoluteness about it but the
movement is curiously unvibrant. With its frequent pauses it
seems only to twitch with life; in 'together, together, together'
rhythm breaks down completely—expressing the numbed exhaustion of a state beyond suffering and opening up vistas of possible
emptiness.

The return to the idea of togetherness in the fourth line quoted
indicates the poem's centre of interest. In 'Possessed' the message is,
as in *More Poems 1961*, that woman too suffers: the lover is told that
she,

> no less vulnerable than you,
> Suffers the dire pangs
> Of your self-defeat.

In 'Ibycus in Samos', where the emotion is a feverish ecstasy
('Sprigs of the olive-trees are touched with fire'), the stress is, more
positively, on the man and woman's oneness in suffering:

> She whom I honour has turned her face away
> A whole year now, and in pride more than royal
> Lacerates my heart and hers as one.

'Uncalendared Love', however, while insisting that their union is an
indissoluble one, yet hints at depths of ambiguous feeling about the
fact: 'together' is a neutral word and points to what may be either
joy or despair.

The transition from the numbness of despair, the final consequence of the White Goddess experience, to faith in a new kind of
love—and, in fact, the closeness of that despair to the freedom of the
new love—are to be seen in the most startling of these poems, 'A
Restless Ghost'. In his affliction the poet no longer yearns to be
restored to the Goddess's favour but to be absolved once and for all
from his love of her. Out of the exhaustion of the old experience the
new love will be born; the poet anticipates different and, it seems,
more intense joy: the hills and coast will shine as never before

> when she is gone indeed,
> Her divine elements disbanded, disembodied
> And through the misty orchards in love spread...

It is as though the despair were a prerequisite of this state of ecstasy.
Though not precisely defined, the nature of its difference from the
old love is suggested in the carefully chosen 'disembodied': it is the
joy of a love that will perhaps transcend physical existence.

The results of this new experience are best studied in 'The
Winged Heart'. The poem starts from the moment of a suddenly
felt release, a sense of miraculous powers bestowed—his 'heart
suddenly sprouting feathers'. He then reports how (in an image for
their past estrangement) the season's drought had concluded in a
four-day sirocco, and how this at last had been broken by the coming
of 'the full honest rain'. The two symbols for spiritual renewal, the
beneficent rain bringing freshness and the sudden winged lightness
of the heart, lie as it were casually alongside each other—Graves
makes no attempt to interweave them. The poem has elegance but
not the neatness which has in the past been the hall-mark of so much
of his verse. The 'open' kind of poem is a departure from his usual
form that reflects most distinctively the new mood. The manner is
correspondingly relaxed:

> How it hissed, how the leaves of the olives shook!
> We had suffered drought since earliest April;
> Here we were already in October.
> I have nothing more to tell you.

This has the ease and simplicity of informal conversation. The fact of their estrangement is accepted, easily and simply, as something inexplicable. The poet's abstention from questioning, reasoning about or protesting against the fact indicates on this occasion neither pain nor despair but contentment; the last sentence says—'there it is, a fact; that is all you can say about it'.

The poet has come to a point where he can surrender himself completely to the unreason of this new 'certitude' in love—careless of the practicalities, improvident for the future. The symbolic description, in 'The Winged Heart', of their transfiguring experience resembles that in 'A Restless Ghost': 'the tranquil blaze of sky etherializing/The circle of rocks and our rain-wet faces'. 'Etherializing' carries the same message as 'disembodied'. The encirclement of the lovers, the enclosing of them within the impregnable security of their miraculous love, is an image that anticipates several images in the later Black Goddess poems. And 'tranquil blaze' renders the fusion of pain and ecstasy that is the essential characteristic of the Black Goddess experience. Other images for it occur in 'Ruby and Amethyst' and 'An Unnamed Spell', the first and last poem in this volume. In the former its mystery is compared to the 'rose-amethyst', which

> Has such a garden in it
> Your eye could wander there for hours
> And wonder, and be lost.

In 'An Unnamed Spell' likenesses to the later poems abound. It leaves no doubt that the paradigm of the lovers' 'royal certitude' mentioned in it is to be found in the illumination vouchsafed to those few who in the Orphic, Jewish and Sufi cults worshipped the Black Goddess of Wisdom. It has been evident for some time now that Graves is a serious student of Sufi lore, and it has been put beyond question by the introduction he contributed to Idries Shah's book on the subject. The language of this poem confirms it: the woman is the possessor of a 'headlong wisdom', and their love harbours a nameless Truth which is the

> Secret of secrets disclosed only
> To who already share it,
> Who themselves have sometime raised an arch—

Pillared with honour; its lintel love—
And passed silently through—

secrecy and silence are the necessary accompaniments to the revelation of this new mystery.

Man Does, Woman Is is the third volume in what, according to his announcement in the brief Foreword, Graves now sees as 'a three-book sequence dramatizing the vicissitudes of poetic love'. Poetic love is love that acknowledges its origin in the Muse, the White Goddess. No mention is made in the Foreword of the Black Goddess, though the volume includes a poem dedicated to her; but his recognition that *Man Does, Woman Is* brought to a close a phase in his writing probably arose from a presentiment that in any poetry he should write in the future she would have a major role to play.

The theme of the man and woman's common fate is in a number of poems taken a stage further. Although the title of one poem, 'Expect Nothing', and, indeed, the poem itself communicate as bleak a message as any in *New Poems 1962*, yet the tone expresses a dour strength which has its source in a perception also informing the more romantically confident 'An Unnamed Spell': that, while the crumbs of comfort that she scatters are meagre, the diet is one on which she as well as he must subsist 'while the *lonely truth/Of love* is honoured and her word pledged' (my italics).

The poet has taken heart from the knowledge that despite repeated estrangements the bond between them still holds and presumably will always hold: there is a 'truth' in love apart from, and unendangered by, the sequence of actual events, painful or not; he has found a new pride in this knowledge. It is a pride in the privileged uniqueness of their fate; this is the feeling that governs the opening lines of 'That Other World':

> Fatedly alone with you once more
> As before Time first creaked.

The poet's pride finds more urgent expression in 'Eurydice':

> My own dear heart, dare you so war on me
> As to strangle love in a mad perversity?
> Is ours a fate can ever be forsworn
> Though my lopped head sing to the yet unborn?

Here his vowed allegiance to their joint fate, whether or not it should bring about the paradisal perfection prophesied by the hero's singing head, is religious in its absoluteness.

The vigorous life in the rhythms of that stanza is characteristic of this volume as a whole. The manner changes from poem to poem but, where the theme is the lover's suffering, the attitude of stoicism reflected in it invariably goes beyond the expression merely of the will to endure, as in *More Poems 1961*, or of exhausted tenacity, as in *More Poems 1962*; it has more of a *positive* strength in it. There is a steely quality in the poet's voice, for instance, when, in 'Bank Account', he peremptorily refuses to consider the possibility of protest against the woman's cruel treatment of him:

> Never again remind me of it:
> There are no debts between us.

The manner of 'Deed of Gift' is in sharp contrast with this but similarly testifies to the poet's assurance. It describes how, after 'unembittered meditation', the loved woman 'gave herself to herself, this time for good'. Forswearing promises of love and friendship that she deemed it unnecessary to keep, she turned now to the accomplishment of her own private truth. But, the poet asks, though to have returned to her true path

> From which by misadventure she had strayed,
> So that her journey was that much delayed,
> Justified the default of duties owed,
> What debt of true love did she leave unpaid?

The tone emulates her 'unembittered', quiet performance of her task. The movement's gentle, measured pace and the unruffled propriety of the diction take from the last line's hint of pain any suggestion of a reproachful intonation; it is mild, uncomplaining, almost neutral in its implications.

Yet it does cause a faint ripple of unease to pass over the calm surface of the poem; the mere use of the question form makes this inevitable. It has been Graves's occasional practice at every stage in his development to conclude poems with an unresolved question. 'Children of Darkness' ended in this fashion; it played an important part in the effect of some of the very best poems of his second period, such as 'Time' and 'Certain Mercies'; and it was a feature of a number of fine poems written in the latter half of the third period—'The Survivor', 'The Portrait' and 'The Straw' are notable examples. The increased frequency of his use of it in the 'sixties confirms its importance to Graves as a technique; in *Man Does, Woman Is* alone sixteen poems end on the questioning note. It seems that in this way of organizing a poem he has discovered a form that captures the quintessence of his outlook on life: it represents his recognition that hardship and, especially, uncertainty are intrinsic to the way of life on which he sets supreme value. Here, for example, in 'Deed of Gift', the question, without modifying the absoluteness of the poet's assent to the woman's behaviour, her withdrawal of her love, yet registers a sense of puzzlement at the difficulty of reconciling the different facets of their relationship—his need of her love, her conflicting loyalties on the one hand to him and on the other to herself. The uncertainty is not in the poet's fidelity but in the love-situation itself. The effect produced by this procedure is akin to irony: it sets against the view of the situation the poem is chiefly concerned to present simultaneous hints of opposite views and other considerations that would have to be taken into account before a final estimate could be calculated.

The explanation for the frequency of the question form in the poems of *Man Does, Woman Is* is not that the poet's awareness of uncertainty has intensified but that he has arrived at a new conception of 'doubt', as something quietly positive—protective, beneficent, bringing luck. It is a state of mind not merely to be endured but to be cultivated by the poet, as spiritually nourishing as (and a kind of) certitude. The first poem in this volume, 'Time of Waiting', is one that announces the attitude which informs the manner of most of these poems. The theme, as Graves describes it in *Mammon and the Black Goddess*, is the poet's 'resolve not to prejudice the future by hasty action' (p. 89): to

> Conclude no rash decisions, enter into
> No random friendships, check the runaway tongue
> And fix my mind in a close caul of doubt...

This may be the moment that precedes the conception of a poem, or that precedes any important action. 'Doubt' here is a state of mind that guarantees, by sealing from extraneous influence, the utter freshness of the new-born poem, or ensures that the new action is in spontaneous accord with the deepest needs of the personality. It is more difficult to maintain than 'to face/Night-long assaults of lurking furies' but it is a pain that generates new life. Comparison of this with the lines on doubt in an early poem like 'Children of Darkness' or those on the illusion of 'certitude' in 'Vanity' will quickly reveal the distance Graves has travelled.

'The Oleaster' illustrates at its finest the firm, challenging stance characteristic of this volume—in this respect recalling *Poems 1953*. Its verse has an aggressive, 'impudent' robustness, for example, in these lines which compare the poet, appropriately, to the tough wild olive—

> The savage, inexpugnable oleaster
> Whose roots and bole bunching from limestone crannies
> Sprout impudent shoots born only to be lopped...

The poem, furthermore, develops the 'open', relaxed form of 'A Winged Heart'. It has two narrative strands. Firstly the poet describes a night's storm and the munificent rain that just before dawn followed upon it. He breaks off, in a diffident manner, and begins to make an apparently unrelated observation about the Majorcan practice of grafting the sweet olive on to the oleaster instead of planting it separately. Again he breaks off suddenly and resumes the first narrative, proceeding to recount how when the rain had stopped he and his love walked out on the road. But here the two strands loosely, as it were casually, twine: they gaze at the waterfalls and the surf but chiefly at the olive-trees—

> Whose elegant branches rain has duly blackened
> And pressed their crowns to a sparkling silver.

As the day has been refreshed by storm and rain so has the bark of the olive trees been cleansed by the New Year snows. The narrative is interrupted for the last time: the poet turns with awkward humility to the woman and compares her to the sweet olive and himself with the oleaster. His is the toughness of the wild olive that enables them to survive storm and is strengthened by winter snows; hers is the sweetness, promising a new miraculous love, of the sweet olive.

'The Oleaster' is also a vivid, suggestive celebration of a near-mystical state of being, akin to the positive doubt soberly rendered in 'Time of Waiting'. Longer than most of its neighbours, the poem is without their terseness yet, paradoxically, like them it leaves an impression of spareness. This is a result of the disjointed progress of the narrative: it is as though each change of direction—signified by punctuation dots—is an involuntary betrayal by the poet of his sense that what he has to say, though simple, is not fully communicable in words, that it is necessary to stop short at a certain point. What Graves *is* saying, eluding direct statement, is not only that suffering is a refining agent directly responsible for the purity and radiance of this new world inhabited by the lovers (one recalls the imagery of 'A Winged Heart' and 'A Restless Ghost'), but also that the pain and the ecstasy (like 'doubt' and 'certitude') are in some way identical. This is conveyed in the description of the olive-trees: the same rain that has 'blackened' (implying sorrow) the elegance of the branches has 'pressed' (implying an intenser pain) the uppermost leaves to a dazzling brilliance. Darkness and illumination somehow go together. This identification is furthered by the association of 'blackened', 'pressed' (a word suggesting not only pain but a shaping activity) and 'silver' with the creative processes of heating and moulding metal.

While 'The Oleaster' is the most successful example of the *dominant* mood of *Man Does, Woman Is*, in these lines it also shows a close relationship with a small group of poems which are the first to present, fervently, rapturously, what for a want of a better word must be called the 'mystical' Black Goddess experience. There are three distinct stages of love, writes Graves in 'Intimations of the Black Goddess': first, the old-fashioned 'affection and companionship'; next, the 'experience of death and recreation at the White Goddess's hand'; and lastly, 'a miraculous certitude in love', 'a new pacific bond between man and woman corresponding to a final reality of love', represented in the Myth as the Black Goddess. 'The Hearth', after summarizing the first two stages, describes the third as a place

> Where an unveiled woman, black as Mother Night,
> Teaches him a new degree of love
> And the tongues and songs of birds.

At Hierapolis, Jerusalem and Rome she was acknowledged as the dark sister of the reigning White Goddess. Her devotees were few and select, for 'she ordained that the poet who seeks her must pass uncomplaining through all the passionate ordeals to which the White Goddess may subject him' before he is admitted to an understanding of her mysteries. Blackness symbolized Wisdom, but in the Orphic Wisdom-cult the Sun was chosen as their 'metaphor of illumination'. 'Throughout the Orient, Night was regarded as a positive power, not as a mere absence of daylight; and Black as a prime colour, not as absence of colour, was prized for capturing the Sun's virtue more than any other.' This may account for the association of blackness with brightness in 'The Oleaster'.[1]

These images belong to a larger complex of images, the burden of which is the ineffableness of the experience they aim to realize. It is the ultimate, wordless truth, the final secret: depicted in turn as intensity of dark and light, silence, the dark forest's centre, reality stripped of false appearances. Love, says the poet in 'The Metaphor', was a 'dead metaphor/For love itself' until it became 'numinous', pervaded everywhere. Then it became a forest enclosing them, and they dared to bring the metaphor to life, to discard its merely temporal garments, and

> So at last understood true nakedness
> And the long debt to silence owed.

Again, in 'The Green Castle', their love is envisaged as a self complete reality, an enclosing silence. As distinct on the one hand from the innocent imagination, 'unclouded/By prescience of death or change/Or the blood-sports of desire', and on the other from the Christian heaven, attainable by prudence, discipline and mortifica-

---

[1] *Mammon and the Black Goddess*, pp. 164 and 162.

tion of the body, this 'seventh heaven' of love, effortlessly beyond desire, is

> a green castle
> Girdled with ramparts of blue sea
> And silent but for the waves' leisured wash.
> There Adam rediscovered Eve...

Green is for rebirth and blue is for eternity.

But the supreme evocation of this experience is the poem entitled 'The Black Goddess':

> Silence, words into foolishness fading,
> Silence prolonged, of thought so secret
> We hush the sheep-bells and the loud cicada.
> And your black agate eyes, wide open, mirror
> The released firebird beating his way
> Down a whirled avenue of blues and yellows.
>
> Should I not weep? Profuse the berries of love,
> The speckled fish, the filberts and white ivy
> Which you, with a half-smile, bestow
> On your delectable broad land of promise
> For me, who never before went gay in plumes.

The new love is presented here as such a perfection of reciprocal understanding between the lovers that it can be greeted only with silence, a silence denoting thought beyond the scope of words. They own a secret knowledge of a mental state so deep, so unconnected with the external world, that it cannot co-exist with—or exist below the consciousness of—even the everyday sounds of the sheep-bells and the cicadas, so incessant that they form an uninterrupting accompaniment to all more ordinary, shallow thoughts. The poet's soul, released from time and space, finds its home in the '*black* agate eyes' of the Goddess, which are both a deep reflecting pool and a forest avenue of trees leading to the heart of the mystery. The treasures that the Goddess bestows in such profusion—they represent love, poetry and wisdom—belong one to each of the seasons, to Winter, Spring, Summer and Autumn respectively: there is no hint here that the turning of the seasons imprisons the poet in a temporal cycle of creation, destruction and recreation.

The poem is an astonishing combination of clear, bare, simple expression and richness of thought. Each statement expands with multiple implications—I have attempted to identify some of those latent in the first stanza. Consider also in those lines the consummate skill with which the verse enacts the meaning: the way in which, with the pauses—each phrase threatening to bring the line to a stand-still—and the falling rhythms within and at the end of each line, it seems to drift towards the silence it describes; and how the sibilant consonants have the effect of intensifying the quality of that silence. Economically and unostentatiously these sensations together create the powerful impression of movement towards a central, inexpressible reality. The extreme spareness of the writing, as in 'The Oleaster', now serves the function for which, it seems, it was ultimately if unconsciously intended—to reflect the poet's humble awareness of just how inexpressible except by bare hints the 'final reality of love' is. Again Graves uses the technique of disjointed progression, but less noticeably and with perhaps a finer effect. The poem does not pursue a consecutive argument but, as it were, walks round the subject, presenting in turn three separate approaches, each of which, however—a pointer merely to a meaning that cannot be fully revealed—penetrates so far and no further. The gap between each view, each stanza, is a tacit acknowledgment of all that it is not possible to say. The connection, for instance, between what is represented as silence in the first stanza and as spiritual release in the second is left mysterious: they may be regarded as nearly alternative versions of the same reality. The transition from the second to the third stanza—'Should I not weep?'—records the poet's awed bewilderment, simple relief, and gratitude for this illumination but not the desire for rational explanation.

The possession of this reality, it can be seen now, has all along been the goal of Graves's poetic efforts. It is that 'Promise of glory, not yet known/In full perfection' of 'Sullen Moods', and then the state beyond conflict which he attempted to define in *Whipperginny*, *The Feather Bed*, and *Mock Beggar Hall*; again, it is the Looking Glass world, outside the usual three dimensions and obeying other than logical laws, gaily celebrated in 'Alice'; it is the realization of the desire, expressed in 'The Felloe'd Year', that the year should 'Be a fixed compass, not a turning wheel'—an experience rendered by a similar image, in 'Instructions to the Orphic Adept', as the 'still, spokeless wheel:—Persephone'; and it is Darien, 'guardian of the hid treasures' of the poet's world. The final possession of this reality is the culmination of Graves's development in this three-volume sequence of the 'sixties: signifying the reward of endurance, the conversion of love's 'difficult achievement' into the accomplishment of the impossible, and the uncontested rule of unreason. A consequence that could not have been anticipated is the peculiar blend of deep calm and buoyancy of the poems which in the next volume celebrate Graves's enlightenment—this is completely new. Even in 'The Black Goddess', the mood while chiefly awed, wondering, sombre, is on the brink of gaiety: the soul is a gorgeously-plumed firebird and, in ecstasy, is 'whirled' down an avenue coloured by exotic 'blues and yellows'.

The message of this poem is the message of all the poems in his next volume, *Love Respelt*, published shortly before (and forming also the last section of) *Collected Poems 1965*. The poetic self they present to the reader is recognizably the fully ripened product of the previous six years, but at the same time has the unexpectedness of a new creation. Although I have dated the beginning of this period from the appearance of *More Poems 1961*, it is *this* group of poems that is the nearest equivalent of *Poems 1926–1930* and *Work in Hand*, which were the first volumes respectively to manifest the two previous changes of direction in Graves's development. Graves claims, however, that now for the first time he is writing the sort of poems he has always been aiming to write, that he has reached the final stage of his development; and, indeed, the poems have an air of finality suggesting that there will be no *radical* change in the future. But he has never been predictable, and he may yet prove himself and his readers wrong.

Finality is the theme of 'Tomorrow's Envy of Today'. With a conviction more absolute than that displayed in any of the White Goddess poems the poet celebrates a love-bond that is unbreakable and complete. Not only do the lovers experience it in the here and now but they are in no danger of losing their hold on it. They conceive of it

> Not as a prophecy of bliss to fall
> A thousand generations hence...
> But as a golden interlock of power
> Looped about every bush and branching tree.

The perfect love, which was 'sister of the mirage and echo' in 'The White Goddess', existing only in the poet's imagination, and 'the new green of [his] hope' in 'Darien' is here a palpable and irreversible achievement.

The poet (in, for instance, 'The Fetter') is more emphatic than before that the vow of love that they at first swore is irrevocable:

> We have taken love through a thousand deaths;
> Should either try to slip our iron fetter,
> It bites yet deeper into neck and arm.

Awareness that lovers are united in suffering, which then became, more generally, recognition of the fact that they are engaged in a joint venture, and finally the realization that theirs is a common fate to which each, though differently, owes total allegiance, has grown to be a conviction that in love man and woman are completely equal; Graves is uncompromising in his assertion (in 'A Court of Love') that

> No man in love, plagued by his own scruples
> Will ever, voluntarily, concede
> That women have a spirit above vows.

Secure in the knowledge that the love they now feel is the ultimate goal of 'a thousand deaths' and that the bond between them has proved unbreakable, the poet can declare without fear that he is 'free at last' ('Gold and Malachite'): free, specifically, from the repeated experiences of death and uncertainty which were central to the kind of love symbolized in the White Goddess Myth. The lovers now, beyond desire, 'disembodied' (as depicted in 'Deliverance'), have been released from time and the mill-wheel of the universe turned by the White Goddess, the inevitable progress through the seasons of love: their 'implacable demon, foaled by love' pastured 'far out beyond the stellar mill'. And their release is final; they

> gasped in awe at our deliverance
> From a too familiar prison,
> And vainly puzzled how it was that now
> We should never need to build another,
> As each, time after time, had done before.

Nor have they thereby exchanged one prison for another—Muse-love for a conventional married relationship: it is their task, says the poet in 'Between Hyssop and Axe', to prove that they can live together

> without succumbing
> To the low fever of domesticity
> Or to the lunatic spin of aimless flight.

The new love exists in a dimensionless region between the two. In the Foreword to *Collected Poems 1965* Graves writes: 'My main theme was always the practical impossibility, transcended only by a belief in miracle, of absolute love continuing between man and woman'. This refers to the conflict between the realistic and romantic sides of Graves's personality that has provided the impetus for much of his mature poetry. Here, advisedly, the sentence describing his position is in the historic tense; for in these last poems for the first time it no longer strictly applies. The belief in miracle has paid dividends: the miracle has happened. Their love is like the 'wild Majorcan cyclamen' which at the poet's request the loved woman drew for him: '(Not yet in season), extravagantly petalled'; though not yet in season it existed and its 'odour/Hung heavy in the room for a long while' ('Wild Cyclamen'). And it is the performance of 'the impossible' that, in the poem of that title, the poet urges upon his love:

> Dear love, since the impossible proves
> Our sole recourse from this distress
> Claim it...

The accomplishment of miracle has at last resolved the conflict between the desire for the impossible and the knowledge of its impossibility; and the realization of absolute love means that the two faces of love, benevolent and malignant, have become one. The wisdom of the Black Goddess is unambiguous as long as it is protected from the shallow, prying curiosity of the waking intelligence. In 'Gold and Malachite' the poet issues this warning to her adepts:

> After the hour of illumination, when the tottering mind
> Has been by force delivered from its incubus of despair

and you are returning to ordinary consciousness, reason will begin to question the whole experience, threatening to destroy it; then, he commands,

> Stop your ears with your fingers, guard *unequivocal silence*
> Lest you discuss wisdom in the language of unwisdom...
> > (my italics)

The lesson of Graves's experience has never before been 'unequivocal'. It is so now because he has at last learned to surrender himself wholly to the wisdom of unreason (of 'mysticism'). 'Hereafter' he asserts in 'What Will Be, Is',

> We make no truce for manifest reason
> From this side of the broad and fateful stream
> Where wisdom rules from her dark cave of dream
> And time is corrigible by laughter.

Wisdom's cave is *darkly*, impenetrably mysterious but it is also a place of such security and freedom, as never before enjoyed by the poet, that he who occupies it can only view life in time with a gay detachment. It is this mood, or variations of it, that prevails in these poems. It denotes a calm so deep and a sense of fulfilment in love so complete that even the mildest of physical reassurances are unnecessary to maintain it:

> As for that act of supererogation,
> The kiss in which we secretly concur,
> Let laughter mitigate its quiet excess.

These lines (from 'The Fetter') in their quiet amusement, embodying a supreme assurance, and their manner of casual elegance are characteristic. Mocking himself for being happy and understating the miracle of it, Graves avoids complacency or unpleasant arrogance, and succeeds all the more in giving a convincing demonstration of spiritual tranquility. Even those poems in which humour is not part of the mood reveal a quality evidently deriving from the same source of tranquillity. 'Ambience' is not the most ambitious of these poems but it is in this respect finely representative.

> The nymph of the forest, only in whose honour
> These birds perform, provides an ambience
> But never leads the chorus: even at dawn
> When we wake to whistle, flute and pipe,
> Astonished they can so extemporize
> Their own parts, as it were haphazard
> Each in his own time, yet avoid discordance
> Or domineering, however virtuose,
> Or long sustained each voluntary of love.
> The rare silences, too, appear like sound
> Rather than pause for breath or meditation...
> Nor is the same piece ever given twice.

This celebrates the poet's new found 'miraculous certitude in love' represented by the Black Goddess, 'nymph of the forest', in the carefully structured syntax and simple yet elegant and fastidious diction of a supremely well-bred prose. The verse flows smoothly and unhurriedly; the first, long sentence forms a beautifully modulated period, avoiding the appearance of neatness on the one hand and intricacy on the other; the tone never deviates from the inflections of conversation, the language is limpid and natural, and the imagery is precise without drawing attention to itself; and yet the total effect produced is, unexpectedly, one of rapture. The rapture is to be felt not as intensity of feeling but as something beyond that—lightness, a 'winged' or airy lightness, expressed by an exquisite delicacy of touch in the poet's handling of his theme rather than by a raising of the poem's emotional pitch. That what the birdsong represents is a miraculous perfection is only the cumulative impression that emerges from the sum of quietly noted particulars: that, for example, it has the gay insouciance of 'whistle, flute and pipe'; that each song is unpredictably free and spontaneous yet neither conflicts with nor dominates the others; that this naturalness is at the same time the perfected skill of the virtuoso; that, finally, it expresses the triumph and exultation of the 'voluntary'. The meaning of the poem is densely compressed without at all appearing so: words like 'ambience' (compare 'Her divine elements disbanded, disembodied,/ And through the misty orchards in love spread' from 'A Restless Ghost') and 'silences', which signify a reality in itself, something deeper than 'pause for breath or meditation' yet including both, contain each a world of thought but nevertheless fit easily into their contexts. The style is that fusion of elements already noted in other poems of Graves's maturity. It is difficult to find a name for the *new* quality in the style which corresponds to the light certainty of mood; the reader is left chiefly with an impression of *order*, an order at once complex and, it seems, effortlessly achieved. The form of the poem answers with such mathematical precision to the structure of the thought that it has become, as it were, a transparent medium for what the poet has to say; furthermore, there are seemingly no stages in the transmission of this thought—the poem is a single, complete utterance.

The burden of these poems is that the new love is a miracle; it is what Graves has always deemed in the nature of things impossible —a love without fluctuations, or a love that transcends them. He represents himself in 'A Court of Love' as 'one who has presumed/ Lasting felicity still unknown in time'. 'Felicity' is one of the keywords. All the poems break new ground, but the most remarkable of them are those which define love as the union of incompatibles: 'Felicity endangering despair', as the opening poem, 'The Red Shower' expresses it.

Graves employs a new imagery of colour to embody this paradox: black (as we have seen, regarded in the Orient as a colour), green, red and yellow. Chapter 15 of *The White Goddess*, 'The Seven Pillars', in which Graves applied his theory concerning the language of myth to Hebrew literature, gives us most of the necessary background information. Much of that book's argument aimed to prove the existence of a Bronze Age sacred tree-alphabet serving also as a thirteen-month, lunar calendar, in which the tree-consonants stood for the months of which their trees were characteristic and the tree-vowels stood for the equinoxes and solstices. In this chapter Graves reconstructed as well a parallel jewel-sequence and a sequence of the tribes of Israel, assigning to each month a jewel and tribe. These recent poems take their colour-emblems exclusively from the jewels of the last month, extending from November 25 to December 22 and the first month of the New Year, which begins on December 24. The dark green malachite is the stone for the last month. This is the darkest month, the last of the dying year, and yet, being one of the two winter rain-months in Palestine, it is also the time of ploughing; so that 'green' carries the opposed meanings of death and renewal. The stone for the New Year month is the red sard, which comes first in the year in honour of the new man, Adam (a variant of a word meaning rusty-red). But the most important stone is the amber. In the lunar calendar there is an extra day, December 23, which belongs to Benjamin; although this is the darkest day, Benjamin's jewel is amber, of the sun's colour, and he is called 'The Ruler of the South', because the sun reaches its most southerly stage in midwinter. More startlingly, this is the same fusion of opposites as is expressed by the dark green malachite: it is given further stress by the fact that Benjamin's tree is hyssop, or wild caper (mentioned a few times in these poems), which grows green in walls and crannies and was the prime lustral tree in Hebrew use. Thus black for death and wisdom, green for spiritual purification and rebirth out of death, and gold-yellow for the sun's illumination combine to communicate the essential paradox—a paradox expressed in the Wisdom cults in the belief that black was a prime colour and captured the sun's virtue more than any other colour.

This conception of blackness symbolizes the identity of joy and despair. In 'The Snap-Comb Wilderness' the poet takes as his image for the new love the black 'irreducible jungle' of a woman's hair, concentrating his vision of it in a memorable phrase, 'Dark as eclipse and scented with despair', the darkness of the eclipse implying the sun as Benjamin's day was thought to imply it. In 'The Red Shower' the mysteriously close connection of felicity and despair is rendered by the image of a red shower of 'live sparks' raining from a (by implication, dark) 'central anvil': at the centre of despair is the fire of illumination. The regenerative power of despair is the theme of 'The Frog and the Golden Ball'. Graves has made of it a fairy-tale allegory with the clear outlines of ballad, and the poem is an attractive blend of the ingenuous tones of ballad narrative and the rich meaningfulness of symbol. A princess, losing her golden ball, asked a 'cold frog' to retrieve it, for which she rewarded him with a kiss. The poem goes on to tell how by her grateful kiss the frog was released from an enchantment and returned immediately to his original 'princely shape'. The *cold* frog is the embodiment of the poet's despair and the well is his element. Although the princess had been promised in marriage to a royal cousin, she now vowed herself to an unworldly love of the frog-turned-prince. Their plight would seem 'past human hope', said the prince, to those lovers

> Who have never swum as a frog in a dark well
> Or have lost a golden ball:

the more-than-human hope which sustained him was a direct product of the more-than-ordinary suffering borne by him in the darkness of his well; it is in the dark that new life germinates. And so, when she asked him what they should do, he answered:

> 'Is magic of love less powerful at your Court
> Than at this green well-head?'—

in which the final stress is on 'green', the green of spiritual renewal. The lines imply that such *magical* love is inseparable from the dark but green experiences of the well.

Unworldliness has been Graves's standard at least ever since the years of Laura Riding's influence. It meant living in the world of the mind, a world of values, rather than according to the dictates of a purely physical existence. As is plainly indicated by the emphasis on the 'impossible' or 'miraculous' or 'magical' nature of the experience he is presenting, he has now discovered a new degree of unworldliness. Founding it on the mystical certainties represented by the Black Goddess rather than on the uncertainties represented by the White Goddess, Graves is absolute in his assertions:

Your vow is to truth, not practicality;
To honour, not to the dead world's esteem;
To a bed of rock, not to a swan's down pillow;
To the tears you kiss away from her black eyes.

('The Vow')

He is equally positive that he and his beloved are alone in honouring
this vow:

none else would venture
To live detached from force of circumstance
As history neared its ending.

('Iron Palace')

The tone is, considered in the context of these poems, not arrogant;
it is more that of one initiated into a mystery. In several instances
the poet describes their love as if it were the consequence of a
specific discipline. In 'Those Who Came Short' he refers to 'our
studies'; and in 'The Vow' the tears in the Goddess's 'black eyes'
'lament an *uninstructible* world of men' (my italics), rationalists who
need proof that to 'walk invisibly' is possible. Achieving a faith in
miracle the lovers have become 'love's exemplars to all mankind'
('Iron Palace') and 'twin paragons, our final selves' ('Conjunction').

Graves has made it clear in recent essays that he has in mind the
Sufi idea of love. He seems to have been in direct contact with Sufi
thought since the early 'sixties, but the experiences it has made available to him and its conclusions concerning the absolute values of
love (the Sufis claim to have influenced the early troubadour poets)
and the primacy of intuition over reason only confirm and extend
earlier experiences and beliefs which he has held most of his life. To
take one example, quoted above in Chapter 4: the description of Laura
Riding in 'Against Kind' as living 'against kind' and yet 'among kind'
is very similar to the Sufi ideal of being 'in the world but not of it',
quoted by Graves in his Introduction to Idries Shah's book. Graves
has held to his view, first formulated in the late 'twenties, of the poet
as the spokesman for unchanging values in a world of compromise,
and of poetry (the reading and writing of poetry) as a way of life,
superior in kind to any other, with unwavering consistency. The
difference between his position then and his position now is only

one of degree, the difference, say, that exists between the poetic trance—on the special experience of which so much of Graves's thought has been based—and the trance of mystical illumination which has developed out of it. Seen in retrospect, the attitudes to the world, to love and to poetry embodied in Sufism which are now at the centre of Graves's poetry form what seems the inevitable culmination of a lifetime of poetic thought.

This is not the time to pronounce a conclusion to Graves's career as a poet. But, taking our cue from the fact that he has replaced 'Leaving the Rest Unsaid', a poem which in token of the unpredictable development of the poet's art ends on a comma, as the last poem in his *Collected Poems* with 'Nothing Now Astonishes' in *Collected Poems 1965*, we may safely assume that his poetry has now reached some kind of *spiritual* conclusion. No matter what his future themes and attitudes, it is unlikely that Graves will cease to be able to say, in the words of this poem:

> Rest, my loud heart. Your too exultant flight
> Has raised the wing-beat to a roar
> Drowning seraphic whispers.

He will continue to 'rest' in the new-found certainties of *Love Respelt* and to hear the 'seraphic whispers' of a perfect state of being never before experienced.[1]

---

[1] Since this was written Graves has published another volume, *Poems 1965-1968*. It is too late to add any comments, except that he shows no signs of failing poetic vitality or of repeating himself. As he has put it in a letter to me, with these poems he has turned yet another corner. The blurb quotes his own description of them: 'Once more, my theme is metaphorical of experiences which, as in classical Persian poetry, transcend ordinary physical circumstance...'

Conclusion

CRITICS who differ over the nature of Graves's poetic achievement seem to agree about its limitations. A common judgement is that in some way Graves has evaded the problems of the twentieth century, forsaking the arena of general concern, where, for example, Pound, Eliot, Empson, Bottrall and Auden have honourably fought, for the less demanding labours, albeit performed with incomparable skill, of the private garden. It is true that his themes are not public and rarely topical, that his imagery, though exact, vivid and richly evocative, is uncomplicated, rural, and traditional and makes very little allusion to the realities of an urban, technologically sophisticated society or, except indirectly, to modern scientific and philosophic thought; he has, in fact, deliberately excluded from his collections those poems in which it does. But his poetry is no less fully engaged with the modern world for having these characteristics. We have a right to expect a contemporary poet to be in some sense 'modern'—that his work should bear the impression of the age in which it is written—even if he is profoundly at variance with the tendencies of that age; it is a question not of themes and images, however, but of sensibility. The quality of a poet's modernity can be gauged less from the amount of direct reference to contemporary history or direct indebtedness to contemporary thought than from the degree of (implicit or explicit) *awareness* embodied in his work of contemporary ideas and events, and the quality of his response to them. By this definition Graves's poetry is modern. He lives in spiritual exile from our civilization, but he rejects its values neither ignorantly nor irresponsibly.

The First World War, which for many societies marked the end of the old stabilities and the beginning of a new era, served also as Graves's initiation into our modern world. His direct experience of the war was the crucial factor both in his personal and poetic development. But, whether they were actively involved or not, it was a test that few writers passed. Graves was one of the few—Blunden and Sassoon, for example, psychologically did not survive—who in the end was toughened and enlarged by it. Slowly his poetry absorbed the impact of violence but, more importantly, between 1923 and 1938 he worked hard at coming to terms with the war's aftermath, the final collapse of the old religious values and social traditions. During the 'twenties he looked for an explanation of himself and his society, ultimately for a new order and new certainties, in contemporary psychology and anthropology, and his later studies with Laura Riding of ancient religion, mythology, philosophy, scientific and political thought were directed towards the same goal. The poetry of these years was written out of an honest, intimate awareness of the 'botched civilization' lamented by Pound and the spiritual wasteland depicted by Eliot. In the Foreword to *Collected Poems 1938*, noting the high proportion of his poems which are close and energetic studies of 'the disgusting, the contemptible and the evil', he interprets this as 'the blurted confession of a naturally sanguine temperament: that the age into which I was born...has been intellectually and morally in perfect confusion' (p. xxiv). At this time he considered it part of the poet's task—or fate—to be exposed to, but not to be destroyed by, such confusion. He comments, in an introductory letter to Ronald Bottrall's *The Turning Path* (1939), on 'the personal and immediate hell of living unfulfilment' reflected in Bottrall's poems, that it is 'a shameful hell, not to be satirized even, and hardly worth the harrowing—yet a hell through which we must all pass with greater or lesser laboriousness according to our sins of vanity'. Both passages refer in the main to the poems of moral criticism, such as 'Hell' and 'Ship Master', directed against either a worthless society or the poet's implication with the motives of that society. He believed, however, that the poet must go beyond negation to affirm a contrary reality. He took seriously the poet's duty to bring order into this intellectual and moral chaos. In 'A Private Correspondence on Reality' between himself and Laura Riding, published in *Epilogue III* (1937), he recalls: 'It was as a poet in search of an integration of reality that you first knew me. The problem for me was at that time the same technical one that faced all my fellow-poets: what to do when the world of thought had grown unmanageable' (p. 121). The 'destructive' poems of Graves's second period were complemented, then, by poems of a 'creative', liberating purpose, which were no less responsive to the contemporary predicament. For they aimed at erecting a structure of values—mental clarity, hard work, commonsense, love—to replace the rotten edifice of Western, Christian civilization.

Graves was more immediately engaged with the problems of modern society during his second period than at any other time. This does not mean that he ceased to be a *modern* poet after that. One of the achievements of that period, I have proposed, was the creation of a style to answer the challenge of twentieth-century experience. It is unrhetorical, direct, taut, emotionally controlled, ironic, expressing intellectual stringency and a tough, sceptical sensibility. When his theme was no longer the haunted house and the 'fallen tower' (weak in the west wall and in the underpinning at the south-eastern angle) of modern civilization, when he turned, in the White Goddess poetry, to a reality not describable in a language of contemporary reference, then this style and manner of response brought with it evidence of previous confrontations with the contemporary world. I tried to demonstrate in my comments on 'End of Play' the close relationship between the moral commonsense informing the destructive part of that poem and the creative affirmation of the concluding stanza: the latter asserts a new, unreasonable faith in the same fierce, strict tone that Graves uses in the earlier stanzas to dismiss the sentimentalities of the old faith. And 'End of Play' points forward in theme and imagery to 'The White Goddess' and other poems of the 'forties.

Graves's achievement is that, although, as he says in the Foreword to *Collected Poems 1938*, educated in 'the anodynic tradition of poetry' and owning a 'naturally sanguine temperament' (p. xxiv), he survived through sheer emotional stamina the trauma of his war experiences and by scrupulous, unremitting hard work remade himself and his poetry; between 1923, when he left the Georgian fold, and 1926 he thereby turned himself into a *modern* poet. The language of desire in Graves has always been in the romantic tradition, but since 1926 his romanticism has been resilient, a moral protest rather than a retreat; and the tough, intellectual vein in his poetry shows the influence not only of Laura Riding but of the Elizabethans, Ben Jonson, the Metaphysicals and the Cavalier poets. As I have argued, Graves's peculiar fusion of romantic emotion, moral realism and a frequently classical elegance and urbanity makes for a more complex effect, a wider range of mood and tone, than is generally granted. His poetry shows that allusiveness, juxtaposition of parts rather than logical sequence, and dislocated syntax, the techniques of Pound and Eliot, did not in the 'twenties constitute the only way of solving the poet's problem 'when the world of thought had grown unmanageable'. In this he resembles Yeats; like Yeats, too, Graves sought meaning and consistency in a personal synthesis of knowledge.

The White Goddess Myth, of course, objectifies a personal drama, but one that takes place within a wider context, contemporary and timeless. It is necessary to insist that the aims of the mythological poetry are continuous with those of his previous work: the synthesis embodied in the Myth originated in the *full* emotional content of his earlier poetry, and is only the culmination of that search for an intellectual and ethical system which had animated his work since about 1923. The mythological poetry, therefore, as much as the poetry of his second period, arose from his intense concern with the spiritual dilemmas of the twentieth century: providing one answer to the radical problems of thought and belief—intellectual confusion, the collapse of absolute values, and religious apathy—that have marked out an age characterized by unprecedented social change and the waning power of the Christian tradition. He has compressed into the one symbol his total response to this situation. The Goddess is the principal of flux itself. She is also, however, a spiritual grace, a changeless certainty, on which the poet can call to defeat flux.

Graves has achieved consistency, despite appearances to the contrary, without sacrificing breadth of interest or variety of mood. The Goddess is at the centre of a complex of meanings. She represents, separately or together, the poet's inspiration, his aesthetic and moral conscience, the spiritual reality in the man-woman relationship (both the ordeal and the ideal of love), fate or providence in the poet's life, a force in history governing human destiny, an alternative to the Christian God, a goal of mystical perfection! Far from narrowing Graves's scope, as is frequently alleged, the White Goddess Theme is no less than 'the single poetic theme of life and death'; which takes in also the question of immortality, 'of what survives of the beloved'. The chief events in her story—love, death and rebirth—are in any religious conception the central experiences of human life. Her relevance extends beyond the particular chaos of modern history: she is the Mother of All Living, the necessary condition of existence, combining good and evil.

However, the mythic pattern does exclude from most of the White Goddess poems certain emotional possibilities. The seasonal, ritual and lunar symbolisms were designed to express the poet's subjection to a recurring cycle of experience, ending in the inescapable defeat of love. In *The White Goddess* Graves states that the main problem of pagan religion—and it is his own—is contained in the meaning of the Druidic letter-name of R, 'I flow away'; it implies the question: 'Must all things swing round for ever? or how can we escape from the Wheel?' (p. 139). As Mr Hoffman says, in *Barbarous Knowledge*, the 'expansion of feeling and intellectual joy which other poets from Shakespeare to Donne and Yeats have known' (p. 219), though not absent from Graves's poetry, are in the White Goddess poems usually presented as transitory states, a tenuous hope created out of despair. But there are exceptions. Early in his third period, in his 'Instructions to the Orphic Adept', Graves described at least one solution to the problem of paganism, a kind of liberation. It was: not to forget past sufferings, to remember at each stage the whole cycle, and thus to transcend them. There were other poems—like 'Theseus and Ariadne', 'The Turn of the Moon', and 'Ruby and Amethyst'—which, in celebrating without reservation the perfection of the female principle, freed the poet's psyche from the prison of a deterministic pattern. To his latest poems, written in honour of the Black Goddess of Wisdom, Mr Hoffman's words no longer apply at all. They proclaim Graves's final release from the wheel of suffering. Without any doubt such poems as 'Ambience', 'Whole Love', 'Iron Palace', and 'Deliverance'—indeed, most of *Love Respelt*—manifest precisely an 'expansion of feeling and intellectual joy'.

We must seek the intrinsic limitation of Graves's work in another aspect of it. It is, surely, to be located in his obliqueness of approach, his practice, mentioned in Chapter 6, of only *hinting the fact*. This strategy points to a centre of disturbance in the poet's psyche which he cannot treat directly, an inability—it is the theme of 'The Cool Web'—to embody in his verse the most extreme emotions ('We shall go mad no doubt and die that way'). The oblique approach is not invariable but it is frequent and indicative of a general caution, at least partly responsible for his habitual use of allegory and emblem and the spareness of his style. It is an odd verdict to pronounce on a poet who portrays himself as a prophet of unreason but Graves has perhaps been too successful in attaining the freedom of impersonality—reason (urbanity, fluency, commonsense) commands too firmly. When, in his letter introducing Bottrall's poems, he asserts that the poet must subject himself to the hell of modern civilization, 'the hell of living unfulfilment', the terms of his assertion betray this compulsion to keep his distance from it: it is a hell, he writes with what strikes one as inappropriate arrogance, 'hardly worth the harrowing'.

Yet there should be no question of Graves's standing. I have avoided classifying his work as either 'major' or 'minor', vague categories usually implying standards extrinsic to literary judgement. One can say, however, that his best poems offer what in any one age only a few poems offer: they exemplify, with the accents of an alert mind and a passionate nature, possible moral stances in the face of contemporary experience—responses of such completeness, sureness and complexity as to satisfy the modern reader's need for a coherent, authoritative attitude to the world in which both he and the writer live.

Bibliography of Robert Graves
1916-1968

I. COMPLETE BIBLIOGRAPHY 1916-1965

Higginson, Fred H. *A Bibliography of the Works of Robert Graves.* London, Nicholas Vane, 1966; Hamden, Ct., The Shoe String Press, 1966.

II. POETIC WORKS (excluding works for children)
A complete list of the first English and American Editions

Over the Brazier. London, The Poetry Bookshop, 1916.
Goliath and David. London, The Chiswick Press, 1916.
Fairies and Fusiliers. London, Heinemann, 1917; New York, A. A. Knopf, 1918.
Treasure Box. London, The Chiswick Press, 1919.
Country Sentiment. London, Secker, 1920; New York, A. A. Knopf, 1920.
The Pier-Glass. London, Secker, 1921; New York, A. A. Knopf, 1921.
Whipperginny. London, Heinemann, 1923; New York, A. A. Knopf, 1923.
The Feather Bed. Richmond, The Hogarth Press, 1923.
Mock Begger Hall. London, The Hogarth Press, 1924.
John Kemp's Wager: A Ballad Opera. Oxford, Blackwell, 1925; New York, S. French, 1925.
Welchman's Hose. London, The Fleuron, 1925.
Robert Graves (The Augustan Books of Modern Poetry). London, E. Benn, 1925.
The Marmosite's Miscellany (under the pseudonym 'John Doyle'). London, The Hogarth Press, 1925.
Poems (1914–1926). London, Heinemann, 1927; New York, Doubleday, 1929.
Poems (1914–1927). London, Heinemann, 1927. A limited edition including nine poems not contained in *Poems (1914–1926).*
Poems 1929. London, The Seizin Press, 1929.
Ten Poems More. Paris, Hours Press, 1930.
Poems 1926–1930. London, Heinemann, 1931.

275

To Whom Else? Deyá, Majorca, The Seizin Press, 1931.

Poems 1930–1933. London, A. Barker, 1933.

Epilogue, 1935–1937. See PROSE WORKS.

Collected Poems. London, Cassell, 1938; New York, Random House, 1939.

No More Ghosts: Selected Poems. London, Faber, 1940.

Work in Hand. With Alan Hodge and Norman Cameron. London, The Hogarth Press, 1942.

Robert Graves (The Augustan Poets). London, Eyre and Spottiswoode, 1943.

Poems 1938–1945. London, Cassell, 1946; New York, Creative Age Press, 1946.

Collected Poems (1914–1947). London, Cassell, 1948.

Poems and Satires 1951. London, Cassell, 1951.

Poems 1953. London, Cassell, 1953.

Collected Poems 1955. New York, Doubleday, 1955.

The Crowning Privilege. 1955. See PROSE WORKS.

Poems Selected by Himself. London, Penguin Books, 1957. Revised and enlarged in 1961 and 1966.

5 Pens in Hand. 1958. See PROSE WORKS.

The Poems of Robert Graves: Chosen by Himself. New York, Doubleday Anchor Books, 1958

Steps. 1958. See PROSE WORKS.

Collected Poems 1959. London, Cassell, 1959.

Food for Centaurs. 1960. See PROSE WORKS.

More Poems 1961. London, Cassell, 1961.

Collected Poems. New York, Doubleday, 1961.

The More Deserving Cases: Eighteen Old Poems for Reconsideration. Marlborough College Press, 1962.

New Poems 1962. London, Cassell, 1962; New York, Doubleday, 1963.

Man Does, Woman Is. London, Cassell, 1964; New York, Doubleday, 1964.

Love Respelt. London, Cassell, 1965; New York, Doubleday, 1966.

Collected Poems 1965. London, Cassell, 1965; *Collected Poems 1966*, New York, Doubleday, 1966.

17 Poems Missing from 'Love Respelt'. London, Rota, 1966.

Colophon to 'Love Respelt'. London, Rota, 1967.

Poems 1965–1968. London, Cassell, 1968.

III. PROSE WORKS: CRITICAL, MYTHOLOGICAL AND AUTOBIOGRAPHICAL

A nearly complete list of the English and American editions

On English Poetry: Being an Irregular Approach to the Psychology of this Art, from Evidence Mainly Subjective. London, Heinemann, 1922; New York, A. A. Knopf, 1922.

The Meaning of Dreams. London, Cecil Palmer, 1924; New York, Greenberg, 1925.

Poetic Unreason and Other Studies. London, Cecil Palmer, 1925.

Contemporary Techniques of Poetry: A Political Analogy. London, The Hogarth Press, 1925.

Another Future of Poetry. London, The Hogarth Press, 1926.

The English Ballad: A Short Critical Survey. An anthology compiled, edited and introduced by Graves. London, Heinemann, 1927.

A Survey of Modernist Poetry. With Laura Riding. London, Heinemann, 1927; New York, Doubleday, 1928.

A Pamphlet Against Anthologies. With Laura Riding. London, Cape, 1928; New York, Doubleday, 1928.

Good-Bye To All That: An Autobiography. London, Cape, 1929; second impression (expurgated: a poem by Siegfried Sassoon is omitted), 1929; New York, Cape ar ' Harrison Smith (an expurgated edition), 1930. Second edition (considerably revised), London, Cassell, 1957; New York, Doubleday Anchor Books, 1957.

But It Still Goes On: An Accumulation. London, Cape, 1930; New York, Cape and Harrison Smith, 1931.

Epilogue: A Critical Summary. Edited with Laura Riding. Contains critical contributions and poems. Deyá, Majorca, The Seizin Press: London, Constable. Vol. I, 1935. Vol. II, 1936. Vol. III, 1937.

The White Goddess: A Historical Grammar of Poetic Myth. London, Faber, 1948; New York, Creative Age Press, 1948. Second (latest) American edition (amended and enlarged), 1958. Third (latest) English edition (amended and enlarged), 1961.

The Common Asphodel: Collected Essays on Poetry 1922–1949. London, H. Hamilton, 1949.

Occupation: Writer. London, Cassell, 1951; New York, Creative Age Press, 1950.

The Nazarene Gospel Restored. With Joshua Podro. London, Cassell, 1953; New York, Doubleday, 1954.

The Greek Myths. Two volumes. London, Penguin Books, 1955; Baltimore, Penguin Books, 1955. Revised in 1957 and 1960.

Adam's Rib, and Other Anomalous Elements in the Hebrew Creation Myth: A New View. London, Trianon Press, 1955; New York, Yoseloff, 1958.

The Crowning Privilege. The Clark Lectures 1954–1955; Also Various Essays on Poetry and Sixteen New Poems. London, Cassell, 1955; New York, Doubleday, 1956 (omitting the poems and adding essays from *The Common Asphodel*).

Jesus in Rome: A Historical Conjecture. With Joshua Podro. London, Cassell, 1957.

English and Scottish Ballads. An anthology edited with an introduction and critical notes. London, Heinemann, 1957; New York, Macmillan, 1957.

Steps: Stories, Talks, Essays, Poems, Studies in History. London, Cassell, 1958.

5 Pens in Hand. (Contents partly the same as *Steps.*) New York, Doubleday, 1958.

Food for Centaurs: Stories, Talks, Critical Studies, Poems. (Includes material from *Steps* omitted from *5 Pens in Hand*, but otherwise different.) New York, Doubleday, 1960.

Oxford Addresses on Poetry. London, Cassell, 1961; New York, Doubleday, 1962.

The Hebrew Myths: The Book of Genesis. With Raphael Patai. London, Cassell, 1964; New York, Doubleday, 1964.

Mammon and the Black Goddess. London, Cassell, 1965; New York, Doubleday, 1965.

Poetic Craft and Principle. London, Cassell, 1967.

Index

Graves's works are indexed in the main alphabetical sequence. Poem titles appear in quotation marks, book titles in italics; parts of books indexed separately (e.g. essays, lectures, chapters) are given in quotation marks, followed by the name of the volume in which they are contained.